Published by Mission Point Press
2554 Chandler Rd.
Traverse City, MI 49696
(231) 421-9513
www.MissionPointPress.com

Cover and title page image by
Winslow Homer, "Northeaster," 1895;
Collection of Metropolitan Museum of Art, New York, NY.

ISBN: 978-1-954786-48-6 (softcover color)
ISBN: 978-1-954786-49-3 (softcover b/w)

Library of Congress Control Number: 2021918096

Printed in the United States of America

GUARDIANS OF THE
$\mathcal{M}$ANITOU $\mathcal{P}$ASSAGE

A Chronicle of Service to Lake Michigan Mariners
1840 – 1915

JONATHAN P. HAWLEY

MISSION POINT PRESS

Contents

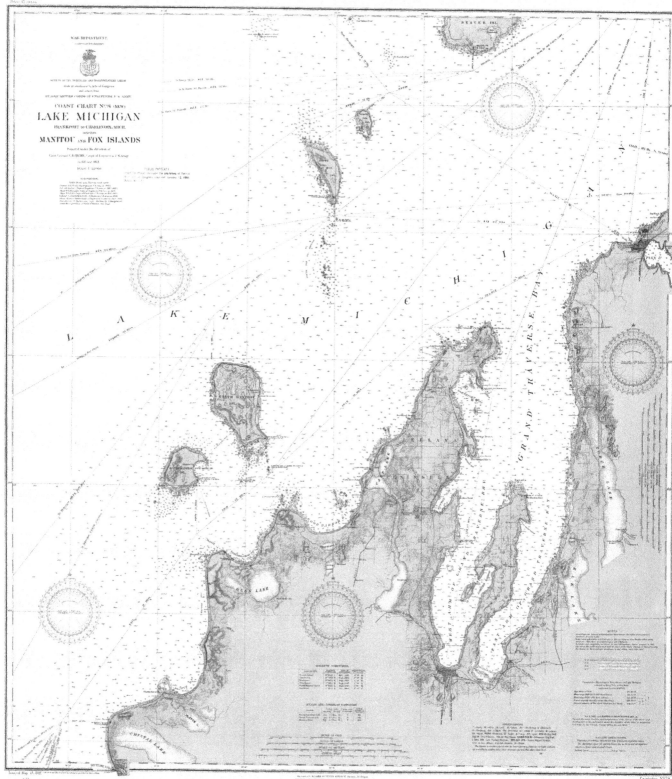

Preface

In the summer of 1876, the United States' centennial year, a fully staffed and equipped lifesaving station was erected within the grounds of the grand national celebration in Philadelphia prior to its permanent siting on the Atlantic coast at Cape May, New Jersey.

As the exhibit was later described by the newly established US Life-Saving Service, the facility was visited by "a multitude of people, whom its unique devices greatly interested. Among them were many persons of distinction from foreign nations interested in nautical affairs, including several officers of lifesaving institutions in other countries, who examined minutely into all the details of our entire system, which some of them volunteered to say was unequaled by any system in the world."

Less than a year later, in the early spring of 1877, the first crewed lifesaving station serving northern Lake Michigan's Manitou Passage began operations at what had long been known from the French presence in the region as Pointe aux Bec Scies, referring to a prevalent species of duck. Since the 1890s, this site has been primarily known as Point Betsie. A second passage rescue station began service on North Manitou Island just two months later, and over the following quarter-century, additional facilities protecting mariners sailing this heavily traveled course were gradually established.

In its first annual report, covering fiscal 1876, the new US Life-Saving Service wrote of having "already accomplished so much for humanity" and of its promise of "even more splendid developments for the future." The Manitou Passage lifesaving stations and coastal lights, of which the earliest established preceded the lifesavers' arrival, are part of that rich tradition.

Imagine for a moment that you're the captain of a schooner sailing the Great Lakes from Buffalo to Chicago, with two other persons aboard and mixed cargo, on a fall evening in 1873. Having come through the Straits of Mackinac and into northern Lake Michigan, you set course to the naturally sheltered harbor at a small island called South Manitou. You are to pick up a load of lumber for delivery to Chicago, which continues rebuilding after its massively destructive 1871 fire.

Still having a way to go to reach the island, and sensing some growing unsteadiness in the wind and sea, you're feeling uneasy. As you watch the rolling seas and the darkening sky, you sight near the horizon a steady white light some eight miles off the mainland coast, on your port side. You know that it marks Skilligallee Rock, and you steer clear of this obstruction.

Well off to your right you soon see a flashing white light that you know is coming from the tall structure at the south end of Beaver Island. Next, off to the starboard, you see a flashing red signal from the southeast end of South Fox Island, providing guidance between it and North Manitou Island, a course through which you must be mindful of scattered shoals. A few hours later, a fixed white light appears off to the left on the mainland, fracturing the darkness. That would be from Grand Traverse Light, erected at the northwest tip of the Leelanau Peninsula to guide southbound ships to the passage between the two Manitou islands and the mainland shore's soaring dunes.

You're on the passage course not only because it is the direct route toward your final port, but also because it offers welcomed shelter from potentially destructive winds you might encounter had you sailed west of the Manitous. You also know, however, that your course should be sailed with care, for it is itself a graveyard of wrecks stemming from its own hazards, primarily hidden shoals. That's why two of the Great Lakes' earliest rescue boats, their oars pulled to disasters by recruited volunteers, had been assigned to the two islands about twenty years previously.

You relax a bit, however, knowing you're getting close to your destination for the night. Had your vessel become enveloped in fog, a common situation at this time of year, you would have listened for the every-minute tones from a steam-powered whistle to guide you toward a safe anchorage. You watch the starboard horizon for a steady white light that assists you, as well as crews of numerous other schooners, into South Manitou Island's naturally protective harbor.

Reaching port, you drop anchor, tie down sails, and catch a night's rest. In the morning, you maneuver your vessel to the wharf to load wood that was cut from the islands' expansive forests, milled, and hauled by horses to the harbor. After a brief chat with other sailors about the weather and conditions on the lake, it's off on the long, open-water sail to Chicago or other shoreline market towns, with no mid-lake refuge.

Fortunately, rain and gusty winds had passed harmlessly overnight, and the long, final leg of the trip bodes well. After delivering the lumber to a Chicago River dock and taking aboard a load of grain, you sail north off the east coast, and likely see a beam from Point aux Bec Scies lighthouse marking your course change to the passage. You will have just the return sail to Buffalo to complete before winter lay up, when the freezing winds would turn your wooden deck into a too-dangerous ice pond. Years go by as you continue to make your living on these lengthy trips, during which you are conscious that wear and tear inevitably takes a toll on an old schooner. Now and then, your thoughts turn to captains you've known whose vessels went missing without a trace.

But now, as merely a reader, you must make a mental shift to the early twentieth century, when you find yourself on yet another imaginary trip. Although there are still a few old sailing ships in the Great Lakes' commercial fleet, you're fortunate to be skippering a steamer moving south off of Lake Michigan's northeastern shore, on another dark and potentially foggy night. Life on the sea is less risky, though admittedly less romantic, than back when most ships were powered only by finicky winds to move them up and down the longest of the Great Lakes.

You're standing watch by the rail, scanning the horizon, observing your ship's progress through the safe but nonetheless still challenging Manitou Passage, where hundreds of vessels travel, day and night, throughout the shipping season, making as many trips as possible between early spring and late fall. There are now more navigational aids, particularly steam-powered fog signals, than were formerly available to you.

As your ship makes her way into the passage, it is comforting to know that North Manitou Island, from which a few lights from shore structures are now visible, is the site of the lifesaving station that was established about twenty-five years ago, in recognition of the island's menacing shoals. You will also be grateful for the recent addition of lifesaving stations at two other passage locations, one at South Manitou and the other on the mainland shore of Sleeping Bear Bay. Not only does the simultaneous existence of these three stations within the passage reflect the numerous disasters over the years that were attributable to its perils, but they substantially increase the opportunity of rescue should you sometime find yourself in serious trouble.

Alternating flashing red and white lights at twenty-second intervals will be visible from a lighthouse situated on North Manitou's southeast point. Its signal is readily distinguishable from a fixed white light you will soon see, coming from a white-hulled vessel anchored in twenty-one feet of water; its side bears the bold identification MANITOU, marking hazardous shoals where vessels were known to wreck.

After passing on your starboard the waterway that separates the two islands, the ship will smoothly enter South Manitou's wide harbor.

A steady white light, said to be visible for about nineteen miles, will appear from a tall, conical brick tower about one hundred feet above water level. There is a steam-powered fog signal here, and nearby on the shore is this island's lifesaving station, its disciplined crew ready for action during the navigation season.

Thinking of fuel, your mind may wander to the backbreaking, mind-numbing job of the lightkeepers tending steam-powered fog signals on South Manitou, blasting throughout day and night for hundreds of hours, some years consuming one hundred or more cords of wood.

Along with the other steamers, before leaving South Manitou your ship's own fuel supply must be restocked for the long trip ahead. Soon you're underway, with the next checkpoint off portside being the tower, light, and fog signal at Point Betsie. There you will also spot a long-established lifesaving station whose crews respond to lake crises south, west, and north of the station, into the passage.

Hopefully, these two imaginary trips, first by sail and then by steamer, have afforded you a glimpse of lake life and travel during much of the past century, and introduced you to the heavily traveled Manitou Passage as well as the vital services provided mariners on these waters.

While one might think of these stations simply in local terms, it should be remembered that the lighthouse and lifesaving station crews served in separate federal agencies, bore different responsibilities, and worked under different personnel policies and leaders. Where stationed near each other, they and their families were typically friends, occasionally friendly rivals, and their services were highly valued within their communities and by sailors on the "Big Lake." Both the trained lifesavers and lightkeepers of the passage stations were effectively "first responders," as today's rescuers are known, particularly on the isolated islands where they were usually the only ready source of emergency assistance.

Lightkeepers, typically isolated, led demanding lives. Keeping a "good light" every night was critically important to the safe travel of ships and the well-being of persons aboard them. The maintenance that lightkeepers were required to do every day for their light and other equipment was essential to their performance, and to the standards demanded by their service's superior officers. As for the lifesaving crews, they daily performed their drills and station duties in order to be ready for rescue attempts that could imperil their own lives while striving to carry out their mission. High drama and monotony were both realities, as US lifesaving stations' surfmen had to be constantly ready to employ their skillful aid in life-threatening circumstances, and able to cope with the boredom of days, sometimes even weeks, that could pass without an appeal for their services.

This memoir is devoted primarily to the role of the US Life-Saving Service in the Manitou Passage, as revealed in two sets of unique federal archival sources: the daily journal entries in which the stations' keepers reported their crews' activities to their superior officers, and the service's top leaders' comprehensive annual reports to their department's secretary and the US Congress. The latter documents were prepared each fiscal year (from July 1 to the following June 30 during the period covered here) by the agency's Washington, DC writers to inform government policymakers of the service's performance, budget requirements, etc., and to promote its public reputation and support.

Preserved by the US National Archives and Records Administration, the Library of Congress, university libraries, and other public and private institutions, these unique records, together with other valuable documents, reveal the history of the passage's lifesaving stations from their formation until early 1915, when they became units of the newly formed US Coast Guard. These sources also illustrate the significant relationships between the national and district US Life-Saving Service offices where the agency's operational policies were developed and overseen, and the individual stations whose keepers and surfmen bore the responsibility for their effective implementation. Quotations have been reproduced as originally written, and thus retain occasional variant spellings and grammatical errors.

This account also includes the history of the passage's lighthouses, whose faithful and resourceful keepers saved uncountable vessels from peril, and the lives of persons aboard them.

The assistance provided by the men of both federal services were vitally important, not only to travelers of the passage, but to the islands' residents who relied upon the service's protection for their livelihoods, and sometimes their very lives.

Manitou, Chicago-built 1893 for the Manitou Steamship Company.
Historical Collections of the Great Lakes, Bowling Green State University.

Manitou Steamship Company Advertisement.
Leelanau Historical Society Museum.

Left: Manitou, Canadian-built, 1903.
Historical Collection of the Great Lakes, Bowling Green State University.
Right: Manitou, Leland-built fish tug, 1912.
Historical Collection of the Great Lakes, Bowling Green State University.

"Manitou": Why and Where

The identification "Manitou" holds profound spiritual significance for the many thousands of North American native people of the Anishinaabek culture and traditions, including the Chippewa (Ojibwa), Ottawa (Odawa), and Bodawatomi (Potawatomi) bands of the northern Great Lakes region. "Manitou" is their "Great Spirit," the Creator of all, always to be deeply respected.

The Manitou identity is also geographically and historically significant, being applied to a substantial number of communities and locations across North America, including the two northern Lake Michigan islands, a lake in the center of North Manitou itself, and another island in Lake Superior. The name also marks numerous roads, and is prominently displayed on both commercial and pleasure boats, as well as a wide variety of service businesses and products. With its qualities of goodness and strength, "Manitou" endures as an element of faith, and is recognized as holding broad commercial appeal.

For forty years between 1855 and 1895, there was also a Manitou County in northern Lake Michigan, comprised of the two Manitous and numerous more northerly islands, including North and South Fox, as well as those of the larger Beaver Island and its cluster of seven nearby small islands. When the county was terminated, the islands were divided between Charlevoix and Leelanau counties, with only the Manitous, the two most southern islands, being placed in Leelanau, the more southern county.

Island Bound Visitors.
Leelanau Historical Society Museum.

Manitou Passage and adjacent shores, 1844 map.
Author's Collection.

Boating enthusiasts may recall a more recent *Manitou* in American history, associated with President John F. Kennedy. *Manitou* was the US Coast Guard's classic sixty-two-foot "Floating White House," which the young president loved to sail on coastal Atlantic waters. Family members and numerous guests were often aboard, including the famous actress Marilyn Monroe.

Maryland-built and launched in 1937 for a Chicago-based auto racer, the boat was designed with the specific goal of winning the world's longest freshwater race, the annual Chicago to Mackinac competition up the 330-mile length of Lake Michigan. The yacht's name was chosen by her original owner to honor the Manitou Passage to which competitors generally raced after passing the landmark Point Betsie Lighthouse, and heading northeast toward the finish.

In 1938, *Manitou* and her crew promptly achieved their winning goal in record time, and also finished second the next year. The sleek boat's back-to-back wins in the 1940 and 1941 Port Huron to Mackinac races on Lake Huron earned *Manitou* more distinction in the yachting world.

Some years after having been sold following these early triumphs on the Great Lakes, *Manitou* was donated in 1955 to the US Coast Guard for training service at its New London, Connecticut academy. Not long after Kennedy's inauguration, the Coast Guard's leaders, knowing of his passion for sailing, identified the beautiful *Manitou* as appropriate for presidential use, and she was outfitted with the necessary accommodations, communications equipment, etc. for the commander in chief. In later years, no longer required by the Coast Guard, *Manitou* was returned to private ownership, having been sold to a group that offered the illustrious boat for charter in the Mediterranean Sea.

John F. Kennedy sailing the US Coast Guard
presidential yacht, *Manitou*.
Author's Collection.

It is noteworthy that the Sleeping Bear National Lakeshore's origins stem from several public policy intentions, embodying both conservation and recreation motivations.

Apart from this interesting presence in presidential history, one of the most distinctive places where the Manitou identity is now protected is Sleeping Bear Dunes National Lakeshore, within which the two islands and more than thirty miles of Lake Michigan's northeastern shore are part of the US national park system.

It is noteworthy that the Sleeping Bear National Lakeshore's origins stem from several public policy intentions, embodying both conservation and recreation motivations. Impetus for its creation, along with that of other federal parks in the late 1960s, was supplied by a distinguished group, the Outdoor Recreation Resources Review Commission, which Congress had established in 1958, late in President Eisenhower's administration, and also by the National Park Service's "Mission 66" study.

Their efforts illuminated the reality that shoreline development was rapidly reducing the public's accessibility to shoreline on the Atlantic and Great Lakes coasts in particular, and that addressing this issue would require the use of federal funds for land acquisition, an objective secured with Congress's enactment of the Land and Water Conservation Act in 1964. Not only was there this growing awareness of the recreational value of the shoreline, but it was very clear that the units of the national park system were concentrated in the West, where they came, over decades, largely from the public domain, an opportunity that did not exist in the eastern portion of the country, where many millions of people already resided and substantial growth was inevitable. Hence, substantial federal investment for land acquisition and operations was required to effectively address the issue.

Thorough reviews of the remaining shoreline areas on the Great Lakes and eastern ocean shores led to the identification of potential sites, numerous of which in the ensuing years were brought into the national park system, each of them by an individual legislative enactment by Congress addressing its specific characteristics.

After a decade of contentious debate over how best to protect the islands and this beautiful coastline, which encompassed previously established state parks as well as private homes, farms, and other properties, both private and publicly owned, Congress passed legislation, signed into law by President Richard M. Nixon in 1970, to secure them for posterity. (Thus, ironically, both Presidents Kennedy and Nixon, strong political rivals who won seats in Congress in the same post-World War II election and whose later tenures in the nation's highest office both ended sadly, albeit in drastically different forms and degrees, deserve recognition in the Manitou Passage story.)

That organic act of Congress, authorizing the national lakeshore's establishment, recognized the need within this extraordinarily scenic natural environment for its managers to be sensitive to both the conservational and recreational objectives inherent in the national park system, as well as to this shoreline's distinctive cultural values and history.

Through the half-century since the establishment of the national park, except for an interruption due to Lake Michigan's recent extraordinarily high level, visitors can take a privately operated ferry from the mainland town of Leland, crossing the beautiful Manitou Passage to explore the once residential islands. Persons going to the north island need to be prepared for longer than expected camping, as a sudden change in weather, as routinely experienced by ships and their sailors through the years, can interfere with scheduled ferry service.

On the two islands, they have the opportunity to experience not only unique natural features, but also to observe structures rehabilitated by dedicated volunteers in a nonprofit group, Preserve Historic Sleeping Bear, and enjoy activities representing the areas' economic and cultural past.

The park not only embraces the Manitou identity, it also encompasses the sentinel dune whose identity was early known to French traders as "L'ours Qui Dort," the "Sleeping Bear." In this endearing legend, of which there are several slightly varying interpretations, a mother bear sought to escape a forest fire by attempting to swim across Lake Michigan with her two cubs. Being stronger, she outdistanced them and climbed the shoreline dune to eternally await their arrival. The Indians who early came upon this distinctive place saw it as the work of the Great Spirit—the Manitou—who raised the north and south islands from the sea in the cubs' memory and in tribute to the mother's lasting devotion.

Given the Native Americans' presence in the broad area's history, it should be noted that archaeological research has yielded indications that both Manitou islands were residential sites in archeological history. North Manitou holds the greater interest to archeologists studying the region's sites of encampments of Paleo-Indians who hunted behind the last glacial retreat.

For thousands of years, indigenous people are believed to have lived along the Lake Michigan shoreline and its bays and inlets, sustained by hunting, fishing, and gathering plants. During much of the nineteenth century, small Ottawa and Ojibwa settlements were situated along the northern Lake Michigan shoreline, their people seasonally migrating up and down the coast as food supplies were available. The people of an Ottawa village situated on the mainland where the town of Leland developed are thought to have visited the islands to fish and trade, and to have used the Manitou Passage to canoe their way along the shore.

Early Ship Travel in the Manitou Passage

Lake Michigan and its two Manitou islands appeared on nautical maps drawn centuries ago. Ship captains and their crews long ago valued the natural refuge the islands provided them from suddenly violent storms, which were most likely to occur at times of seasonal change as streams of warm and cold air collided over the lake, mounting destructive seas. But there was also the risk that ships sailing the route could face powerful adverse winds and currents that would drive them onto hidden shoals where, as a classic phrase expresses their fate, they would be "pounded to pieces."

Close to 350 years ago, the French explorer Robert Cavalier Sieur de La Salle took note of hazardous shoals off the island and mainland coasts where a ship stranded several hundred yards offshore would be quickly destroyed, particularly in the storms of late fall or an early winter, imperiling the survival of all on board.

Michigan Territory's early Indian agent, Henry Rowe Schoolcraft, referred to a loss of a flotilla of canoes in the passage. While the facts of this report are unknown, contemporary writer Jerry Dennis conjectures, "Probably they were caught in a squall. They come up quickly here, and gain force as they funnel between the islands and the mainland. Fifty canoes, each carrying two, and probably three or more, people. Gone without a trace."

Historian Milo Quaife referred to a diary entry describing a northbound sailing of the *Felicity* (or *Felicitous*) during the month of November, 1779, when the ship's captain, upon arriving off the Manitous, commented, "We cam [sic] to anchor under the lee of the Northmost these islands it looking very blak to North I did not think it prudent to proceed farther, for there is several shoals off from Wabashans point which would be impossible to avoid in a dark night."

As commerce grew, with respect to vessels southbound on the lake, Quaife stressed, "The absence of natural harbors made the navigation of Lake Michigan particularly hazardous for the early mariner. From Green Bay and the Manitous southward there was not a single place of refuge, so that vessels were compelled to anchor in the open lake to receive and discharge passengers and cargo and in case of storms to flee 200 miles or more before shelter could be found."

In 1822, fifteen years before Michigan's statehood, a territorial map showed several landmarks along the northeast coast of Lake Michigan, including a single island identified as "Manitou I," and two notable features of the mainland coast, Sleeping Bear Point and Gravelly Point, the latter being an early designation for Point Betsie.

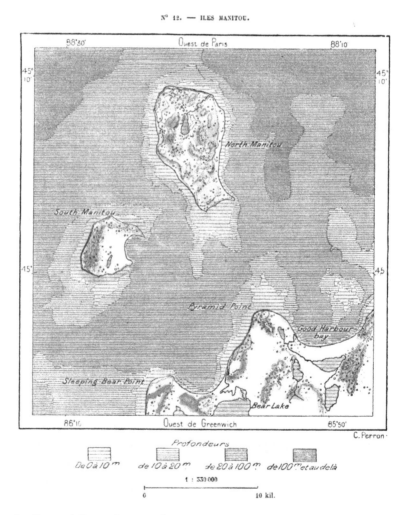

Charles Perron's Late nineteenth-century French Map, "Manitou Isles," 1892.
Author's Collection.

Another early description of the perilous passage comes from an account of an 1838 trip by a noted Frenchman, Francis Comte de Castlenau, who described feeling like a "plaything of the giant waves that pushed us toward the immense bank of sand [Sleeping Bear Dune]." Having previously experienced storms on such tempestuous waters as the English Channel, the Newfoundland coast, and even on long ocean voyages, he added, "Nowhere have I witnessed the fury of the elements comparable to that found on this fresh water sea."

An original wood-engraved and hand-colored map of the Iles Manitou, including the mainland shore from Sleeping Bear Point to Pyramid Point and eastward into Good Harbor Bay, was published in 1892 by renowned French cartographer Charles Perron as one of nearly ten thousand maps in nineteen volumes of *Nouvelle Geographie Universelle*, which he and his associate Élisée Reclus produced between 1876 and 1894.

Particularly noteworthy are the map's horizontal lines and shaded areas revealing the depth of the water around the islands and off the mainland; the lighter the tone and the greater the spread between the lines, the shallower was the water, thus illustrating the risky and the safe areas of passage.

Describing the passage course as a "notorious graveyard," writer Mark L. Thompson projects that current understandings of the losses near the Manitous "probably represents only a small percentage of the actual total."

Claimed by Lake Michigan.
Leelanau Historical Society Museum.

We can presume that wrecks whose loss was unreported at the time, and the remains of others that were said at the time to have "gone missing," will emerge as the technology for deep exploration becomes more effective …

Author Benjamin J. Shelak observes that if all five Great Lakes' tolls are combined, more than ten thousand vessels have been destroyed and some thirty thousand people have died on them, yet he acknowledges that those numbers may fall "far short of the totals." As for the contents of the Lake Michigan graveyard, he cites the route's diverse cargoes including "lumber, coal, gravel, iron ore, china, railroad ties, automobiles, general merchandise, hardware and machine tools, liquor, juke boxes, marble, Christmas trees, and perishables such as grain, fruit, and salt." He writes that three locomotive engines rest on the bottom, two of them having come off a two-master during an 1851 storm, and another that was intentionally pushed off a barge two years later to avoid its capsizing.

We can presume that wrecks whose loss was unreported at the time, and the remains of others that were said at the time to have gone missing, will emerge as the technology for deep exploration becomes more effective, and as they are revealed through the changing lakes' levels working against their shores' sandy banks. LaSalle and other early chroniclers of travel would be surprised that an official underwater preserve now protects the Manitou Passage's discovered wrecks for recreational divers' exploration and enjoyment.

A recent example of an extraordinary discovery is the finding in 2019 of the remains of a small Wisconsin-built schooner, the *W.C. Kimball*, in the depth of the Manitou Passage. Missing for about 130 years, she was sailing northbound from Manistee to her Northport home with a cargo of salt and other items when she disappeared. Amazingly intact, she lies in several hundred feet of water, with her apparently unharmed dinghy just off her stern. The likely, and certainly chilling presumption of her disappearance, is that she was caught in an early spring snowstorm sweeping across the lake, sinking gently to the bottom under the increasingly heavy coat of ice as her crewmen froze to death.

Migration to the Lake Country

The 1825 opening of the Erie Canal proved to have an enormous impact upon the settlement and economic development of the Great Lakes region. The number of inhabitants in Michigan had exploded to nearly four hundred thousand by 1850, with much of the growth reflecting persons traveling primarily from New England and other eastern areas as well as from western European countries. For nearly all of them, travel on Great Lakes vessels was a key part of their journey to their new homesites in the lake country or farther into what was then "the alluring West."

Fur trading, which had been an active economic activity throughout the northwestern Great Lakes, disappeared early in the nineteenth century with the collapse of the European market. But in the early 1840s, steam-powered ships hauling passengers and cargo gradually began to emerge within the Lake Michigan commercial fleet. The islands' abundant forests and bays afforded refuge as well as sites for docks to realize the area's economic potential and lead to settlers' arrival.

In 1833, a steamship is said to have completed the entire trip from Buffalo to Chicago in twenty-five days. Twenty years later, that long voyage was accomplished in just four days.

Steamers had begun regular service between Buffalo and Chicago in the early 1840s, delivering grain from midwestern farms to eastern cities, and conveying travelers and goods to emerging communities in the nation's heartland. Thus, a promising new economic base gradually emerged on the lakes in the form of commercial shipping.

The canal's opening reportedly cut the cost of transporting a ton of freight from Buffalo to Albany from one hundred dollars to less than eight dollars, a reduction that encouraged new immigrants from the eastern US and from European countries, including persons from Scandinavia, Germany, and Ireland, to homestead in the Great Lakes region, including the Manitous. As land was cleared by the cutters, newcomers saw the opportunity to create farms. A new trade economy was born, with surplus agricultural products being sent to eastern markets, and manufactured items from eastern and foreign sources were sent westward.

Researcher Mark Thompson writes that there were 493 ships on the Great Lakes in 1845, only twenty years after the canal's opening. By 1860, there were 1,457 ships in the fleet, and close to double that number just ten years later. After initially consisting primarily of schooners and less numerous wind-powered ships with other rigs, steam technology was increasingly adopted by the laker fleet.

Historians Lawrence and Lucille Wakefield wrote, "By far the busiest place in the Grand Traverse region during the 1840s and early '50s was South Manitou Island. Strategically located on the main waterway for traffic between Chicago and Milwaukee and Buffalo, its harbor was an invitation to passing ships." As storms presented Great Lakes captains with serious threats to their survival, it was not unusual for as many as fifty boats to seek shelter in South Manitou's natural harbor, and it was also a welcomed fuel stop for woodburning steamers.

The Westmoreland *Story*

While the grounding of the schooner *Free Trader* in 1835 and the loss of two of her crew constitutes the first recorded wreck in the Manitou Passage, much more is known of the catastrophe which struck the *Westmoreland* on December 7, 1854, illustrating the peril that even steam-powered vessels could confront on this route, particularly from mid-fall to mid-spring. She was bound from Milwaukee to Mackinac Island with thirty-four passengers and crew aboard, ferrying various supplies, among which was thought to be a substantial amount of gold destined for Fort Mackinac's accounts.

With towering, frigid waves rolling across her deck for hours, the *Westmoreland* became weighed down with ice to the point that her hull began to leak. Bailing virtually nonstop, the crew tried desperately to prevent the incoming water from flooding her boiler and extinguishing her fire. After getting within sight of the South Manitou Island Lighthouse and the island's natural refuge, the bailing crew became overwhelmed. Having lost power, she was unable to withstand the strong north wind and the battering waves that pushed her southward, away from the protection the passage afforded and into the broadly exposed waters of Platte Bay.

The steamer was gone, never to be seen again for a century and a half, when about a decade ago wreck hunter Ross Richardson discovered her remains on the lake bottom. She had carried three lifeboats, but they proved to be tragically inadequate. Nineteen persons climbed into the two smaller boats, and others climbed into the larger boat, which immediately flipped over as it was being lowered, tossing its occupants into the freezing waters. One of the smaller boats also overturned as it neared shore, killing two more men, raising the disaster's toll to seventeen.

Upon reaching the isolated shore, the survivors then faced other challenges in December's brutal weather, some of them walking nearly fifty miles south to Manistee where they could board a ship to Wisconsin, two trekking north to Mackinaw City, and others finding temporary shelter in a cabin.

In his comprehensive 1992 compilation of Great Lakes shipwrecks, author David D. Swayze identified about fifteen reported wrecks that occurred in the vicinity of the Manitou islands prior to the mid-1870s. A notable example is the grain-loaded nine-year-old schooner *Jennie & Annie,* which was driven aground offshore and pounded to pieces near Empire, Michigan, in a mid-November 1872 gale and lost seven of her ten-member crew. Varying lake levels and migrating sand uncovered and recovered portions of her structure through the years.

The *Westmoreland* and *Jennie & Annie* wrecks bring to mind the general description provided by Orange Risdon, who conducted a resurvey of this stretch of mainland shoreline in 1850. He described the high-clay and sandy Empire Bluff and Sleeping Bear ridge as being "not of much value [except] ... as an outlet to the country interior," where he referred to some "good land." But between those towering headlands, and within sight of the national lakeshore's scenic Pierce Stocking Drive, lies one of its natural recreational attractions, North Bar Lake. Risdon described it as "very deep with bold shores and if the bar was cut across and poles driven, it would make a good harbor." Sailors confronting storms in the passage might have welcomed this additional refuge, but the surveyor's suggestion apparently passed unrealized. Visitors to this idyllic protected lake, popular for summer swimming, are cautioned today that it is too shallow for diving. The outlet through the sandbar between North Bar Lake and Lake Michigan comes and goes with the latter's cyclical changes.

Nineteenth-Century Island Life

The initial settlers on the Manitous were men attracted by the opportunity to cut and sell cordwood to fuel the steamers which began operations on Lake Michigan in 1837, a year following statehood. Their days and nights surely must have been rough and lonely. Writer Margaret Fuller, who toured the lakes in 1843 expecting the islands' wilderness to present something of an appealing lifestyle, was shocked by the "unkempt persons" and "slovenly dwellings" of the island's only residents, the woodcutters. Soon thereafter, traveling journalist Thurlow Weed observed, "There were neither animals nor birds and even reptiles were seldom seen; in the absence of all these, even the mosquitos, finding no one to torment, come not to the Manitou Island."

In the mid-1840s, woodcutter Nicholas Pickard came to North Manitou, and gradually became the island's major land owner. Docks were built on both sides of the island, from which wood was sold to steamers that were increasingly cruising Lake Michigan. Until about 1880, when the construction of railroads first made coal available in the lake country, steamship captains depended on the harvested forests of both islands, their vessels consuming enormous quantities of logs on each voyage. On the increasingly common round trip between Buffalo and Chicago, a ship might consume 150 cords or more, a cord being a stack eight feet long, four feet wide, and four feet tall.

Quite a sled load.
Leelanau Historical Society Museum.

Resupplying at a midway port was an essential way to make the long trip, as the space that otherwise would have to be used for fuel storage would significantly reduce the amount of profitable cargo that a ship could carry. Hence, the Manitou Islands were not only refuge for ships caught in storms while traveling the lake between the northern Mackinac Straits and its southern ports, but an essential component of the maritime economy.

As the Manitous' woods inevitably fell victim to the lumberjacks' saws and vessel owners turned to coal as an economical fuel alternative, the cordwood business wound down. South Manitou's timber resource is thought to have been exhausted by 1847, though a notable legacy yet survives at the island's southwestern tip, an extraordinary cluster of giant white cedars. Wind-blown sand chewed up saw blades, prompting lumbermen to leave those trees standing. As the valued resource disappeared, cutters began to shift their attention to the mainland's timber. A trading post that had been operating on South Manitou moved to Glen Arbor in 1848, where a dock and sawmill were later constructed.

Woodcutting, farming, and fishing were the prevailing occupations on the Manitous through the residential decades. On the south island, the 1870 US census included seventy-six people, thirty-four of whom were children age fifteen and under, residing in fourteen dwellings. Eleven of the families were recorded then as farming, three as laborers, one as a retail grocer, and another as a wood merchant.

A German immigrant, George Hutzler, who had arrived in 1850 and was joined by his family six years later, was one of the earliest homesteaders on South Manitou. Those persons who came during the following two decades were generally engaged in farming. As the years went by, orchards, primarily apples and pears, were also established, and the island's isolation eventually made it an attractive site for the experimental cultivation of seeds.

Its harbor area was an active place, with its village, general store, blacksmith shop, dwellings, and outbuildings serving visiting mariners and residents of both islands. A post office opened on the island in 1879, and a school soon thereafter, both of which were operating until World War II.

In 1860, larger North Manitou was the residence of 270 people, compared to just seventy-three on South Manitou. Among the north islanders were a butcher, several fishermen, a carpenter, a wood merchant, a coal dealer, a boardinghouse operator (whose keeper was destined to later lead the island's lifesaving station),

East Side – North Manitou 1908

Top: "Big Wheels" timber transport on North Manitou.
Leelanau Historical Society Museum.

Bottom: North Manitou east dock.
Leelanau Historical Society Museum.

eight fishermen, and twenty-three laborers. Most of the laborers were likely employed in its wooding facilities as the number of steam-powered ships traveling Lake Michigan expanded. North Manitou's first school, built of logs in 1895, served thirty-six children.

Early North Manitou school house.
Leelanau Historical Society Museum.

In a memoir of his childhood years on North Manitou in the early twentieth century when the population had declined, Glenn Furst, who was the stepson of Ernest Hutzler, the keeper of the island's lighthouse, wrote of his older brother and sister walking four and a half miles to and from the fourteen-pupil school each morning and night, along the coastline or through the inland woods. When his siblings were off to school, there was no playmate for him. He could see the South Manitou lighthouse about four miles away and long for his companions there.

For the few residents by that time living on North Manitou, the pains of isolation and loneliness were an unavoidable reality. He remembered being told of a man who had been found frozen to death on the passage's ice, having become lost when he apparently lost sight of the tower's small "winter light" while walking the twelve-plus miles across the ice between the mainland village of Leland and the island.

When the north island's light was automated in 1928, his family clearly welcomed Hutzler's 1928 transfer to South Manitou to be keeper of its less-isolated station, where he had served previously as an assistant keeper for many years. In his memoir, Furst recalls his stepfather saying years later that given the challenges his family had faced, accepting the appointment as lightkeeper on North Manitou was his life's "biggest mistake."

As on the south island, as the lumber business faded, farming gradually became North Manitou Island's dominant economic activity, with crops such as potatoes and cabbage being grown there, and in later years, a variety of orchards were also established on the islands.

Above: Winter takes a toll.

Leelanau Historical Society Museum.

Above right: Boating was important to islanders year-round.

Leelanau Historical Society Museum.

Right: Winter fishing off South Manitou Lighthouse.

Leelanau Historical Society Museum.

Over time, however, agriculture proved not to become the sustainable, long-term economic base for which most residents of both islands likely hoped. The coming of railroads and improved highways serving the northern Michigan mainland, connecting more productive farms with major-market cities, gradually undercut the economic competitiveness of the isolated islands' farms. In the decade between 1860 and 1870, the islands' combined populations fell from 342 to 167, and then to 106 by 1890. The trend continued, and by World War I, most residents of the Manitous had moved to the mainland for a less isolated lifestyle and more secure job prospects.

It was, however, a time when tourism was becoming increasingly important to the economy of northwest Michigan. Steamers of the Manitou Steamship Company, Northern Michigan Transportation Company, and other lines sped the length of Lake Michigan, taking passengers between Chicago and the expanding resort ports. Three times a week during summer, the vessel passed through the passage, stopping at various towns along the way to drop off or board passengers. As one would expect, the *S.S. Manitou*, advertised as "The Greyhound of the Great Lakes," was the fleet's queen.

The Passage Receives U.S. Navigational Aids

As early as 1789, the nation's first year under the Constitution, the need to provide protection for sailors and their ships' cargoes along the Atlantic coast was recognized by the US government. Congress enacted legislation, signed into law by President George Washington, to assume responsibility for the existing scattered lighthouses and for newly constructed lighthouses and other coastal works. The administrative responsibility for lighthouses, their function being to support commerce, was assigned to the Department of the Treasury, of which Alexander Hamilton was first in charge.

The first lighthouses on the Lake Michigan shore were constructed in 1832 at the emerging southern ports of Chicago and St. Joseph, Michigan.

Many years passed, however, before the increasing settlement of the Great Lakes country, with the commensurate growth in its marine traffic, led to appeals for navigational aids on the inland seas. Before statehood, Wisconsin's territorial governor had called for federal funds to improve Lake Michigan's harbors and to construct lighthouses to mark the harbor entrances, which were typically at sandy mouths of rivers that drained into the lake, and to also warn mariners of hidden shallows that could destroy their ships if they sailed too close to shore.

The first lighthouses on the Lake Michigan shore were constructed in 1832 at the emerging southern ports of Chicago and St. Joseph, Michigan. In that same year, the first lightship to be stationed on the lake was moored at Waugoshance Shoal, marking a northern mainland point and cluster of small islands extending several miles into the lake west of the Straits of Mackinac.

Five years later, a search was undertaken by a navy officer to identify possible locations on the lake for additional coastal lights. The south end of South Manitou Island was identified as an appropriate location. Federal funds for the lighthouse's construction were approved, enabling the district superintendent to issue specifications in July 1839 for the construction of the first lighthouse within the Manitou Passage, marking the island's natural harbor of refuge and its emerging business opportunity for refueling steamships.

Lost to history until recently found among archives, the extremely detailed construction proposal specified that the lighthouse was to be built of stone or hard brick, with the foundation being sunk three feet or more for the structure's stability in the presumably sandy shoreline. The light's components would be placed in a round, thirty-foot tower, eighteen feet in diameter at the base and nine feet at the top, the thickness of its walls diminishing upward from three feet to twenty inches. The dwelling, also of stone or hard brick, was to be thirty-by-twenty feet, with an attached fourteen-by-twelve foot kitchen. An outhouse and well were also to be provided.

The facility's stationary light was to be produced by the then-common system, bearing the last name of its Swiss physicist inventor, of eleven oil-filled Argand lamps, each equipped with fourteen-inch reflectors containing six ounces of silver. This seemingly substantial station offered guidance to Passage mariners for a decade or more.

At the time of its construction, lighthouses were still the immediate responsibility of a treasury department official known as the "Fifth Auditor," whose lackluster performance was the subject of much criticism from the rapidly expanding maritime industry …

At the time of its construction, lighthouses were still the immediate responsibility of a treasury department official known as the "Fifth Auditor," whose lackluster performance was the subject of much criticism from the rapidly expanding maritime industry and eventually resulted in a major restructuring of lighthouse management. That came in 1852 with the creation of the US Lighthouse Board, which was composed primarily of military officers determined to expand the country's coastal lights and improve their operation. This body supervised the construction and maintenance of lights and other emerging aids to navigation for over half a century, until lighthouses were placed under more civilian administration by the Department of Commerce in 1910.

In that same year of 1852, a light was built on the northwest mainland point that separates Grand Traverse Bay from Lake Michigan to guide vessels to the north entrance of the Manitou Passage. This first Grand Traverse light was installed in a relatively low tower, situated close to shore and adjacent to a separate keeper's dwelling.

With lake travel continuing to grow, the nearly twenty-year-old lighthouse on South Manitou was replaced in 1858 by a white brick building that housed a fourth-order Fresnel lens, set sixty-four feet above sea level to increase the visibility of its fixed light. The station was also equipped with a bell to alert ships sailing in fog of their hazardous, shallow location.

Known by the name of their distinguished French designer, physicist Augustin Fresnel, lenses of his truly revolutionary design featured a configuration of reflecting and refracting prisms to produce a beam about eight times more powerful than the reflector-based system that the US had used previously. Of the total 320 lighthouses that then existed on the ocean and Great Lakes coasts, only a small fraction had been equipped with Fresnel lenses, which had been used for years in Europe. Not only were the lights produced by the lenses much more effective than reflectors, but their oil consumption was cut in half or more.

Under the board's leadership, the use of Fresnel lenses quickly became standard policy in American lighthouses. Just under a decade later, at the start of the Civil War, 486 lights were in service, all with lenses, and by 1876 that total had been raised to 637 lights, and also thirty lightships.

First-order Fresnel lenses, the largest and most powerful type, were installed at critically important points on the ocean coasts. Generally, midsized lenses of the fourth and fifth orders, as well as a very few third-order lenses, were placed in lighthouses along the Great Lakes.

Also in 1858, with the six-year old Grand Traverse Light's visibility having proven inadequate and its foundation deteriorating, that structure was replaced with a taller brick building, with its lantern located above the dwelling. The fixed white light emanating from a fifth-order Fresnel lens, which was soon replaced by a larger fourth-order model, was positioned forty-seven feet above the lake's high level.

The lighthouse board completed one more important construction project in that busy year of 1858, a brick lighthouse and attached tower at Point aux Bec Scies (the then-common French spelling), a distinctive mainland promontory about twenty miles south of South Manitou Island. The light's primary function was to guide northbound ships toward the passage and to mark the location where southbound ships leaving the passage's protection would set courses for down-lake ports. First lit on October 20, 1858, the light became nightly operational in early 1859. The station's distinguishing characteristic, displayed from its fourth-order Fresnel lens, was a fixed white light varied every ninety seconds by a distinctive white flash. The pattern was modified later to a revolving white flash every ten seconds.

A lighthouse was constructed in 1867 at the southeast end of South Fox Island, northwest of North Manitou. Its flashing red beam, exhibited from an attached square tower in which the light was placed sixty-eight feet above the lake, guided ships sailing to or from the passage through an eighteen-mile course of varying depths.

In 1871, a one-hundred-foot brick tower was built at the South Manitou Island Light Station to replace the 1858-designed lamp room situated atop the keeper's residence. Raising the light by nearly forty feet to further increase its visibility, the new tower was equipped with a more powerful, third-order Fresnel lens.

Further attesting to the South Manitou station's important role for passage mariners, in 1875 the station became the site of Lake Michigan's first steam-powered fog whistle, blasting for four seconds each minute. The official *Light List* advised mariners that "in case of accidents to the steam fog-whistle, the fog-bell struck by machinery would be sounded." (In later-constructed fog signal facilities, duplicate equipment typically was installed to avoid interruptions by an equipment failure.)

In 1891, a fog signal was installed at Point aux Bec Scies in a new structure immediately north of the lighthouse. It was built with iron sides to protect the building from the intense heat buildup caused by burning of wood or coal to generate the steam pressure that powered the whistle, originally a five-second blast

South Manitou Island Light
and Fog Signal Station, ca. 1885.
Leelanau Historical Society Museum.

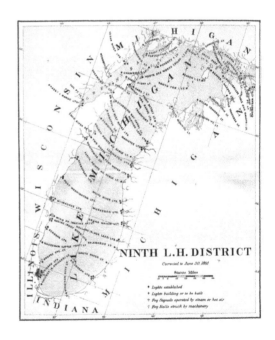

Map of Lake Michigan
lighthouses, June 30, 1891.
Author's collection.

followed by ten seconds of silence, then another five-second blast followed by forty silent seconds.

Similarly illustrating the increasing recognition of the importance of navigational assistance in foggy weather, a steam fog-whistle also was installed in 1900 at the Grand Traverse station, blasting unequally once every forty-five seconds: a three-second blast followed by twelve seconds of silence, then a six-second blast followed by twenty-four seconds of silence.

Just as every light's pattern (its characteristic) was unique to its service area, so too was the timing of its fog signal blasts, assisting sailors at night and in the fog to know their position and course. Mariners in the passage were heavily dependent upon keepers' maintenance of their station's equipment, day and night. During the decades before fog horns could be powered by electricity, an hour might pass before fire-built pressure became sufficient to sound the horn, making for nervousness among mariners groping their way through the lake's offshore soup.

Superintendents regularly inspected the stations and evaluated their equipment to ensure the accuracy of their light, the operation of their fog signal, and the thoroughness of the station's upkeep, awarding stations with outstanding performance a sought-after pennant.

Until a technician could reach isolated stations to make major repairs, keepers were forced to rely upon their own creative abilities to keep their stations' vital equipment operational. Given that a missing light or whistle's silence could prove disastrous for a ship and those aboard it, the keepers' skills were essential. Through more than a century of light stations' operations by resident crews, their performance was truly legendary.

Concerns as to the adequacy of lighthouse coverage within the passage were still being raised in the late nineteenth century, despite the significant navigational aids that were in place. For example, in its 1892 report, the lighthouse board discussed the "immense commerce" between the Straits of Mackinac and Green Bay, which utilized three different courses, the choice depending entirely upon prevailing weather conditions. Acknowledging that the two northernmost passages were already served by lights at White Shoal (about twenty miles west of Mackinac), Squaw Island (the most northern of the islands in the group around Beaver Island), and Seul Choix Point (on Lake Michigan's north coast), the board counseled that the substantial vessel traffic in the passage north of North Manitou Island lacked adequate light service.

North Manitou Island Light and Fog Signal, ca. 1900.

Leelanau Historical Society Museum.

With South Fox Island Light being seventeen miles away, the board proposed that a light and fog signal be constructed at the north end of North Manitou Island, saying it would be valuable to vessels passing between South Fox Island and North Manitou Island.

Six years later, when a lighthouse finally was erected on North Manitou, it was not at the initially recommended site but at the island's southeastern tip, where dangerous shoals extending from both the island and the mainland's Pyramid Point lined a sailing course less than two miles wide. The new station's light alternately flashed red and white every twenty seconds during the navigation season, and the crew operated a steam fog signal when needed. A small winter light was provided during the less actively sailed months.

Despite the north island station's navigational benefits, seamen continued to deem the passage inadequately protected. The lighthouse board and the Department of Commerce and Labor responded to the concerns in 1907: "In recent years, owing to the deeper loading of the lake steamers, a shoal has developed southeast of North Manitou Island. With the exception of this shoal this

is the safest passage through Lake Michigan and is largely used. Owing to the close proximity of Pyramid Point to the eastward it is impracticable for masters to accurately locate the position of their vessels in thick weather."

The proposed remedy was the stationing of a light vessel on the easterly and southeast shoal. The department soon approved an appropriation for the establishment of the recommended navigational aid. The wooden-hulled, one-hundred-foot-long LV 56, more commonly known as *Manitou,* as these ships displayed the name of their current station on their sides, was first anchored off North Manitou's shoal in 1910. The ship's lighting apparatus consisted of three oil-burning lanterns hoisted up each of her two masts. She was also equipped with a steam fog-whistle and a hand-operated bell.

An officer and seven men, each with a specific responsibility such as lamp trimming, were on board; the crewmen generally served for two months on, then one month off, while the officer rotated with a colleague, each serving one month on, then one month doing shore duty. Lightship personnel dealt with unique circumstances—not only lengthy confinement and isolation from shore, but a vessel rocking up and down, this way and that, while being chained to the bottom.

Lightship service at North Manitou continued for twenty-five navigational seasons, three different vessels being stationed there. Five-ton permanent mooring sinkers and chains held the ships on station during the navigational season, and then they were laid up for the winter at mainland ports such as Frankfort and Charlevoix.

Meanwhile, the island's own lighthouse continued operations until 1935. Soon thereafter, however, its fog signal was washed into the lake. The light tower suffered the same fate in 1942, and the brick keeper's dwelling was lost to the inland sea in the early 1970s.

The lightship service was replaced in 1936 by a steel structure mounted on a concrete- and rock-filled foundation set on the bottom in the middle of the passage. Manned by a resident crew that rotated every two weeks until it was automated in 1980, the isolated crib displayed a red flashing light every fifteen seconds and sounded a horn every twenty seconds from its mid-passage site when needed. Now privately owned and awaiting a future use, the structure is closely visible from boats going to the Manitous from Leland.

The light stations provided mariners with vitally important navigational assistance for many decades. Those which still serve as official aids to navigation operate automatically, so there are no on-site residents. While hundreds of shipwrecks are scattered on the lakes' bottoms, far more vessels managed to avoid destruction and the loss of their crews' lives by virtue of lighthouses' warnings of dangerous shoals, and their guidance toward harbors of refuge during hazardous weather conditions.

Great Lakes lightkeeping records and the stories dedicated keepers passed to their descendants are a valuable legacy of lonely service that was essential to the survival of ships and thousands of lake seamen. The lives of those serving on a lightship or on islands such as the Manitous, separated from the mainland that they could see in the distance but reach infrequently and briefly, were a challenge.

As North Manitou descendant Furst wrote, "One of the first letters an assistant or keeper would write upon arriving at North Manitou light station was a letter to the Superintendent of Lighthouses requesting a transfer to a shore station." The head-quarters' response was predictable; the request would be filed for consideration when an opening was available. The applicant likely would give up after several years, moving off the island and seeking other employment on the less-isolated mainland.

Rescue Boats Are Assigned
to the Great Lakes

As essential as lights and fog signals were for the safety of vessels traveling the Manitou Passage, as lake commerce rapidly expanded in the middle of the nineteenth century, appeals mounted for government-provided rescue facilities for seamen, their ships, passengers, and cargoes.

In the late 1840s, the US government had finally established primitive lifesaving stations at dangerous spots along the Atlantic coast, long after public policymakers became aware of the heroic rescue stations positioned along the rugged coasts of England and Holland. Other than this initial federal response, the only aid had come from nongovernmental organizations that had constructed small boathouses and other small buildings along the coast to shelter the survivors of near-shore groundings who managed to reach land alive.

Also, lightkeepers at some ocean shore locations were gradually equipped with small boats in which they could attempt to save sailors from ships they observed to be breaking up in shoreline surf. Not until well into the nineteenth century did Congress finally approve significant federal funding to expand lifesaving service at hazardous locations along the northeastern American coast.

As for the Great Lakes, the initial federal response to increasing disasters there came later, starting gradually in the mid-1850s, as the pace of settlement and associated commerce on the inland seas rapidly expanded. The rapid increase in the population of Lake Michigan cities itself speaks of the huge growth of lake travel that occurred during several decades before and after the middle of the century, when Chicago's population was just under thirty thousand. By 1860, Chicago, the youngest American city with a population above one hundred thousand, had 109,000 residents. Ten years later, its population was just under 299,000. In 1880, the city had swelled to 503,000, and by 1890 its population was almost 1.1 million.

Milwaukee's population rose during the same four decades, from twenty thousand to a little over 204,000. Meanwhile, the count in Muskegon, on Lake Michigan's eastern shore, went from less than one thousand to more than 22,700. The growth of marine traffic during the period was similarly notable.

The federal government's first response to the dangers of the Great Lakes was the acquisition of Francis Metallic surfboats, named for their inventor Joseph Francis, who produced them in his New York factory. Composed of corrugated iron that was pressed into the proper shape by equipment he had designed, these open, double-ended, non-self-bailing surfboats measured from twenty-six to twenty-seven feet in length and a maximum six feet in width. Given their considerable weight, they could only be stationed at sites where they could be quickly launched and gotten underway by six or eight muscular oarsmen.

Between the late 1840s and early 1850s, just under fifty of these boats were placed at scattered points on the Great Lakes, each under the responsibility of a local resident. Two dozen boats were assigned to Lake Michigan (more than at any other lake), two of them being positioned in the Manitou Passage, one at South Manitou, where it was the responsibility of Lightkeeper Alonzo Slyfield, and the other at North Manitou, where private pier owner and wood seller Nicholas Pickard assumed its responsibility under bond. As custodians were expected to bear the costs of their care, maintenance varied widely, but Pickard built a rare boathouse, the only surviving such structure, at his North Manitou post.

Hence, at these islands and other widely dispersed sites elsewhere on the Great Lakes, this initial government-provided life-saving presence amounted to a boat, a man in charge, and anyone he could persuade to help him undertake rescues. When the fishing was really good and its profits especially enticing, it wasn't always easy to convince reliable volunteers to abandon the promising fishing grounds and row a boat into dangerous seas.

The limitations aside, these boats were for some wreck mariners the difference between life and death. (A treasured Francis metallic boat which was assigned to the Saugatuck lighthouse for many decades has been restored by local historical society volunteers, and is viewable in adjacent Douglas, Michigan.)

Lightkeeper Slyfield's
South Manitou Rescue

South Manitou's Lightkeeper Slyfield's memorable performance on a stormy June night in 1854, when he spotted the brigantine *J.Y. Scammon* being battered just offshore by gale-force winds in the Manitou Passage, provides a memorable example of a rescue that could be mounted by a sole responsible individual with a small boat:

> *I saw the doomed vessel slowly nearing the beach, and knowing she would soon be ashore if her anchors did not fetch her up, and [be] among the breakers that were dashing and boiling and foaming while against the shore, and perhaps drown the crew, I came to the conclusion that something must be done to get communication to them. The thought came to me like a flash to write a note and send it to them in a bottle. I then took a small bottle in my hands, held them aloft, and made signs to the crew to send me a small line, which they soon understood, and fastening a line to a buoy and throwing it overboard was but a moment's work. It soon reached the shore. I attached the bottle containing the note and it was hauled on board, and the passengers, as well as the crew on board, were not long in learning my design, and a shout of joy went up from every mouth. The note was, 'Can I render you any assistance? If so, send word by bottle.' The answer came back by the same trusty little messenger, saying 'Our big chain has parted, and the small one will not hold us long. Look out for us ashore.'*

His account continued, "I patrolled and in about an hour after that, the brig came on broadside. The men launched a spare spar over the rail, an end resting in shoal water. The mate mounted it and slid down, and wading through the water, was helped ashore. Next followed four ladies, who came ashore in about the same manner, the mate and I assisting them as they came in reach. And so all the crew were safely landed, much to their joy."

Both the gratitude of the women rescued and a touch of irony mark the end of that story. Slyfield, who had spent his early career as a doctor in southeast Michigan but had curtailed his medical practice there due to his own illness, had moved his wife, Alice, and their young family to isolated South Manitou upon learning of the opportunity for steady employment as the lightkeeper. Upon returning to the station after this creative rescue, he learned that while he was performing his rescue, Alice had given birth to an eight-pound son.

Perhaps she had something to say about that, such as, "So where was the doctor when I needed him?" At South Manitou, and more extensively at his subsequent long tenure at Point aux Bec Scies Lighthouse, his medical experience was called upon, necessitating many miles' travel, sometimes in hazardous conditions, to treat seriously injured or ill residents. Members of his family would do their best to keep the light burning properly during his absence. Thus, "Doc" Slyfield served the people of his surroundings, on land and lake, with two highly valued skills.

Lake Crises Heighten Appeals for Surfmen

The Great Lakes, according to the US Life-Saving Service, "present peculiar and distinctive characteristics. They are a cluster of seas, enormous in their extent, containing about 80,000 square miles, and frequented by an immense commerce. Their American coastline is nearly 2,500 miles in length. Excepting for certain periods at the opening and close of navigation, during the spring and fall, their waters are generally tranquil, though at times swept by sudden and violent storms."

The description continued, "Their natural harbors are few, and these are mostly narrow and lie at the mouths of small rivers, from which piers and breakwaters have been built and jut for a considerable distance. Unlike our other coasts, they are closed to navigation by ice for five or six months of the year." Not mentioned in that statement was the fact that the months of early spring and late fall posed the greatest risks to the lakes' commercial mariners, who commonly sought to maximize the return on their financial investment by sailing at those times.

Summing up the realities, particularly of Lake Michigan, the service cautioned, "It has regular shores; no islands except in its northern portion; few harbors and bays, and is subject to severe storms at certain times of the year."

It took devastating storms in 1870-71 on the eastern coast and Great Lakes to provoke Congress and the executive branch to address the rising incidence of disasters on the inland seas. Records indicate that more than two hundred persons lost their lives on the Great Lakes during that winter, when more than 1,100 wrecks are said to have occurred. It was becoming clear that without new leadership at the top level, and trained station crews ever ready for action, the calls for expanded protection of the nation's mariners would not be met.

A response came in the spring of 1871, when Congress passed legislation appropriating $200,000 for the employment of paid surfmen, to be hired and trained under the direction of experienced station keepers. To administer the expanded federal effort, the secretary of the treasury appointed Sumner I. Kimball, a department lawyer, as head of the Revenue Marine, to which the responsibility for lifesaving stations was initially assigned. Kimball proved to be an outstanding selection, bringing to the position both his respected capabilities and a commitment to fiscal responsibility.

A commission soon was appointed to advise Congress as to coastal locations, including on the Great Lakes, where "commerce and humanity required the establishment of lifesaving stations." The investigation, which found the nation's existing operations inadequate in multiple respects, lent support for Kimball's determination to thoroughly reorganize the nation's lifesaving functions and facilities, and vastly strengthen their management.

One early recommendation addressing travel in the Manitou Passage was the establishment of a fully staffed lifesaving station at Sleeping Bear Point, a goal not to be achieved, however, for more than a quarter century.

One early recommendation addressing travel in the Manitou Passage was the establishment of a fully staffed lifesaving station at Sleeping Bear Point, a goal not to be achieved, however, for more than a quarter century. Attempting to bring effective management to the fledgling US lifesaving operations, Kimball and his leadership team developed a classification system for proposed stations, based upon their individual circumstances. So-called "complete" (or "first class") lifesaving stations typically would be constructed along isolated coasts with flat beaches and offshore bars, and far distant from population centers where crewmen to conduct a rescue might quickly be found. These stations would be staffed with paid crews and well equipped for marine rescues: a surfboat, rocket and mortar apparatus for firing a line to a vessel stranded offshore, a life car (a hatch-covered, tube-like enclosure used to bring as many as a half-dozen persons to land from a ship stranded offshore), and other essential items.

These complete stations would house the crew as well as afford temporary quarters for persons rescued off wrecked vessels, and contain the necessary cooking utensils, bedding, and so forth. Their construction was to be aimed primarily at the mid- and south-Atlantic coast, and at a few locations on the Great Lakes "where such protection seemed requisite," the service explained.

Lifesavers, top to bottom.
Leelanau Historical Society Museum.

Seven men would be employed at a complete station: six surfmen (the number of pulling [i.e., rowing] positions in a surfboat) and the keeper, who would handle the long steering oar. The men were to be known by numbers for the purposes of efficient command, No. 1 being the most skilled and trusted man (he and No. 2 would hold the stroke positions in the boat). He would be capable of taking charge of a rescue, or of the station temporarily, in the event of the keeper's absence or incapacity to serve.

In addition to his critical boat management requirements, the station's keeper was responsible for the maintenance of the station's property, and of property recovered from a wreck until it was retrieved by a ship owner. The keeper bore the responsibility for recruiting and managing his crew, and for leading and evaluating their unending daily drills on land and lake to bring their performance to the standards demanded by the agency's periodically visiting inspectors.

A complete station's complement of surfmen was later expanded to a total of seven, so that one of them, generally No. 7, would be left to man the station, aware of his crewmates' location when they were responding to a crisis. That man was also expected to receive shipwreck victims, protect the station's property, and potentially to organize an attempt to rescue his crewmates in the event their response to a wreck endangered their survival. (Later, the service sought unsuccessfully to win approval for the employment of an eighth surfman, primarily to assist in launching and retrieving boats in treacherous surf.)

The second category, lifeboat stations, would be similar in concept to the Francis boat precedent, but under better management and situated far more widely. They would be established at sites where a self-righting and self-bailing boat could be readily launched, such as harbor entrances, or at narrow or crowded waterways where collisions or other accidents might be anticipated.

There would be no hired surfmen at lifeboat stations, the presumption being that enough able-bodied males would be resident in the immediate vicinity from which a keeper could recruit volunteers for rescues. As housing for rescued persons would likely be available nearby, these smaller stations would be designed to accommodate only the boat and some equipment.

...lifesaving functions officially became the US Life-Saving Service, a distinctive agency of the US treasury department.

In proposing this class of station, Kimball and his colleagues indicated that compensation should be paid to volunteers for services rendered at each shipwreck. Initially amounting to three dollars per rescue only when a life was saved and without regard to the risks the surfmen themselves took in attempting the rescue, these payment policies proved to be a recurring issue.

As for the development of an agency headquarters and staff, in fiscal 1876, spanning July 1, 1875, to June 30, 1876, the government's geographically spreading lifesaving functions officially became the US Life-Saving Service, a distinctive agency of the US treasury department. In the following spring, when Rutherford B. Hayes succeeded President Grant, Kimball continued his leadership as the agency's general superintendent. He was destined to lead the service through more than four decades, its entire history, achieving a uniquely long and distinguished tenure in government.

"LEMONADE LUCY"

President Hayes is not only remembered for having prevailed in the hotly contested 1876 election that was settled by a congressionally created commission only days prior to Inauguration Day, but also for his wife's being the nation's first first lady to hold a college degree. More relevant here, however, is her coming to be known as "Lemonade Lucy."

The story stems from the presidential couple's having barred alcoholic drinks from the White House, a prohibition which provoked much critical banter within the Washington social circle. Some persons apparently were voicing doubt that official dinners and receptions at the president's home would continue to be enjoyable under such strict terms. The secretary of state wondered aloud how foreign diplomats could be expected to attend events under the teetotaling policy.

A creative steward is said to have come to the critics' rescue by fashioning a sherbet-like drink, roman punch, composed of beaten egg whites, sugar, and lemon juice, which disguised a tasty amount of Caribbean rum. Initially infused in oranges to hide its banned content, it was later served in glasses, but with its rum apparently never being revealed to the hosts. Presumably reflecting growing public interest in the innovative marine rescue program, the punch's service quickly came known about town as the White House's "lifesaving station"!

Building a Professional Lifesaving Program

General Superintendent Kimball reported that not as much progress had been achieved in opening new stations during 1876 as anticipated, owing to "unexpected and unavoidable delays in obtaining sites" and in getting new construction underway. The only complete stations then in operation on Lake Michigan were at Point aux Bec Scies, with Thomas E. Matthews as keeper, and at Grand Point au Sable, more than sixty miles farther south on the Michigan shore. The service planned to have only one other complete station on all of Lake Michigan, and it was still under construction at Evanston, Illinois's Grosse Point; when operational, its surfmen, uniquely, were students at adjacent Northwestern University.

Respecting the precedent of the Francis lifeboat on North Manitou, Kimball and his team reported that a lifeboat station would be established at Pickard's Wharf. The station was reported in 1876 as finished but not equipped, and its keeper not yet selected. Eight other lifeboat stations were planned to be established at sites around Lake Michigan. The following fiscal year's report indicates that the North Manitou Island facility had opened on June 23, 1877, with resident Daniel Buss as keeper, and not long afterward had an employed crew of six men. (Where volunteers had proven difficult to recruit at some Great Lakes locations, stations were permitted to hire some surfmen. Within two years, however, sufficient appropriations had been secured to permit the employment of regular crews at all stations on the lakes where necessary, enhancing the stations' potential for service.)

As liaisons between the Washington headquarters and the individual stations, district superintendents were provided an annual salary of $1,000. Assistant superintendents would earn $500 a year, and station keepers just $200 yearly. The frugal Kimball was doubtless pleased to inform the department and Congress that because the Lake Michigan district's initial superintendent had served only for the last month in the fiscal year (at that time, federal financial years started on July 1 and ended the following June 30), his service's cost had been a mere $85.15!

The $200 annual keepers' rate derived from 1854's very limited program. Thrifty though he was, Kimball was deeply troubled that this amount was still in effect in 1876. He and his senior administrators insisted that it was "never sufficient" and had become "glaringly inadequate" over the ensuing twenty years with the erosion of its purchasing power.

"Unless an adequate compensation is provided for these officers, the service must inevitably suffer, and the country be disgraced."

Viewed on the basis of the typical eight-month active season on the Great Lakes (as well as in some other areas), a station keeper's annual rate of $200 would amount, monthly, to significantly less than the forty dollars a month received by the surfmen he recruited and led during the eight months when the crew was required to live at the station. If needed to respond to a wreck during their station's four-month inactive period, surfmen were paid three dollars for that effort. The requirement that surfmen pay for their meals and uniforms did not offset the obvious inequity in monthly compensation. (The purchasing power of forty dollars and $200 in the mid-1870s would today slightly exceed $1,000 and $5,100, respectively.)

The treasury secretary reported in 1876 that he shared the general superintendent's concerns, recalling that "in 1871, it had been only barely possible to secure proper men" at the $200 annual rate, and adding that the service's ability to retain them had been eroded as their prospects for an increase had not been realized. He added, "This hope has almost ceased to exist, and the superintendents of the districts represent that the difficulty of obtaining good keepers verges upon impossibility." He warned, "Unless an adequate compensation is provided for these officers, the service must inevitably suffer, and the country be disgraced."

The service's report raised the sensitive issue of lifesaving station keepers' compensation compared to that of the US lightkeepers, whose agency, housed in the Department of Commerce, was funded through a different appropriations measure. The service pressed Congress that lifesaving keepers' pay should equal that of lightkeepers "whose virtues are mainly comprised in the somewhat passive duty of vigilance...the unsleeping watch of a lamp," as they expressed it, their compensation averaging about $600 a year.

Kimball's reasoning that his own agency's keepers, who bore the same risks as their surfmen, is aptly expressed in the foreboding maxim: "You have to go out, but you don't have to come back." They deserved to be paid at least comparably to their lightkeeping brethren. This issue was particularly sensitive at sites where lighthouse keepers and rescue stations were situated side by side.

The 1877 report again criticized the $200 figure: "The renewed recommendation for its increase is made under a painful sense of exigency, derived from the knowledge that it is no longer possible to keep or obtain competent men upon the old terms in such positions, and the gloomy anticipation that with the inferior officers who must succeed them, injury and calamity to maritime interests are pending, involving the dwindling of the service and the shame of the country."

Pleading its case, the service wrote, "The cannon demands the cannoneer, and the lifeboat requires the lifeboatman." It added that the service is "in fact, virtually a profession, requiring regular and sedulous instruction and practice, and the existing law should be so amended as to render it fully efficacious."

In 1878, keepers of lifesaving stations finally received an annual salary increase to $400. The relentless Kimball's 1880 report renewed his concern that surfmen's pay rate was still inadequate, supported by a new justification: the substantially higher compensation being offered by Great Lakes steamer and schooner operators, who were aggressively recruiting reliable crewmen. Kimball pointed out that seamen then were making two dollars per day during summer service on the Great Lakes, and double that in the autumn, with their meals provided, while the lifesavers received approximately $1.33 per day which, after allocating forty cents for their board, left only ninety-three cents for all their other needs. He put forward his case:

"Heroes on 93 cents a day, especially if they have large families to support, however full of human kindness or prone to daring exploits, will inevitably yield to the plump $2, or the fat $4 per diem of the Lake schooner or steamer," warned Kimball, adding, "with the flesh-pots of the cook's galley thrown in by way of garnish. The consequence is that all the best men will be drawn from the stations by the Lake marine, forcing the employment of raw, crude, unskilled, or commonplace surfmen to fill the deserted places."

The service's appeals continued a year later, insisting that the pay of station keepers was indefensible when compared to that of lightkeepers:

On bad nights, the keeper, a brave, live, faithful man, is out with the patrols to make sure that there is no shirking. On him rests the unceasing care to see that the work is done; to shore up the under-paid, perhaps disheartened men to the nightly task of risking health, life, and limb in the watch for ships in danger. At wrecks, as in a recent instance, he takes the steering oar and guides the surfboat through miles of seas which make the boldest crew white.... For all this, $400 a year! Meanwhile, $800 a year, and two assistants at $400 each, for the adjacent lightkeeper, ensconced aloft in his solid chamber, near the lens, when death and tempest walk the strand with the patrolmen.

It took unceasing appeals such as this on behalf of lifesaving station keepers—often emphasizing the seeming unfairness compared to their brethren at the lights—to wrest an increase to $700 a year in the mid-1880s, and eventually to $1,000.

The service also took issue with a provision under which enrolled volunteers (men who regularly participated in a lifeboat station's training drills, and thus could be counted upon to serve effectively in a rescue effort) would be eligible for ten dollars only if lives were actually saved in the mission. This quickly proved to be counterproductive to the recruitment of volunteers, as it denied compensation not only for their training time, but for rescue efforts that did not result in a saving of life, even though they could result in volunteers' own injury or death. Nor did this policy recognize that potential candidates who had other jobs, and families to feed, might lose their regular job's pay when called away for a rescue.

Another objective of Kimball's, as presumably crafted by the service's group of skilled Washington writers, was to extend pension benefits and disability compensation to keepers and their crews. The report emphasized, "these crews are composed of poor fishermen, who live scantly, and find a main means of support in the slender pay they receive as surfmen. Grown old or become disabled in the service, they sink into penury or dependence, and when they lose their lives...in attempting to save others, or when they die in the course of nature, their death, after all their valuable and heroic service, leaves their families in poverty and want."

The lack of pensions for retired, longtime lifesaving station keepers clearly left them in difficult straits, as illustrated by a long-time Point aux Bec Scies captain in his nineties who, having retired after more than forty years of federal service, was mowing lawns to meet his needs.

The service's eloquence continued, "It should be borne in mind that they are the very flower of their class—hardy and able seamen, dexterous and courageous, matchless in managing boats in heavy seas and in the perilous neighborhood of wrecks, and of such approved integrity that the property of mariners and passengers, and the cargoes of vessels saved by their efforts, suffer no loss at their hands."

"It is because he does this that, grown veteran or infirm, or falling on the battlefield, we recognize his right and the right of his family to support at the expense of the public he guards."

Summing up the service administrators' compensation concerns, the report argued, "The soldier, in this age, is known, and is only justified, as one who professionally stakes his life in the defense of his fellow citizens. It is because he does this that, grown veteran or infirm, or falling on the battlefield, we recognize his right and the right of his family to support at the expense of the public he guards. These life-saving crews—these storm-soldiers—render a similar service, and no less dangerous and noble, and they deserve the same substantial recognition."

Surfboats and Lifeboats: Debating Their Respective Merits

In the service's 1876 report, Superintendent Kimball and his colleagues extensively discussed the respective qualities of surfboats, which had served effectively for years on the Atlantic coast, and of heavier and more durable lifeboats. Boats of both designs would be used for many years by lifesaving crews, and debate over their respective advantages and disadvantages was destined to continue for decades. A station's preference would often depend on where a rescue was best initiated from: if from a beach, a boat would have to be hauled down the sand, in which case the lighter surfboat was advantageous; or if from a ramp or harbor launch, a heavier boat could be more easily deployed.

Acknowledging the differences of opinion among various experts as to whether self-righting and self-bailing lifeboats were preferable to the "best surf-boats," Kimball took note of rescues from two severe gale-wrecked ships by the Grand Haven, Michigan lifesaving crew, which had used an "improved surf-boat" rather than "the excellent self-righting and self-bailing life-boat." The station reported, "The management of the surf-boat by the surfmen employed upon our coast is superbly skillful, and they believe that the little craft in their hands will safely ride through any sea in which any life-boat can live."

However, the service's officers believed that "the weight of opinion...was in favor of the self-righting and self-bailing boat where its use is practicable," based on its qualities that would enable crewmen to survive a capsize, and its greater strength that would withstand an impact with a ship's hull or wreckage during an attempted rescue. Kimball foresaw that "if a self-righting and self-bailing boat can be devised, capable of being used at our stations, it will, after the surfmen have become thoroughly familiar with it, supersede the surf-boat on the severest occasions."

The superintendent of the Lake Michigan district, where lifeboats had been furnished to all its lifeboat stations on account of their greater buoyancy, capacity, and self-righting and self-bailing capabilities, had reported that their "crews rendered assistance to distressed ships when the most powerful tugs and steam craft refused to go out of the harbor, declaring that no vessel could live in the heavy seas."

He cited an instance in which a crew had "rendered aid to a vessel when thousands of people standing upon the docks declared that there was nothing made by man that could go out through the surf and sea then raging, and return with safety." He added, "The people here are beginning to regard the self-righting and self-bailing life-boat as one of the wonders of the world."

His colleague who had charge of the stations on Lakes Huron and Superior, however, said the following with respect to their surf-boat stations: "The keepers and crews…are continually recounting the wonderful qualities of their particular boat in heavy surf. They all have been thoroughly tried." He wrote of a personal experience when he had to go many miles from a station to Whitefish Point where he could catch a steamer, thus avoiding a four-day delay:

I was not able to walk, and the wind was blowing a gale directly off the lake. The surf was very high and furious. I ordered the surf-boat out. The keeper could not believe me in earnest; but was soon convinced that I was. The boat was taken to the beach, headed out, two men placed in the bows, the rest strung along her sides; and when a favorable opportunity came, the order to launch was given; but the effort was a failure; the boat was thrown ashore with a half pitch-pole. The second attempt ended like the first; but the third time the men were mad and determined, and she was successfully taken through the surf, and from there to the Point (eight miles). She did not ship two barrels of water. This crew will stake all they have on that boat. The men at all the stations are anxious for occasions to distinguish themselves.

By the end of 1876, a surfboat of improved design, featuring air cases, cork fenders, and sailing rigs, had been developed by the service's two construction superintendents and was beginning to be provided to all the recently built complete stations. The new boat would be sent to older stations when they needed to replace their current one.

Cork-vested crew poses boat-side. *Leelanau Historical Society Museum.*

Summarizing the continuing debate over the boats a year later, the service concluded that "the life-boat is better for some occasions, and the surf-boat for others," the most common determinant being a station's location. A lifeboat was used in harbors where a ramp or mechanical means could be used to directly launch a heavy boat, while the lighter surfboat would be more appropriate for hauling on a beach and launching into the pounding surf toward a wreck.

During the four decades in which stations of the US Life-Saving Service served Manitou Passage mariners, both types of rescue craft were extensively utilized. Initially powered by oars and muscles (and in some models, sailing rigs), they were later equipped with small gasoline engines. Variations among the models were attributable to the decisions and skills of their designers and builders. The earliest surfboats generally had flat sterns; these gradually gave way to double-ended designs, which were deemed easier to control in a following sea.

The Sheridan Family Tragedy

A notable tragedy which surely saddened residents throughout the passage occurred in icy waters in mid-March 1878, a quarter century before the establishment of South Manitou Island's lifesaving station. Lightkeeper Aaron Sheridan, his wife Julia, and their infant son, the youngest of their six boys, were returning from a trip to the mainland in an island fisherman's small sailboat that capsized within sight of the shore in a sudden storm. Aaron, who had lost the use of his left arm in the Civil War and secured the keeper's position after his recovery, had nobly served the island station for about a dozen years, aided by his wife, who had become his official assistant when the fog signal's arrival extended the keeper's duties.

Although the boat's owner was saved by islanders who had heard their cries for help, the three Sheridans were drowned, their bodies lost in the lake. It is said that the surviving children searched the beach for days, looking for their parents and baby brother. One could speculate that had a lifesaving crew been stationed on the shore of that island, as it would be many years later, the outcome, resulting from the sail's sheet possibly being tied to the craft rather than handheld during the storm, might have been less devastating. Doubtlessly, the tragedy was an influence on one of the surviving sons, who grew up to follow in his parents' footsteps, light-tending on southern Lake Michigan.

Proposing a Sleeping Bear Point Lifesaving Station

In its 1877 report, the service renewed its 1873 recommendation for the establishment of a manned lifesaving station at the mainland's Sleeping Bear Point, and that June, Congress took the initial legislative step of authorizing its establishment as well as thirty-seven other stations throughout the country. But although the agency expressed its appreciation for a gift of private shoreline for the station's construction, no further action was taken at the time. In fact, twenty-five years would pass before two additional stations were finally established to serve the passage, the one at Sleeping Bear Point and one on South Manitou Island, both of which began operations in August 1902.

Nonetheless, the 1878 legislation played an important role in the development of our country's lifesaving capabilities. As the service commented a year later, the measure provided for "the definite organization of the service into a national establishment," which led to the organization's increased prominence, prestige, and performance. As an example, two years later the service would call for the establishment of a complete station at Frankfort Harbor, just five miles south of Point Betsie, to better serve that port's growing marine traffic.

Sleeping Bear Point Lifesaving Station, ca. 1902.
Author's collection.

South Manitou Island Lifesaving Station, ca. 1902.
Author's collection.

General Superintendent Kimball's Persuasive Command

The writers of the service's official annual reports, based upon the station keepers' own journal entries and the district superintendents' views, were known for their expression of Kimball's mission. Kimball used his professional writers' talents to craft documents that would interest the public and draw Congress's attention to his agency's needs and achievements. In the following example, the 1880 report promoted pending congressional legislation to support his insistence, sometimes over politicians' self-interests, that politics in general, and party affiliations in particular, would play no role in the appointment and employment of officers and crews of the lifesaving service:

> When the wrecked vessel is swept fore and aft by the winter seas, and haggard sailors and sobbing women and children are clinging to shroud and bulwark, the man who can best take out the life-boat through the breakers to their rescue is the man of all men for this service.... The gunner that can cast at the first fire the shot-line over the breaking deck when the stormy night is blackest, and there is nothing to guide his aim but the spot of light made by the ship's lantern in the rigging amidst the rending surf and overleaping spray, will be proclaimed by the sufferers his wreck craft brings to shore the man this service demands, though every caucus on the coast denounces his politics. If a patient be in mortal danger, and to save his life a capital operation is to be performed, we send for the surgeon. We raise no question of creed or party—we want only the surgeon, and we want the best. When the wreck is beating into ruin on the lee shore, the case is equally one of life and death, and equally, to the exclusion of every other consideration, is the highest professional ability required.

Daily Station Life

Consistent with policies Kimball had laid down when he had first taken charge of lifesaving within the Revenue Marine, anyone over the age of forty-five years was barred from being enlisted as a surfman; anyone over the age of fifty-five years was barred from being reenlisted unless he was found physically fit for duty, and every keeper over fifty-five years of age was required to be examined by a physician annually, on or before the first of September.

Rigorous daily drills and exercises were set forth in regulations for all manned lifesaving stations. The orders were: Mondays during the first month of the active season, practice with the beach rescue apparatus, and also examine and overhaul all apparatus and gear; Tuesdays, practice with station rescue boats; Wednesdays, practice with signals; Thursdays, practice with beach apparatus; Fridays, practice resuscitation; and Saturdays, clean the house. The rules stated that whenever a drill was prevented by wreck duty, storms, or high surf, it had to be acknowledged in the keeper's journal and rescheduled as soon as possible.

Launching from the beach.

Leelanau Historical Society Museum.

Keepers of the two passage stations, as elsewhere along the nation's coasts, daily filled out a form, known as a journal or log, to report on their station's activities. The document began with the day's wind condition; the weather's general character and the condition of the surf at midnight, sunrise, noon, and sunset; as well as barometer and thermometer readings at the same intervals.

Next provided were the names of the individual surfmen who had performed the beach hikes to both the right and left of the station (assuming the topography made going both directions possible), between the hours of 8:00 p.m. and midnight; midnight to 4:00 a.m.; and 4:00 a.m. to 8:00 a.m., as well as in additional hours if dense fog or other dangerous conditions necessitated daytime patrolling. Service regulations required both regular surfmen and volunteers to sign articles binding themselves to the faithful performance of their duties, notably advising them to be mindful "of what will be required of them in respect to patrolling the beach." Lest there be any doubt as to the importance the service attached to this particular duty, its regulations stated that "any failure or neglect in its performance on the part of any surfman, coming to the knowledge of the Department, will be punished by dismissal from the Service, and his prohibition from future employment therein."

Another provision mandated that "unauthorized absence without a satisfactory reason, and intoxication or neglect of duty, will be punished by the instant dismissal of the offender from the Service." Any surfman leaving before his enlistment term's expiration would be labeled a deserter, and forfeit his due pay.

By the mid-1880s, General Superintendent Kimball was making notable progress in his quest to create and sustain an agency that not only would perform to his own high standards, but would also deepen its mission's support in Congress and the administration. Accountability from bottom to top was fully in place, a reminder that a station's keeper and crew were not freelancers formulating their own policies, but on-the-ground (and water) workers of a federal agency whose senior officers maintained control via the daily logs through which station keepers reported their crews' operations, good or bad, up the chain of command.

As an example, one day in the mid-1880s, Keeper Matthews penned the following in his Point aux Bec Scies journal:

Called the men together and directed their attention to the rules relative to watch from the top of the station house and that getting to the leeward of the lookout house and sitting on the railing and laying their heads down on their arms was contrary to rules. [Surfman] Rohr said he would sit down when he got tired, and was insolent and insubordinately inclined and as it was not the first offence on his part I concluded it was necessary to make an example of him. I informed him that he was discharged and in presence of the rest of the crew he defied me to discharge him. I gave orders that he would not be called for watch duty in the morning. But before his watch [time] he came to my bed and asked me to let him take his watch, that he was sorry for his conduct. I said no, not in that way would the matter be settled, but after breakfast I would muster the crew and in their presence if he would apologize for what he said and asked to be reinstated I would overlook the offense this time and give him back his place. He made the apology as desired and was reinstated.

The log also called for answers to a series of specific questions: "Is the house clean? Is the house in good repair? Is the apparatus in good condition? How many members of the crew (including the Keeper) were present? Who was absent, and why?" The form also asked for the number of vessels of specific types: "barks; brigs; schooners; steamers and sloops" that had passed the station that day.

The last section of each day's report, "General Remarks," required the keeper to describe the day's major activities. Their writings would include any circumstance that called the station to action; the results of specific drills such as the breeches buoy, boat, and signal flag practices; repairs made to the station, its boats, or other equipment; any surfman's failure to perform as regulations required; and the punishment the keeper had imposed upon an offender.

The agency's regulations emphasized, "As the efficiency of a life-saving station depends upon the good training and discipline of the crew, the strictest attention must be paid by the members thereof to the directions of the keeper on all occasions, and implicit obedience to all lawful orders from superiors will be exacted of them."

When not present at stations, regular and volunteer crewmen were expected during inclement thick weather to be watching for a signal to assemble. Upon seeing the signal for assembly displayed from the station's flagstaff, or hearing the signal gun go off, they were to go immediately to the station.

Regulations banned station crews from engaging in salvage activities, "it being part of their duty, as Government employees,

North Manitou lifesavers in beach cart harnesses.
US National Archives.

to assist without charge in saving property from wrecked vessels, so far as it can be done without interfering with the duty of saving life, which must always be the paramount consideration, or injuring the effectiveness of the appliances for prompt service at any moment."

The regulations also included explicit directions for various activities, including boat training, restoring the apparently drowned, flag signaling, and practicing use of the beach apparatus. Boat practice consisted of launching and landing through the surf, and a minimum of a half hour's exercise of the men in handling their oars.

The early 1880s saw the beginning of a donation program that was much appreciated throughout the service's long history, especially at isolated stations—traveling libraries. This initiative began with the donations of books about lifesaving, especially the much-heralded English crews' experiences that could assist in instructing American station keepers and their crewmen. Over time, the libraries included a variety of books about travel, adventure, fiction, and other topics, including worship.

The service later described the appeal: "When it is recollected that for the most part these stations are at isolated locations on the beach, selected solely on account of the frequency of wrecks in their vicinity, that the main part of the life of the crews who inhabit them is made up of long seasons of irksome and weary waiting indoors, and that they must for the most part while away this dreary monotony as best they can, it is easy to imagine how welcome these little libraries will be to the hermit groups of lifesavers, and how eagerly they will be seized upon for relief from the dull routine of the existence to which they are condemned."

The Essential Role of the Lyle Gun

Always striving to provide the lifesavers with the best-available equipment, the service's 1877 report advised Congress that breeches buoy equipment enabling the crews to remove individual crewmen from a stranded vessel had been supplied to most stations. Where and when its use was feasible, the new equipment would relieve crews of the burden they faced in hauling heavy life cars over beaches to wreck sites far distanced from the station. The carts' loaded weight totaled about 1,700 pounds, of which the smallest car itself contributed 225 pounds.

Lyle gun, faking box, and shot line, Point Betsie Lighthouse Museum.
Author's photo.

A major weight reduction was achieved with the substitution of the breeches buoy equipment for the life car, and an additional reduction was gained by the adoption of a new gun invented by army lieutenant and engineer David A. Lyle. This cannon could fire a nineteen-pound projectile from the beach to a vessel stranded several hundred yards offshore. A light shot line, having first been wound in a faking box to prevent tangles, was attached.

With a connection between shore and ship thus achieved, a much stronger line would then be pulled to the wreck, facilitating a rescue attempt by breeches buoy, avoiding the risk to lifesavers' own lives if attempting to save the ship's crew by surfboat in rough sea. Lyle's last name forever identified this gun, which itself weighed about two hundred pounds and was kept in the station's car, ready for action. It would be pulled down the beach to the disaster by the crew, or sometimes by horse over a long distance.

The beach apparatus drill was required twice each week to make the implementation of this lifesaving, multistep process as routine as possible under the pressures attending actual wreck circumstances.

At the drill site, which would be about seventy-five yards from the station's wreck pole, which simulated the mast of a stranded vessel, an anchor would need to be set in the sand to hold the Lyle gun in place. With each member confirming his specific duty in the procedure, within five minutes the crew was required to set up all the requisite gear and fire a gunshot to the target.

Gunpowder was to be used in every beach apparatus practice, and all keepers were required to specifically report each drill's results, including the amount of gunpowder used and the time required for the simulated recovery of a wreck victim. A surfman's failure to fulfill his task could result in his dismissal.

The shot would propel a projectile and attached line to the pole. In the drills, a person would then be retrieved from the pole by the breeches buoy, in essence a life ring with a pair of shorts attached in which the rescued person would ride.

In an actual rescue attempt, the line would be recovered by the stricken vessel's crew, thus connecting the rescuers with the vessel. (Sometimes several shots were required, with the shot line having to be retrieved and properly readied for refiring.) Once the link to the vessel was secured, instructions would be sent out to the victims of the wreck, telling them what they had do to facilitate their rescue by breeches buoy, and the fired lightweight shot line would be replaced by a hawser, over which the buoy would be sent out and pulled to shore.

An alternative rescue device through many years until it lost favor was also initiated by the Lyle gun's shot. This was the use of the station's eleven-foot, four-inch long, hatch-covered galvanized life car, which would be pulled through the surf to shore from a wreck, saving multiple (sometimes very cramped) people in a single trip. Its principal disadvantage, however, was the considerable burden it added to the beach trip for a wreck.

Drills and actual rescues were based upon the surfmen's numbering, No. 1 being the keeper's top-ranked crewman, while No. 7 was generally the newest crew member. In practicing the procedure for resuscitating the apparently drowned, for example, the keeper was to practice on No. 1; No. 1 would work on No. 2, etc., with No. 7 working on the keeper. The performance concluded with the keeper's opening the medicine chest and questioning each man about the uses of its contents.

Breeches buoy rescue drill.
Leelanau Historical Society Museum.

Beach Patrols: An Essential Duty

The service emphasized the essentiality of beach patrolling throughout the night—an unending duty at every manned station, and a routine procedure when daytime weather circumstances could threaten vessels not visible from a station's lookout tower.

Lacking today's technology, commercial sea captains of old, trying to maneuver safely through fog or storms, had little means other than straining to hear the sound of surf against the shore, or glimpsing the warning of a surfman's lantern or flare to realize that they were about to be grounded. The potential loss of the ship, her valuable cargo, and the crew's precious lives hung in the balance.

"The vigilance of the life-saving patrols, nightly guarding the beaches, detects vessels either sailing too near the shore or standing directly into danger..."

Men on patrol were to carry a lantern and two or three red lights. If they discovered a wreck or vessel in trouble, they were to burn a red Coston flare, which would alert their station and the ship's crew that the vessel's plight, being too close to shore, had been discovered.

The flare was a device which was invented by a young woman, Martha Coston, who, after her husband, a chemist, had died in 1848, was confronted with making a living for herself and her four children. Looking through his notes, she discovered his attempts to develop a means of signaling between ships, and between ships and land. She spent about a decade and achieved the goal that he had been unable to reach; her invention proved to be an enormously significant lifesaving device in numerous applications.

Made by the Coston Company, the flares, with which all US Life-Saving Service stations were equipped, was one of the stations' most effective tools to save lives, thousands of which were also saved through the device's military applications, such as signaling by Union forces during the Civil War, signaling between US Navy vessels, and similar uses by numerous other countries.

All crews at Great Lakes stations were required to maintain constant watch from daylight to dark from the station's lookout,

Faithful patrolmen warn off a vessel by Coston flare.
Sturgis, MA library archives.

and the watchmen could not leave the elevated platform until being relieved of their duty.

As described in the service's 1881 annual report, "The vigilance of the life-saving patrols, nightly guarding the beaches, detects vessels either sailing too near the shore or standing directly into danger, and in such cases the patrolmen at once fire their red Coston signals, whose vivid flame warns the navigators of their peril, and enables them to wear ship [i.e., alter tack] in time. Thus, the patrolman becomes a sort of perambulating beacon, flashing in aid of navigation."

In that single year, the service reported forty-five instances in which vessels had been warned in this fashion, and by altering course had been saved from fully or partially wrecking. It should be remembered, although the lifesaving service stations' responses to catastrophes on the Great Lakes and ocean coasts constituted the most dramatic examples of their value to mariners, in a far larger number of situations, crews were able to prevent wrecks and strandings that threatened their ships, crews, and cargoes by signals while on patrol or watching from lookouts.

Kimball called numerous times for expanding the number of surfmen at each station, terming the addition of one man "indispensable," and observing that at least two more could be usefully employed. Particularly concerned about the burden on the existing crews of the nightly beach patrols, he stressed that "no man ... ever gets a whole night's sleep during the eight months of station duty," since from dawn to dark, the beach had to be walked in both directions every night. "It hardly needs to be said how wearing such a life is to the crews," he lamented.

The service poignantly described the challenges of a beach patrol in areas such as the Manitou Passage stations as "long, dreary, obscure, lonesome, sinister, difficult, perilous. It lies along a waste of foot-detaining sand, whereon to walk is to trudge laboriously, frequently ankle-deep; at times to stumble over stones, or wreck-wood washed up by the sea, or to sink suddenly in spots of quicksand. Often the surf shoots seething across the path, or the sentinel wades knee-deep into the bays beyond, or cuts which trench through into the sand hills. The fitful lights and shadows of a lantern alone mark the somber way."

Volunteer Heroism in Glen Arbor

The service's 1880 report describes in vivid detail the November 1879 rescue, by five townsmen, of two "forlorn survivors" of the wrecked schooner *W.B. Phelps.* The action occurred about a mile east of the mainland village of Glen Arbor, on the coast of Sleeping Bear Bay, more than two decades prior to the establishment of the Sleeping Bear Point station.

Heavy snow and a northwest gale the previous evening had driven the schooner aground, stern first. As the service described the ensuing events:

Her centerboard being down broke up her decks so completely that only a small fragment of them remained on the extreme forward part of the vessel. On this fragment, hardly sufficient for a foothold, her mate and one of the sailors remained all night; the vessel being covered with ice heeled over with her lee rail under water, the rail upon her weather side all gone, and the sea pouring across her between the stem and stern like a cataract.

It was only at daybreak that a citizen of Glen Arbor discovered the two miserable survivors clinging to the bows. The alarm he gave brought to the scene a number of townspeople, who sledded to the spot an old leaky flat-bottomed fish-boat, the only craft obtainable, which was at once launched by William A. Clark, Charles A. Rosman, John Tobin, Welby C. Ray, and William W. Tucker. The effort these brave men made to reach the wreck was soon baffled, the terrible sea and wind driving back the boat, half filled with water, with her crew drenched. Amidst the cries of the two men on the wreck for help, the boat was dragged about twenty rods to windward to get the advantage of a strong current, and the same crew, with the exception of Willard W. Tucker, whose place was supplied by Howard Daniels, made another attempt and succeeded in reaching the stern of the vessel, to which they made fast by a line and surveyed the situation. The two sailors were away from them in the bows, unapproachable on the windward side of the hull by reason of the terrible sea, and inaccessible on the leeward side on account of the great mass of spars, timbers, sails, rigging and deck plank, which hung over the whole length of the bulwarks and thrashed and bounded in the water constantly, menacing approach with destruction. The prospect of rescue was therefore gloomy, and as the boat was fast filling, it was concluded that what could possibly be done must be decided on shore, to which the crew then returned, with their boat stern foremost, not daring to turn it for fear of the heavy seas.

The service narrative relates that the men, soaked and covered with ice, ran to their homes to change clothes, leaving one person on the beach so the sailors on the wreck would not think they were being abandoned. With John Blanchfield having replaced Howard Daniels, the strategy then chosen by the courageous volunteers became to try to maneuver the boat into the midst of the wreckage, which was crashing up and down, and to attempt to get the two men across it.

Somehow managing to avoid having their boat crushed, the rescuers were able to get to within about sixty feet of the victims. They threw a line to the stranded mate, who tied it around himself and used it to crawl to within fifteen feet of the rescue boat and onto a piece of decking. The rescuers were then able to get close enough to haul him into their boat. The other man, who was further weakened by his ordeal, got his leg caught in the debris and was unable to free himself. One of the rescuers jumped from one piece of debris to another until he was able to grab the man by the collar and haul him onto the same decking, from which he was hauled into the rescue boat.

The rescuers then shoved off from the wreckage, with their boat filled with water. They nonetheless managed to get to shore, to the cheers of the gathered crowd. The mate is said to have shouted, "Thank God! I shall see my children again!" Having been on the frigid wreck for some twenty hours, the two were taken to a hotel to recover.

In appreciation of this heroic achievement, the US Life-Saving Service awarded its prestigious gold medal to five rescuers, saying, "No men ever better deserved the token by which the nation commemorates such deeds of valor and charity."

The US Life-Saving Service Reaches the Passage

The first US Life-Saving Service station manned by a resident crew on Lake Michigan began service on April 23, 1877, at Pointe (the "e" would soon fade from use) aux Bec Scies. Its crew was called upon to respond to emergencies not only on the broad waters directly west of the station, but also to crises southward toward Frankfort, and northward into Platte Bay and the southern Manitou Passage.

Records indicate that the station was initially equipped with a New York-built, twenty-five-foot pulling (rowing) surfboat of clinker (i.e., lapstrake) design, featuring overlapping cedar planks on oak frames, and a square stern comparable to those on fishing boats along the Atlantic shore. As were some other surfboat models, it was equipped with sailing rigging.

Another surfboat was assigned to the station in 1882, and in 1887, a Dobbins lifeboat, named for David Dobbins, the superintendent of the service's district covering Lakes Erie and Ontario, who was well known for his designs of safe and effective rescue craft. He devoted many years to the design of rescue craft that were sufficiently strong, capable of both self-righting and self-bailing, and light enough to be transported by carriage on a beach and launched into heavy surf—a formidable challenge, to say the least. Over time, numerous boats featuring his initiatives, as well as subsequent products by other notable designers seeking to achieve these objectives, were assigned to Great Lakes stations.

The service's lifeboat station on North Manitou Island opened two months later, on June 23, 1877, at the site of the Francis boat's assignment two decades previously. Given the care it had received, the Francis may have been usable for a brief period. One of several surfboats constructed in the early 1870s by a Detroit builder, specifically for use on the Great Lakes, it could have been assigned

Casting off in the service's sailboat.
Leelanau Historical Society Museum.

to North Manitou; the station's watercraft in its earliest years is uncertain. However, as the following event makes clear, a surfboat was on station there by early 1880.

A surfboat of a specific New Jersey design, known as a Long Branch, after the place it was manufactured, was newly assigned to the station in 1882 and 1884. Such boats were twenty-six to twenty-seven feet in length, and weighed a little less than one thousand pounds, or about double that when measured with oars. They could accommodate up to ten rowers. Also, in 1886 the station was assigned its first pulling lifeboat, a Dobbins design.

North Manitou's Rescue of the Ida Keith

North Manitou Island Lifesaving Station.
Leelanau Historical Society Museum.

On April 10, 1880, only days after North Manitou Island's station opened for the season, the Chicago-based schooner *Ida Keith*, crewed by nine men, was sailing to Buffalo with a load of corn when she stranded on shallows about four-plus miles south of the station during a northeastern, gale-blown snowstorm. The lifesavers went down the shore, where they could see what was needed, then returned to the station, gathered their equipment, and headed back to the schooner by surfboat. As the service subsequently reported:

> *The captain of the vessel sent word ashore on a shingle that he did not wish to land but desired a boat to be sent out to him. Two shots [from*

the Lyle gun] were fired, the second being successful [i.e., the projectile had carried the line from the surfboat to the schooner] and the boat was pulled partway out by the line, which then parted and the boat then drifted back to the shore. It was by this time too dark to fire another shot; the life-saving crew then built a fire and patrolled the beach until morning. Prepared to fire another shot, the crew received a message by shingle from the captain of the schooner, requesting them to await the quieting of the sea. At 10 a.m., the storm fortunately lulled, and soon afterward the life-saving crew rowed out and landed the ship's crew. The vessel was subsequently got off.

In short, the sailors aboard the schooner were saved, as well as the cargo and vessel, and no surfmen were injured or lost. Though not as dramatic as it had started out to be, this rescue, one of the earliest surviving accounts by the North Manitou crew, had succeeded. Not always would that be the case, nor would such activities be a daily life feature at their (or any other) station.

Point Aux Bec Scies's Famed J. H. Hartzell Rescue

On October 16, 1880, one of the most dramatic rescues by a Great Lakes lifesaving service crew was undertaken by the men of the Point aux Bec Scies station from a grounded schooner, the *J.H. Hartzell*. It was the service's first wreck of the fiscal 1881 year to occur within the agency's service area involving a loss of life, and were it not for the one person's death, its full, extraordinary story might not have received the leadership's attention it did, or its details be so thoroughly retrieved today.

About seven miles south of the station by boat and, under the prevailing conditions, unreachable from there by surfboat, the schooner was about two miles south of the Frankfort harbor, her intended destination. By land, she was about ten miles from the station, much of it over steep and treed dunes. As the service related, "The scene on this occasion was in every respect extraordinary, and few narratives could surpass in interest the soberest recital of what took place that day abreast of and upon the wooded steeps in the neighborhood of one of our western towns." (At the time of this event, Lake Michigan was viewed as a western water body, and a gateway into the expanding country.)

Point Betsie Lifesaving Station, ca. 1912.
Author's collection.

However, a rapid wind shift from gentle southeast gusts to gale-force southwest blasts, accompanied by a mix of snow, hail, and rain, dealt his plan a fatal blow.

Although the disaster occurred several miles to the south of the Manitou Passage itself, the story features life-savers who were expected to respond to disasters of ships sailing both within and near it. In this instance, the wreck occurred off the entrance into Frankfort Harbor, about five miles south of the station itself.

One of the lifesaving service's most compelling early Great Lakes rescue accounts, this story not only reveals the extraordinary challenges that the Point aux Bec Scies surfmen and volunteers who raced to assist them faced in this rescue, but exemplifies the harrowing circumstances for which these surfmen and their colleagues at other Great Lakes stations were prepared.

On her down-lake trip from L'Anse, in Michigan's Upper Peninsula, the *Hartzell* is said to have enjoyed favorable winds until shortly after anchoring off Frankfort in the wee hours of the morning. She was loaded with 495 tons of iron ore to be delivered to the Frankfort Furnace Company inside the town's harbor. Exercising reasonable caution, her captain decided to wait for daylight before trying to sail into the harbor through its narrow, pier-lined channel. However, a rapid wind shift from gentle southeast gusts to gale-force southwest blasts, accompanied by a mix of snow, hail, and rain, dealt his plan a fatal blow.

An attempt to sail the ship to safety further offshore failed, owing to the rapidly deteriorating wind and sea conditions. As the service's narrative relates, she "would not obey her helm, and began to drift in, seeing which her master let go both anchors and set his signal of distress." But she "continued to drag, and soon struck upon the middle bar, about three hundred yards from shore," where she was hard aground, her bow toward shore. Then, "the seas at once crashed over her, and the awful staving and rending usual in such cases began." The vessel was described as being "directly abeam [of a] range of wooded sand-hills or bluffs, almost precipitous, and several hundred feet high, known as Big and Little Bald Hills.... The yawl [dinghy] was carried away, the deck-cabin wrenched asunder and scattered to the breakers, and the vessel began to founder. In a couple of hours all that remained for her crew was to take to the rigging."

Lydia Dale, a cook who was aboard possibly as a passenger rather than working the trip, had been seriously ill. The service's official account continues that as the ship began to break up:

She was very weak, and it took the united efforts of four men to get her aloft into the cross-trees of the foremast, across which planks had been nailed. Upon this species of platform she lay, wrapped up as well as possible, with her head supported on the knees of one of the sailors, and, as they stated, rapidly grew delirious. A little while after the men had got aloft, the vessel sank in sixteen feet of water, the stern resting upon the bar and the forward part in deeper water. Later, the mainmast gave way and went over, remaining attached to the foundered hulk by some of the cordage, and thrashing and plunging alongside with every rush of the seas. The foremast, with the men upon it—one of them, the captain, clinging to the ratlines, about ten feet above the water; the remainder fifty feet aloft in the cross-trees, with the recumbent woman—swayed and creaked ominously, some of the wedges having become loosened, and seemed likely to go over at any moment.

"It was a horrible feature of this shipwreck that the vessel, now an utter ruin, had a short time before been loitering to and fro in the fresh breeze, with no anticipation of disaster...."

As the service observed, "It was a horrible feature of this shipwreck that the vessel, now an utter ruin, had a short time before been loitering to and fro in the fresh breeze, with no anticipation of disaster.... So suddenly and fiercely had the tempest risen that within an hour [it had] destroyed her, and placed in deadly jeopardy the lives of the wretched company that clung to her one tottering spar."

The wreck could soon be seen from the town, and a young boy, the son of a fisherman whose family lived in a cabin close to the south pier, was one of the first to see the ship and told his father about it. The father immediately rushed into the village of South Frankfort, on the harbor's south side, spreading the word. Many residents joined him in getting atop the hills to where they could better see the wreck. As a crowd arrived opposite the stricken vessel, they laid driftwood along the dune's face, spelling a message of hope to the victims aboard: "LIFE-BOAT COMING."

Meanwhile, a young man named Woodward had started on horseback for the distant Point aux Bec Scies lifesaving station. When thus informed, Keeper Thomas Matthews ordered out the beach car and rescue apparatus. Soon thereafter, the car containing the Lyle gun, breeches buoy, hawser, hauling lines, and other essentials left the station dragged by the horse, with five lifesavers helping to move the heavily loaded car as rapidly as possible.

"... the way was so difficult that the men and the horse, tugging and straining at the cart together, could only make ten or fifteen yards at a pull without pausing. This violent toll was pursued amidst the roaring of the gale, which now blew almost a hurricane ..."

The station's sixth lifesaver, who was making his beach patrol, would join the rescue party as it moved toward the scene. The account continues:

The expedition had set out upon a terrible journey. The Point au Bec Scies station is upon the lake-shore, north of Frankfort, south of which town the wreck lay, and the intervening river and the harbor piers making out into the lake from the town made it impossible, in any case, to arrive at the wreck by following the line of the coast. The only way was to make a circuit through the woods and around the rear of the town, where the bisecting river could be crossed by a bridge in that locality, and the beach south of Frankfort gained. The shortest route, not less than seven or eight miles long, but to gain this it was necessary to travel two miles from Point au Bec Scies along the beach, and the beach was now submerged by a swashing flood constantly bursting against and washing away the steep banks of the lake shore, battering the escarpment with inter-tangled masses of logs, stumps, and trees, and of course rendering the way impossible. The expedition was therefore compelled to lengthen the detour by taking an old trail or cart-track, which had been pioneered by the Point au Bec Scies light-house construction party several years before for the transportation of materials. This road wandered through the woods, along winding ravines and up steep, soggy sand-hills. Across these acclivities the way was so difficult that the men and the horse, tugging and straining at the cart together, could only make ten or fifteen yards at a pull without pausing. This violent toll was pursued amidst the roaring of the gale, which now blew almost a hurricane, and the rushing of the storm, until about a mile's distance from the station had been accomplished. By this time the men, despite the bitter cold, were hot and wet with their efforts, and the horse, steaming with exertion, trembled on his limbs and could scarcely draw. There were at least nine miles more of their disheartening journey before them, and the party was already sorely spent.

Reaching a road didn't offer the men much relief, as "the difficulties of an ordinary country road, in the rougher regions of the west, are quite indescribable, and thus far the way was not even a road, but a rude cart-trail, made years before, already half-choked with a dense undergrowth, and cumbered here and there with fallen trunks of trees." The account notes that the load of rescue equipment being dragged by the men and the horse through ruts, etc., weighed a thousand or more pounds. To make matters worse, they faced constant driving rain.

However, they were lucky then to encounter several persons willing to help, one with a horse and buggy, into which Keeper Matthews climbed, attempting to get to the wreck site more quickly, and another person with a team of horses whom he directed to proceed to the station and bring its life car and other items to the scene, as well as the surfman who had returned to the station from his beach patrol.

Struggling through woods, ravines, and other barriers, the valiant party, amazingly covering approximately ten miles in about two hours, reaching Frankfort Harbor, going around that basin and traveling over the sole bridge that spanned the River aux Bec Scies, having covered the "rough stretch" of about ten miles in two hours—an achievement, reflecting, in the service's words, "the ardor of the rushing march of this train."

Matthews had reached an elevated coastal farm, Greenwood's, from which, looking over the lake, he could see the wreck being pounded by stormy waves. He was heading back to the cart, intending to go through the farm toward the site, when a local resident on horseback called to say he would show him a shortcut.

The account proceeds, "The party followed him through a ravine about a quarter of a mile. The way then led up the overhanging hillside through the brush, and the tug with the loaded cart was terrible. So steep was the ascent that man and beast had fairly to climb, and almost to hoist the cart after them. Nothing could have been done but for the aid of a crowd of sturdy townsfolk who had assembled there, and, anticipating the arrival of the lifesaving party, had cleared away with axes and handspikes a great deal of the undergrowth and fallen trees." It took the efforts of twenty-seven strong men, including the lifesaving crew and town volunteers, helped by several horses, to pull the loaded apparatus cart to the summit. Another challenge awaited them there, a line of woods and numerous fallen trees that blocked their way across the summit to the shore's side. But, in the report's words:

The obstacle seemed to inspire all present with a sudden electric energy, and gave occasion for a striking and admirable scene. In an instant, and as by a simultaneous impulse, all hands, citizens and crew, flung themselves upon the wood with axes and handspikes, and

"...So steep was the ascent that man and beast had fairly to climb, and almost to hoist the cart after them."

The first person rescued was the ship's mate. The official narrative reads, "His jaws were set, his eyes vacantly fixed, and the expression on his face dazed and frightened."

a work began which resembled a combat.... In some places, men were showering terrible blows with axes upon standing timber. In others they were prying and lifting aside great fallen trees with all their branches, shouting in chorus.... In an incredibly short space of time the way through the wood was cleared, and the mortar-cart loaded with apparatus was dragged forward to the brow of the hill.

The rescuers then confronted yet one more dilemma, getting that heavy cart down safely without losing control of it, to a more level spot from which its contents could be utilized. A storm was blowing sand up the slope, and a mix of snow and rain was also falling. Having spotted a ledge about 250 feet down the slope from which the rescue operations could be launched, the cart was slowly lowered with the use of its own whip-line and the efforts of surfmen and others managing to keep it from careening down the slope. When the line that was helping to restrain the descent proved to be too short, it was quickly released from the fallen tree to which it had been tied, and men grabbed ahold of it, kept their feet in the sand to create drag, and rode the load to its destination.

The cart was quickly unloaded and the Lyle gun was prepared for firing. On the second shot, the line fell right across the fore-rigging from which the men in the rigging could retrieve it, and after considerable working with lines that were being swept by the roiling sea, breeches buoy operations were ready.

Meanwhile, the wreckage was nearly sunken, but fortunately her masts were still standing. The crew aboard could hear them creaking as the hull swayed back and forth, threatening doom for the nearly frozen and seemingly unconscious woman.

Given the conditions, particularly repeating wind blasts, it took considerable time to get the breeches buoy out to the ship's mast. Upon its arrival, a man could be seen getting into the contraption and starting for shore, a process that took sixteen minutes, according to a bystander. The first person rescued was the ship's mate. The official narrative reads, "His jaws were set, his eyes vacantly fixed, and the expression on his face dazed and frightened." He was given brandy that seemed to revive him, whereupon he muttered, "Save the others," before being taken away by townspeople.

The report indicates that the woman may have earlier expressed fear of the breeches buoy, but further use of that device would have presented another problem, as the tree on shore to which the buoy line was connected was slipping in the sand. Keeper Matthews decided then to utilize the life car, which could be towed out to the mast like a boat, relieving some of the strain on the line. Several people could be brought to shore at a time, rather than individually. Thus, the life car was attached to the lines and hauled out to the ship.

"The crowd [was] confident that the woman would be brought this time, and [was] stupefied when only the two men appeared."

On its way out to the wreck, it turned turtle, but having righted itself, continued to lurch wildly. When, finally, it reached the hull, the fallen mainmast suddenly rose up on a breaker and smashed down on the car, throwing it ten to fifteen feet in the air. Miraculously, the men working the line from the shore hauled in the slack, and the car then hung perpendicularly about twelve feet below them. With ropes around their waists, two men managed to get down from the crosstrees and into the car. Then a third man lowered himself to where he could close the hatch door, and the car began its trip back to the shore, where they were promptly asked about the woman. The report states that they seemed "to have given evasive answers, to the general effect that she would come ashore in the next trip of the car."

Having been somewhat damaged from its battering, the car was hammered into shape and sent on its way back to the ship. Her captain could be seen gradually making his way toward his men further up the rigging. The captain made an attempt to rouse the woman, but without effect. Then the second mate and captain managed to get into the car, and it was pulled to the shore and its hatch cover quickly opened.

The narrative continues: "The crowd [was] confident that the woman would be brought this time, and [was] stupefied when only the two men appeared. There was an instant burst of fierce interrogation, to which the captain and mate appear, like their predecessors, to have rendered equivocal answers. The effect of their replies was that the woman was the same as dead, and that she would be, or might be, brought to shore at the next trip."

However, that outcome was not to be realized. The crowd on shore, having seen people moving about the mast and giving rise to their expectation that the woman would be coming next, eagerly surrounded the car as it again arrived, and when the hatch was opened, two more men emerged.

In this case their failure to make the effort would hardly be less than criminal. Its only extenuation would be the consideration of the terrible and perhaps insurmountable difficulties of the task.

A cry of many voices then rose. "Where's the woman?" It was followed by a momentary silence, in which men were seen bent over the open hatch and groping about with their arms inside the car. Then someone shouted to the crowd in a terrible voice, "They haven't brought the woman!" The dark air resounded with a roar of curses, and amidst the din men were heard yelling that they never would have laid hands to the hauling lines if they had known that the woman was to be left upon the wreck to perish.

The rescued men insisted, when sharply questioned by Keeper Matthews, that the woman was dead, and he judged that sending the car to the wreck yet again for confirmation of her state posed unacceptable risks to anyone going to the ship. The service's subsequent report generally confirms that view, as follows:

Her death ... from previous illness and current exhaustion, is not unlikely, and if dead, the men perched aloft with her upon a mast rocking in its step, and every moment likely to fall, must have felt it useless, as it would have been physically impossible to have lowered the heavy and inert burden of her corpse twelve feet down into the car, and felt that their exertion was justly due to their own preservation. Another possibility is, that when they left she was not dead, but insensible or in a dying condition, and that they felt that her insensibility would make it impossible to save her. In this case their failure to make the effort would hardly be less than criminal. Its only extenuation would be the consideration of the terrible and perhaps insurmountable difficulties of the task.

The following morning, the mast had fallen, and the woman had disappeared. Seventeen days later, her body was found on the beach near Frankfort. Upon inspecting her remains after that lengthy delay, the coroner concluded that she had drowned.

The *J. H. Hartzell* crew left town quickly, doubtless aware of criticism voiced by some residents who asserted that the crew had scandalously abandoned Lydia Dale, and none of the sailors were present at the inquest. Affidavits from the last four crewmen asserted that at the time, the departed was "quite dead, which does not seem unlikely."

That said, in its report the service acknowledged, "It is, and doubtless will always be, an open question in what condition the

Portion of mural at Point Betsie Lighthouse Museum.
Author's photo.

hapless woman was left upon the mast. Whether dead or alive, her desertion caused great excitement at Frankfort for some time afterward, and it is certain that on this topic opinion was considerably divided. No common conclusion appears to have been reached, nor is it likely that such unanimity would be possible from the evidence."

But as for the community volunteers' role, the service wrote: "They were a miscellaneous throng—blown together, one might say, by the winds—fifty or sixty farmers, lake-sailors, lumbermen, roustabouts, plain townsfolk of several varieties, and bound by no engagement, and without even a moment's conference, they massed themselves as one man under the orders of the keeper, obeying him with the subordination and steady constancy of trained soldiers. Before such behavior the language of commendation fails."

Captain Matthews reported several days after the event that the station's life car was "badly damaged" by its battering in the rescue. There was little rest for the weary crew, as at daylight just three days after their exhausting rescue, the Point aux Bec Scies crew discovered an abandoned schooner, the *Anna Maria,* about two miles from shore.

Going out to her, they found that her deck's load and cabin had been swept away two days before, when she was caught in a "terrible gale" off Two Rivers Point on the Wisconsin side of the lake. Possibly a victim of the same storm that took down the *J.H. Hartzell,* they found her dismasted, filled with water, and with her steering mechanism and anchors rendered useless. Seven of her crew had been taken off by a passing schooner, and another man had been lost overboard. The lifesavers sent a message to Frankfort reporting their discovery, where arrangements were made for a tug to go to the vessel and haul her to South Manitou Harbor.

Two years later, still mindful of the crew's ordeal in the *J.H. Hartzell* rescue, Captain Matthews reported that he and his men had worked four days to open a wagon road through the wooded dunes between his station and the state road (now M-22) for moving the station's rescue apparatus to Frankfort. Their efforts preceded a mid-1920s joint project of the point's lifesavers and lightkeepers to improve the road and gravel its surface for automobiles.

Similarly, Matthews reported a year later that he and five surfmen had taken axes and a crosscut saw to clear a footpath over the hills along the shore so that beach patrols could be completed when the surf was too high for walking the beach.

The *J.H. Hartzell* crisis pointed to the desirability of a future lifesaving station's being sited to be able to respond more rapidly to strandings or other disasters occurring south of Frankfort, or when vessels were trying to negotiate the approximately two-hundred-foot-wide, one-thousand-foot-long harbor channel in troublesome winds. As the episode had starkly revealed, the harbor and lake southward could be reached by Point aux Bec Scies's lifesavers only with great difficulty, and given the weather conditions, it was certainly possible that ships could be in trouble simultaneously, north and south of the point.

About a year later, two visiting officials and one of the station's surfmen undertook to cover the route that the crew had taken in hauling the station's rescue apparatus to the *J.H. Hartzell* site. With schooner and steamer traffic increasing significantly, it was not unusual for about one hundred vessels to be sailing this coast on a mid-season day. The officials' evaluation of the route presumably lent support for the proposed establishment of a station between Point aux Bec Scies and thirty-mile distant Manistee, Michigan.

Noteworthy Events
of the Early 1880s

On April 20, 1881, Point aux Bec Scies's Keeper Matthews reported that one of his surfmen had found a bottle on the beach containing a flyleaf from a book on which was written in pencil, "The boat is breaking, the Captain's washed overboard," along with the signature of a crewman from the steamer *Alpena*. Two months later, Captain Matthews reported that a "common liquor flask" had been found by the station's patrolman with a slip of paper bearing the penciled message, "On board the [*Alpena*]...she has broke her port wheel, is at the mercy of seas, is half filled of water, God Help us, Captain [Napier] washed overboard." On the back was written a Chicago street address and this request: "The finder of this will please communicate with my wife and let her know of my death."

One morning the next month, when a thick fog that hung over the lake was finally beginning to lift, the Point aux Bec Scies's lookout spotted the peak of a schooner's foresail about six miles north of the station, drifting slowly northward. He then noticed that a "propeller" (as steam-powered ships were sometimes called) which had been heading toward the schooner had changed course, heading south toward his station. The keeper and crew launched a small boat and rowed out to meet the steamer, where they were told that the schooner *Advance*, carrying pine shingles to Chicago from Manistee, had collided with another vessel, the impact crushing the *Advance's* port bow. Rapidly becoming waterlogged, she had been abandoned by her crew.

The lifesavers returned to the station, one of them going on to Frankfort to get a tug. The surfmen loaded their boat with axes and other tools that they might need, and in the morning they rowed out to the *Advance*, which by then had drifted about seven miles away. The keeper reported finding her deserted, with her large anchor's chain fouled around the windlass (a type of winch with

April, 1881
Alpena

May, 1881
Advance

a rotating drum), the water level having risen above the top of the device. With her jib boom gone and her sails hanging and flapping around the hull, she was, in the keeper's own words, "a bad mess to clean up."

But working for a couple of hours, the station's crew made her ready for being towed, and then set two sails and headed toward Frankfort, meeting the tug just before 6:00 p.m. The tug took the schooner in tow, but around three hours later, as they approached Frankfort's south pier, the schooner hit bottom. It was clear that her deck load would have to be removed to lighten her. The lifesavers, working all night and using a small scow, transferred the shingles to the pier. They were then able to move the vessel to safety, three hundred feet inside the pier's end.

The keeper telegraphed the *Advance's* captain in Manistee, telling him that his schooner was in Frankfort, and sent four surfmen back to the station in the surfboat, keeping the other two to watch the vessel until the captain could come to Frankfort. When he arrived, the keeper learned more of the story. The captain told him his ship had been run into by another vessel, the *Fleetwing*, which was also somewhat damaged by the collision, but had taken the *Advance* in tow. But when the *Fleetwing* also began taking on water and had to drop the tow, she took the *Advance's* crew aboard. Towing only her yawl, the *Fleetwing* was able to reach shoal water, where the crew returned to the yawl, reached shore, and set out for Manistee.

In an important policy decision, the service thanked Congress in its fiscal 1882 report for having enacted legislation providing benefits to men disabled while performing their duties, and also to widows and orphans of those who perished while fulfilling their lifesaving responsibilities. Presumably for cost savings, the lifeboat station's occasional volunteers were not covered.

This benefit made it essential that examinations of men were conducted prior to the start of their service. Any recruit was required to produce for the station keeper a certificate of examination, either by a medical officer of the Marine Hospital Service or by another qualified physician if MHS personnel were not available (the common situation in northwestern Michigan). The report was expected to show the candidate's exact physical condition and attest to his qualifications to perform a surfman's duties. Not only did that establish a baseline against which to measure claims for compensation under the statute, but it also helped to raise the physical capabilities of the applicants.

In these years, the revenue steamer *Johnson* would pull up to the crew-built wharf at the isolated North Manitou station, bringing an assistant district inspector and medical examiner to assess the keeper's health. Being on the mainland, Point aux Bec Scies personnel sometimes were evaluated by a local doctor, unless an examiner came by ship moored offshore of the station or in Frankfort Harbor. Occasionally, the examinations were done by a doctor in Manistee, which necessitated a thirty-mile trip each way.

September, 1881
Columbia

In the fall of 1881, the beach patrols from Point aux Bec Scies were searching for victims and personal effects of the September tenth nighttime foundering of the eight-year-old Canadian steamer *Columbia*, off Frankfort. Traveling from Chicago to Collingwood, Ontario, on the south coast of Georgian Bay, she had experienced gale-force winds that caused her cargo of grain to shift. Careening onto a side, she became impossible to control. Her passengers and crew got into small boats, some of which were immediately swamped or capsized by the heavy sea. Of the twenty-three persons aboard, fifteen or sixteen were drowned.

According to a report in the *Cleveland Herald*, "The town of Frankfort is in a state of excitement never before witnessed. Business is entirely suspended for the time being, and the beach is daily thronged with the inhabitants of the place with a view to picking up whatever wreckage of value washes ashore, and also to secure pieces of the boat for mementos of the appalling disaster. Bodies of persons who met watery graves are continually coming ashore, and are picked up by men engaged to patrol the beach, who bury all that are not claimed or identified."

A news story from Meaford, Ontario (near Collingwood) quoted a source saying that "the people of Frankfort behaved nobly towards...the survivors, who were cast upon their shore naked and penniless, feeding, sheltering, and clothing them without the expectation of renumeration or reward." Over a month later, the Cleveland newspaper reported that a Frankfort fisherman had found the *Columbia*, his nets having fouled in her wreckage about three miles off Frankfort.

Point aux Bec Scies's Keeper Matthews had reported to his superiors that his surfmen's duties after the disaster would include watching, day and night, for dead bodies and property, of which they had learned when they observed pieces of a steamer's hurricane deck, bedding, and water casks drifting to the north past the station. Ultimately, three bodies were found by his crew, as well

November, 1882

Montauk

as trunks, life preservers and other items that were retrieved and given to agents of the vessel's owners.

Shortly before the island station's seasonal shutdown at the end of November 1882, Keeper Buss and his crew dealt with what would become a typical crisis for them. A schooner had been wind-driven onto shallows, where, as Buss soon recorded, she would become "a total wreck." She was the *Montauk*, bound with a load of coal from Buffalo to Chicago and caught in a northerly gale and blinding snowstorm.

She had stranded off the island's north end, about three miles from the station at roughly three in the morning, but was not observed until daylight by a fisherman whose shanty was almost opposite the wreck. He sent a man to inform the keeper, who, finding the sea too rough to launch a boat, took two men and hiked about a mile and a half down the beach to better determine the situation, reaching the schooner at about eight thirty. Her distress signal hoisted, she was in danger of breaking up "some distance out from the shore, with the sea making a clean breach over her."

Buss directed the two men to return to the station and, with the help of the rest of the crew, to use his own large sailboat to get to the stranded ship while he went along the beach to signal the sailors on board that help was coming. It took the crew some time to rig and ballast the sailboat, but after "an extremely rough journey," and "watching their chances between the seas," the crew arrived at the wreck at about eleven that morning. and succeeded in taking all eight men off the vessel, bringing them to safety and caring for them for four days.

With their ship and her cargo a total loss, the rescued *Montauk's* sailors said they "felt that they had been lifted from the grave," the schooner's remains lying about thirty-five feet below the surface.

Lifesaving Services
During the Next Decade

Turning to the final twenty years, when the passage waters were served only by the far-separated North Manitou Island and Point aux Bec Scies stations, it should be kept in mind that wherever they served, US lifesavers were tasked to protect vessels, their passengers, crews, and cargo, and were also regarded as willing and able responders to emergencies their landed neighbors confronted.

Station keepers' daily logs, when read a century or more later, reveal circumstances of people's lives quite different from today's realities. The records of the services performed by these first responders of their time and place often determined outcomes of life or death. It should not be forgotten that the risks the surfmen had to bear, the strength and skills they provided, and even the long days and nights they spent faithfully watching and waiting to be needed, were a valued contribution to people's lives in northern Lake Michigan, on and off the water.

At North Manitou Island in early 1882, the US revenue steamer *Johnson* brought the service's assistant inspector and medical examiner to the wharf for the purpose of the mandatory examination of the keeper, island resident Daniel Buss. The station operated that fall from November 3-30, 1882, with an employed crew of six men, and reopened for the active season in early May 1883.

Between 1882 and early 1915, the end of this chronology, the service assigned the station four pulling surfboats, two pulling lifeboats, and in the last year of that span, a doubtless much anticipated motorized surfboat.

Records indicate that in 1882, an approximately twenty-seven-foot-long Squan surfboat was assigned to North Manitou. These boats were known by the name of the New Jersey town where they were built; in this case, Squan Beach.

Builders at that time generally embraced a popular so-called

Jersey design identified with the mid-Atlantic coast, the craftsmen's products varying according to their personal skills and preferences. Jersey boats were clinker-built, not double-ended, as were the dominant later surfboat designs. They instead featured a flat, sloping stern thought to be helpful in managing a boat in a following sea. They typically had six thwarts (seats) for the rowers, and some were outfitted for sailing, an asset when a station crew had to travel a long distance.

The Point aux Bec Scies station opened with a twenty-five-foot Blackburn surfboat (its New York maker's name), built of cedar planks and oak frames. A twenty-seven-foot Long Branch surfboat was assigned there in 1882, and a Dobbins pulling lifeboat in 1887. Throughout its history under the US Life-Saving Service, the station was assigned eight rescue boats, the final one coming in 1912. This one was a motorized adaptation of the popular self-bailing, but not self-righting, Beebe-McClellan surfboat, designed by Lieutenant McLellan of the Revenue-Marine and Frederick Beebe, whose Long Island yard built most of the boats that were used widely for decades.

At one o'clock in the morning on a dark and rainy September day in 1882, the Point aux Bec Scies lookout saw a torch being displayed from a steamer, indicating that the persons aboard were trying to communicate with the station. When the surfman promptly answered by waving his lantern, showing how close the vessel was to the shore, the steamer immediately bore away to the west, avoiding an imminent, possibly fatal, grounding.

Similarly, at North Manitou Island on a foggy May night the following spring, the station's patrol discerned the topmast of a schooner heading straight for the island's beach. He quickly burned his Coston flare, which was seen by those aboard, the vessel being so close that the surfman could hear men running on the deck to manage her sails and alter her course. Only a minute later, he reported, the schooner would have grounded offshore or smashed onto the beach.

On June 15, 1883, the island crew responded to a plea for assistance from the sailors aboard the Milwaukee-based schooner *South Side*, who were unable to raise the vessel's heavy anchor and its sixty fathoms of chain. A common request received from ships not equipped with a powered windlass, four surfmen were dispatched by small sailboat to the vessel, where they labored for two hours until freeing the schooner. The captain was very thankful for the

June, 1883
Southside

crew's assistance, which made possible the timely delivery of her cargo of wood.

About a month later, on July 7, Keeper Buss reported that as he was about to close the North Manitou station to go to dinner, the first mate and cook from the schooner *Golden West* suddenly appeared. They reported that their ship, sailing to Buffalo from Chicago with eight crewmen and two passengers aboard, was ashore on the island's northwest coast, about six and a half miles from the station by land, or about nine miles by water. The mate wanted to get to the mainland by boat, where he could telegraph for a steam-powered tug to free the vessel.

Buss and the mate were unable to find someone to make the trip, and the mate told him that the ship's captain wanted to see the station's keeper. Buss, his crew, and the two men from the schooner got underway in the sailboat at about 2:30 p.m., arriving there about 7:00 p.m. They determined that she could be gotten off the bottom by throwing some of the cargo of corn overboard. The captain wanted to wait for morning before doing it, so, leaving the sailboat for the schooner's crew in case of need, Buss and his men went to shore at about 8:30 p.m. in the schooner's yawl, Buss having been asked to return the following day "with as many men as he could get." They arrived at the station at about 11:00 p.m. Returning to the ship the next morning, they went to work, and by late that afternoon were able to dump most of the corn.

The lifesavers did not get back to the station until about 2:00 a.m. With the aid of a passing steamer, the *Golden West* was freed with only her rudder damaged, and towed into South Manitou Island's protected harbor for repair. Its captain wrote appreciatively to the lifesaving service, saying that the North Manitou crew's efforts had saved his vessel.

At Point aux Bec Scies station, Matthews's entry on November 27, 1883, only a few days prior to closing for the inactive winter season, recorded the discovery of a three-master, northwest of the point, flying a distress signal. He sent a surfman to Frankfort to arrange for a tug to respond to the schooner, and when the tug passed by the station, he sent out three surfmen to assist in the recovery. The tug towed the ship into South Manitou Harbor, just before "it commenced blowing another terrible gale from the south, causing even steamers to run for shelter."

The fall of 1883 brought severe gales to northern Lake Michigan, presenting challenging working conditions at Point aux Bec Scies.

July, 1882
Golden West

As an example, on November 15, Keeper Matthews wrote that amidst gale-force winds and snow squalls, at 3:30 p.m., a three-masted schooner had been sighted northwest of the station, about three miles from shore. "She was standing to the southward under reefed foresail and fore staysail," he later penned, reporting that "it was blowing a heavy gale from the N.W. and a very heavy sea running, and [in] blinding snow squalls, could not see the vessel [except] between squalls."

"At 4:30 p.m., she appeared to be heading in for this station and rolling terribly and made but little headway; as well as we could make out, they were trying to beach her," he concluded. By 5:00 p.m., with darkness coming on, the ship's crewmen were burning torches, and Matthews judged she would strike the beach some-where between the station and Frankfort. He dispatched a surfman to a farm about a mile north of the station, where a team of horses could be obtained, and by 6:30 p.m. they were ready to haul the beach cart toward Frankfort via the state road, as it was the only way to move it southward, the beach having been interrupted by deeply carved gullies that extended back to the trees.

With the cart, the no. 1 surfman, and four others taking the road route, the keeper and his two other men followed the beach as best they could, trying to watch for the vessel. At one point, Matthews burned a Coston flare, attempting to prompt a response from her, but none was seen. The station's two groups met at a place then called Norwegian Creek, about halfway to Frankfort, and followed the "old stone road" to town, which they reached at 9:00 p.m.

They learned then that the ship apparently had passed Frankfort Harbor, unable to navigate the entrance under the dangerous conditions. Matthews telegraphed the keeper of the Manistee station to remain on the lookout for a disabled vessel. With no further opportunity to render assistance, Matthews later recorded, "We started back for the station where we arrived at 12:20, all of us pretty well [whipped] after our tramp of 12 to 14 miles through the snow."

Acknowledging that perhaps he should have led his men farther south, he explained under the conditions of a heavy surf running and freezing snow falling, whatever could have been done at some distant point for the schooner's crew would have had to be accomplished more quickly than his men could provide.

As the active season at the point drew toward its close, Matthews advised his superior officers that he had placed at Frankfort, to be used only in case of a wreck during his station's seasonal shutdown, the following items: one five-oared surfboat; five cork vests; five pulling oars, and one steering oar "to be housed in a sawmill free of charge."

Also that year, responding to the increasingly obvious need, the service recommended to the treasury the construction of a station at Frankfort Harbor, but noted that land titles and acquisition funds were needed.

On the evening of November 15, 1883, strong winds and heavy snowfall drove the *Monitor*, a Detroit-based schooner with a six-man crew, onto North Manitou's southern shore about four and a half miles from the lifesaving station. On account of stormy darkness and the site's being beyond the beach patrol's turnaround point, the vessel was not discovered until the next morning, when the keeper's wife spotted her.

The lifesavers launched their boat and headed for the wreck, but before they got there, a fishing boat located closer to her had rescued the crew and put them aboard the passing US revenue steamer *Andrew Johnson*. The lifesavers and some crew from the steamer thereafter boarded the schooner in an effort to save items of property, but found everything heavily covered with ice. Several days later, they succeeded in removing the vessel's sails, rigging, and other items. The *Monitor* remained on the shore until the following spring, when she came free, but by then was in very poor condition.

Charges of serious neglect were subsequently placed against Keeper Buss for not having gone to the wreck for close to two hours after its discovery, and also against the patrolman who had the morning watch, for having abandoned his observation post before "it was fairly light enough to see the length of his beat, the result being that at daylight there was no one up at the station but the keeper's wife."

Keeper Buss opened his island station for the 1884 spring season on May 1. His crew spent the day preparing the station's beach apparatus and twenty-six-foot surfboat, and cleaning the station and grounds. He dutifully reported having received the following articles: eleven weekly transcripts of journals; four articles of engagement; twelve reports of changes of crews; forty sheets of writing paper; twelve long envelopes, white; twelve small envelopes, white; twelve large brown envelopes; six blotters; one property return book; three pen holders; and eighteen writing pens.

November, 1883
Monitor

Supplies such as these were routinely required to be inventoried, and the service would not tolerate their being wasted.

At Point aux Bec Scies, Keeper Matthews recorded an early-season event the next day, when a surfman had left for the midnight to 4:00 a.m. southward beach patrol with a sense that bad weather was coming. After walking for about a quarter mile, he spotted what he took to be a light immediately to his side, just as a snow squall burst upon him. Turning to look again for the light, "he discovered something coming right onto the beach, [with sails flapping]." The surfman called out to the vessel, whose captain jumped off and came to shore. "So wet and cold that he needed assistance, the surfman took him to the station, where he was given dry clothes and warm drinks."

May, 1884
Hope

They then returned to the boat, which turned out to be the small schooner *Hope* from Grand Haven, loaded with rags and scrap iron, going from Charlevoix to Milwaukee. A surfman went for a tug the next morning, which arrived in the early afternoon, and the lifesavers ran hawsers between the schooner and the tug, and removed about five tons of rags and iron. Four hours later, the tug was able to pull the schooner off the beach, and Matthews and a surfman went to Frankfort with the schooner to retrieve the station's lines.

In mid-July, Buss's island crew began to build a forty-by-forty-foot pier in front of the station, devoting many days that summer to the project.

Later that month, by order of the district superintendent, Keeper Buss and three surfmen went to Leland for their required medical inspections. However, this would prove to be Buss's final month of service.

On August 30, 1884, James Flynn took charge of the North Manitou Island station, succeeding Buss, who was discharged from the service following completion of the investigation into the circumstances of his crew's delayed response to the *Monitor's* disaster the prior fall. The surfman charged with neglect of duty for having left abandoned the lookout post unjustifiably was also discharged.

Keeper Flynn soon had the crew undertake construction of a road to the island's north point for the purpose of affording the crew more efficient access to that storm-prone area. Maintaining the road, however, would prove a persistent challenge.

Maintenance was also the task at Point aux Bec Scies, as Keeper Matthews soon had his crew building a platform in front of the boathouse, the prior one having floated away during the night. Matthews advised his superiors, "I fear [the] station house will have to be moved back at least 100 feet, 150 feet would be better." He said that the surf had cut away about eight feet of the bank in front, so that the surf came within twelve feet of the house. "I think there is no doubt but the surf will reach the house in the fall blows," he added, urging that the structure be moved as soon as possible.

Indicating that a Frankfort business was equipped to move it, Matthews estimated that with his own crew helping, the job could be done for $100 to $150. Until then, he said he would have to move the beach apparatus and surfboat, etc., whenever a gale-force wind and surf arose, as the launch platform very likely would be carried away.

On May 16, 1885, the North Manitou crew was alerted by a resident to assist the islanders in putting out a fire in the woods about a mile from the station. The surfmen took every bucket they had, working for about six hours until the flames were extinguished. Several houses and barns were saved, along with their contents, for which the residents voiced their gratitude. One of them said, "Everything would have been swept away but for the lifesaving crew."

Records indicate that at this time, a twenty-two-foot, nine-inch Dobbins double-ended boat was in use at the North Manitou station, and a similar craft then served at mainland Point aux Bec Scies.

In mid-July of 1885, Keeper Flynn and two crewmen were enjoying an afternoon sail in a small boat when they observed a vessel ashore about nine miles southwest of the station. They turned to shore so that one of the surfmen could quickly return on foot to the station to alert the men on duty, while the captain and his other crewmen sailed as quickly as they could to the stranded steamship, the *Comanche*.

July, 1885
Comanche

A few hours later, the crew arrived from the station, having rowed the surfboat to the wreck. The steamer's captain said he wouldn't need their assistance until the next day, as he was sending for a steam pump. The wrecking tug *Williams* arrived from mainland Manistee as expected, having picked up the surfmen, who assisted the vessel's crew in unloading coal, but the steam pump initially wouldn't operate properly.

The surfmen continued their labor the following day, during which the revenue cutter *Johnson* also signaled the station for a boat to come to pick up supplies of shellac, white lead, and oil. After the crew had again assisted with the unloading of coal from the *Comanche*, the schooner was finally freed, and the tug towed her into South Manitou Harbor. In the course of this effort, the lifesavers had made thirteen trips between the station and the *Comanche* by surfboat, their oar pulls having covered a total of about 120 miles.

That morning, some tension apparently had surfaced among the crew, perhaps fueled in part by the crew's exhaustion. In the keeper's words, one surfman had "refused duty on account of words between him and the Keeper and ordered [the] Keeper to put him ashore. Keeper put him ashore and went to the wreck with four men."

According to the North Manitou station's log for July 28, 1885, several experienced surfmen had "deserted the Service." Sheer exhaustion may have contributed to their offense. Whatever the issue, the men apparently soon had a change of mind, and resumed their duties.

October, 1885

William T. Graves

George W. Adams

Near midnight on the last day of October, in the midst of a major snowstorm, the steam-powered *William T. Graves* had the schooner *George W. Adams* in tow when both vessels went aground about nine miles southwest of the North Manitou station. Manned by eight seamen, the two ships were carrying grain from Chicago to Buffalo. Such towing was an increasingly common practice on the lakes, as sail-powered ships were gradually losing their competitiveness to steamers which were faster and better able to maintain schedules. Quite commonly, aging schooners were stripped of their rigging, etc., and converted into barges.

The lifesavers used their supply boat to go to the scene. As no assistance was then possible, they returned to the station, but early that evening, when snow squalls and higher winds arose, Keeper Flynn sent a surfman five miles down the shore to a point from which he could maintain watch through the night for any signs of distress from the two vessels.

At about 10:00 p.m., upon hearing whistles from the steamer, the surfman burned his Coston flare, both to respond to the steamer's signal and to call his fellow crewmen to the vessels, which they reached in about two hours. Finding the schooner to be leaking, they went to work manning the pumps until morning, when the ship's mate thought he could manage her with his own crew, the wind having shifted somewhat. But not until almost a week later could the schooner be freed with the aid of tugs after a portion of her cargo had been tossed overboard. The steamer, however, was beyond saving; she went to pieces about two weeks later, along with the rest of her cargo.

Charles Lysaght, a surfman under Flynn's command, succeeded him as keeper of the North Manitou station in 1886, when Flynn was transferred to Grand Point Au Sable, near Ludington, Michigan.

On June 14, 1886, as dense fog was descending upon the island, the crew heard whistles of distress. They pulled south in the surf-boat for about five miles to the island's point, where they found a stranded coal-filled steam barge, the *Sparta*. Just before grounding, the eleven-man *Sparta's* crew had managed to cast off two ships under tow, whose crews had been able to drop the anchors and avoid becoming stranded themselves. Shortly before the lifesavers arrived, the steamer had worked herself free, so the rescuers began sounding for sufficiently deeper water and then ferrying lines to the other ships, thus enabling the group to get underway.

Two weeks later, the *Iron Duke*, a large steamer towing a schooner, had stranded in dense fog near Pointe aux Bec Scies. The steamer, with twenty-three persons aboard, was carrying a load of wheat. Its whistle sounded a warning, and the schooner cast off and anchored in deeper water. At the request of the steamer's captain, the point's surfmen rowed about five miles to Frankfort, where they telegraphed for a tug. They then returned to the steamer, and after four hours of hard work shifting cargo, she was refloated with the aid of several fish tugs.

In his journal of September 25, 1886, the point's keeper advised his superiors of a potentially dangerous equipment problem, in a similar tone (but not spelling or grammar) to that used by the service's headquarter publications:

> *This night very dark and rainy and the patrol have much difficulty in getting along the beach from station to key post [where the surfman would record his completion of the route]. The Buckeye lantern is a failure so far as burning in a gail [sic.] of wind; in fact, they will not burn in a moderate gale. Such a night as last night it is no joke to be left in total darkness while patrolling the beach. It is impossible to relight a lantern out on the beach when blowing and raining even in ordinary gale. If men are expected to [complete]their patrol they must have a light.... The very worst weather is the time that a patrolman has no light and must grope his way among fallen timber*

June, 1886
Sparta

June, 1886
Iron Duke

and driftwood, sometimes on his hands and knees. We had no falt [sic] to find when we were allowed mineral, sperm or lard oil. We have good brass railroad lanterns and all that is needed to give us a first class light at all times in all weather is about 3 gallons of mineral oil per year.

During high northerly winds early that October 1, the North Manitou crew observed a distress flag flying from a vessel that appeared to be aground about six miles away. As Keeper Lysaght and his men approached her in their supply boat, they found her to be at anchor.

October, 1886

B. B. Icsman

Coming upon three of the ship's crewmen who were trying to get to shore in a small boat amidst high waves, they took them into the rescue craft and went to their vessel, the barge *B.B. Icsman*, which was headed for Lake Huron's Drummond Island. Her sails were torn, and she was leaking and becoming uncontrollable. She carried no cargo, but four passengers and a crew of seven men were aboard. The lifesavers immediately headed to South Manitou Island, six miles away, where they secured the service of a steamer to tow the stricken vessel back to the harbor's protection.

That October, three North Manitou crewmen were sent to Leland to obtain provisions, because the people with whom they had been boarding during the summer were leaving the island. The men needed provisions to last until their station's scheduled closure for the season on November 30.

A mid-November snow found the point crew once again searching the shore for bodies. A wreck survivor had reported to a resident that his vessel had gone to pieces in the storm south of the station. They found lumber and masts, rigging, decking, and a cabin all mixed together on the beach and in the surf. One body found under the wreckage was carried to shore, but the crew's extensive search revealed no other victims' remains.

A woods fire threatened a North Manitou house that fall. Being the only organized responders upon whom the island's residents could call for help, the crew mustered to attempt to save the structure. The records of the US Life-Saving Service contain countless reports of such acts of service beyond their traditional seacoast duties.

The fall of 1886 marked two particularly notable developments at other stations on the Great Lakes. On November 7, a Lake Michigan lifesaving crew performed a unique service when the men of the St. Joseph station skillfully employed their breeches buoy to haul the lightkeeper to the tower on the north pier. Due to a storm-caused break in the pier, the lifesavers had previously brought the keeper from his post to shore by boat, and also had prepared for the novel buoy technique if stormy weather made it impossible for the lightkeeper to reach his post by boat. (While rivalry often marked the relationships between the men of the two services, especially where their stations were closely situated, the two crews typically were quick to lend each other a hand when the need arose.)

In the other incident, sadness surely had spread all along the lakeshore among the lifesaving community, along with a true sense of "there but for the grace of God go I," with news that three Grand Point Au Sable crewmen, one of them Keeper Flynn, had lost their lives in the line of duty on November 29, just eight months after Flynn had departed North Manitou Island. The service lauded the two "competent and trustworthy surfmen" and their "faithful and gallant keeper," who had responded to a distress signal from the schooner *A.J. Dewey*. For two years, their widows and children under sixteen years of age would receive the amount that the deceased men would have earned, due to the legislation Congress had enacted to compensate families of such tragedies.

Repairs to the North Manitou keeper's dwelling were under contract in fiscal 1887. John H. McKenzie was appointed keeper on March 7, 1887, succeeding Charles Lysaght, who had transferred to the White River, Michigan station. (Lysaght later transferred from White River to the Grand Point Au Sable station, where Flynn, his captain at North Manitou, had lost his life.) Such assignment shifts among the stations within the Lake Michigan district were quite common.

Just two months after his arrival, McKenzie and his crew were called to duty when a sailor arrived at the station in the late afternoon of May 12, 1887, to report that the schooner *Henry Fitzhugh*, of Vermilion, Ohio, had gone aground the previous night in heavy fog on the island's south coast, about nine miles from the station. The lifesavers headed for the schooner, finding her on a rocky bottom and in great danger were the weather to worsen. Boarding her and taking soundings indicating that the bow portion was not on the rocks, they tried to free the ship by using her mainsail and heaving on a line from the bow and an anchor they had set in deeper water.

When this strategy failed, several surfmen went about twelve miles to the mainland to telegraph for a tug from distant Manistee.

November, 1886
A. J. Dewey

May, 1887
Henry Fitzhugh

Upon returning to the wreck, however, the lifesavers spent a full day shifting much of her cargo of grain and other heavy equipment in an effort to float the vessel. That night, the men also tossed sixty to seventy bushels of wheat overboard, whereupon the schooner finally lifted off the rocks. The surfmen then sailed her to South Manitou's safer anchorage. Once again, the lifesavers had provided rigorous service for which the captain was very appreciative.

In mid-June, the North Manitou crew discovered a fishing sloop having a difficult time rounding the island's northern point and feared that she might capsize. When she soon did roll over, the lifesavers immediately launched the surfboat, and when reaching her, they found a man clinging to the overturned hull while it slowly drifted farther from shore. The crew took him into the surfboat and dragged the hulk to the beach, where they turned it over and found a loose plank which had caused her to fill with water and capsize. The men towed the boat to the station and made the necessary repairs, much to the gratitude of the owner, an island resident who had been in poor health for a long time and would have lost his life but for the surfmen's timely action.

On an early July morning, a heavy fog over the lake lifted and a surfman discovered a steamer ashore at the island's south end, about five miles distant from the station. He promptly notified the keeper, and the surfboat was immediately launched and rowed to the scene. The vessel was found to be the coal-loaded *David Ballentine* of Milwaukee, with a seventeen-member crew and three passengers aboard. The lifesavers promptly took soundings around her, then assisted the ship's crew in shifting cargo to the stern so that her bow would rise. With the engines running, the ship then was able to back off the shoal without sustaining serious damage.

At 8:30 a.m. on September 11, the small steamer *John Cowan* from Frankfort, destined for South Fox Island, lost steering while approaching a North Manitou wharf, stranding in shallow water. Within five minutes the lifesavers pulled alongside in the surfboat and landed her two passengers and freight, then set out lines from the vessel to the wharf. The two crews, assisted by the ship's power, were then able to float her off and bring her to the wharf.

On an early October morning in 1887, the schooner *Pulaski* was observed by the North Manitou station's lookout to round the island's north point and drop her two anchors, but in the prevailing gale-force northwest winds, the anchors, having landed on a soft underwater shelf, would not hold. The vessel was bound for

July, 1886
David Ballentine

September, 1886
John Cowan

October, 1887
Pulaski

Manitowoc, Wisconsin from Sandusky, Ohio with a load of coal. The lookout alerted the keeper, and the crew promptly headed for the schooner in their supply boat, where they learned that she had lost some sails and was already waterlogged. The seas were rolling over her deck and threatening to wreck the station's own boat, so the keeper ordered several men to take it back to the station.

Working together with the vessel's seven-man crew, the surfmen and keeper manned her pumps to free the schooner, and then retrieve the anchors with her windlass. The ongoing gale drove the boat to a spot where they could reanchor her, but as the wind became increasingly powerful and waves were sweeping the deck, the men working the pumps began to lose their footing. That night one of the two anchor chains snapped and the schooner began to drag the remaining anchor toward the beach. The ship's yawl was made ready, and by the time it was lowered for use, the schooner had begun to hit bottom. All the people on board were able to land without incident in the yawl, but by midnight the schooner had been totally wrecked.

Two weeks later, General Superintendent Kimball received a letter of thanks from the owners of the *Pulaski*, thanking Keeper McKenzie and his men for their valuable services in staying by the ship and rescuing her crew.

The year 1887 closed with another tragic event that surely brought sadness to the lifesaving community and many area residents. The sixteen-year-old son of Harrison "Tip" Miller, the legendary keeper of the Pointe aux Bec Scies lifesaving station who had served previously both as the lightkeeper and the lifesaving captain on Lake Michigan's Beaver Island, drowned only a half-mile south of his father's station while trying to pull a capsized small skiff through December's cold surf. Having found the son's body, the station's crew mounted determined attempts to revive him by artificial respiration, sadly to no avail. The irony of his loss must have been shocking.

Surfman Peter Olsen was promoted to keeper upon the North Manitou station's opening in April 1888, John McKenzie having been transferred to the lifesaving station at South Haven, Michigan. Olsen would hold the island post for eight years. During that year, a keeper's dwelling was added to the North Manitou station, its surfmen no longer being dependent on private quarters.

A mid-April Pointe aux Bec Scies report notes that the distant South Manitou Light was visible for the first time that year, and that the lake appeared free of ice. But a day later, the keeper reported, "too much ice on beach to launch boat for practice."

In midafternoon on May 14, the island station's lookout saw a vessel stranded on the southeast point, about four miles south of the station. The lifesavers were quickly underway by surfboat, soon reaching the troubled schooner *Morning Star,* which was sailing from Charlevoix, Michigan to Chicago with a cargo of cedar posts and a crew of eight. After unsuccessfully trying to heave the schooner off the bottom by pulling on an anchor they had placed in deeper water, the surfmen then assisted the ship's crew in shifting the cargo toward the stern, which by lightening the bow enabled them to free her, undamaged, from the shoal. The lifesavers then helped to replace the cargo and repair some sails, earning her captain's appreciation for their timely and efficient service.

Two days later, the Pointe aux Bec Scies watch called the keeper's attention to something floating in the lake about two and a half miles away. He was unable to identify it with his binoculars, so the men launched the surfboat and after a substantial pull, found it to be a large pine tree with limbs sticking up from the water, which had made it look like wreckage.

The service's 1888 annual report featured an extensive appeal for an increase in surfmen's pay, which had not been raised since the rate of fifty dollars per month, over eight months of the year. That rate had been set in 1882, with no provision for subsistence, clothing, or other work expenses. The service asserted that "the growth of our commerce has made the duty of the men much more arduous by increasing the number of wrecks and casualties and by multiplying many small services that cannot be enumerated in detail. The demands of the discipline now enforced are also much greater, as [both] an absolutely regular watch and patrol" were now required.

The agency's message continued in a familiar tone:

> It is probably safe to say that there is no other class of men engaged in duties at once so tedious and perilous as those which these faithful guardians of the coast perform in maintaining the unremitting night patrol throughout the rigorous season of the year. But their labors are not confined to this routine of watch, patrol, and daily drill. Summoned in the dead of night, or by day in the midst of their ordinary toil, to a duty higher than these, by an alarm that a vessel is ashore, they take their places at the boat-wagon or the apparatus-cart for

May, 1888
Morning Star

a supreme effort with a courage of determination that has...made them celebrated throughout the land and added to the nation's glory.

"Their bravery and fidelity are made more effective by the possession of a degree of skill only attainable by long experience," the report observed, adding, "Trained from childhood [as] to the handling of boats in heavy seas, they will go out to a wreck through a surf that would daunt the ordinary sailor and instantly capsize or swamp a boat in less experienced hands."

In pressing their case, the service stressed the uniqueness of the lifesavers' occupation: "Conditions are imposed upon their employment to which the ordinary wage earner is not subject. They must not only be expert in the management of boats, being selected because of this by the keepers, who are themselves men of tried ability and experience, but must pass a rigid physical examination proving themselves to be thoroughly sound in body. They must also give up the pleasures of home and family life, and dwell at the isolated stations where they are subjected to rules of severe discipline. If derelict they are immediately discharged."

With these realities in mind, Kimball and his small management team warned, "While enthusiasm for the philanthropic work, and downright love of the Service may hold many to their employment, it is easy to foresee that it will be impossible to maintain the present high standard of efficiency if this obligation of the Government is neglected." The pay issue was particularly acute in the Great Lakes region, the service adding, "In the spring of this year, thirty-one percent of the surfmen in these districts left to engage in other pursuits."

There would be no holiday for the crew on 1888's July 4, as the station's watch discovered a steamer possibly aground on North Manitou's southeast point. Keeper Peter Olsen was notified, and the men responded by surfboat to the vessel, the *Lawrence*, which was traveling from Mackinac to Chicago with a load of general merchandise and passengers. Having boarded her to be of assistance if needed, Olsen remained there until her captain managed to work the vessel free.

Then the fishing-tug *John Cowan*, out of Grand Haven, caught fire with four men aboard while anchored on August 1 in Platte Bay. The Pointe aux Bec Scies surfmen pulled eight miles in their surfboat and towed the wreck into shoal water, where the fire consumed the wreck, its crew being taken to the station in the surfboat.

July, 1888
Lawrence

August, 1888
John Cowan

August, 1888

Alaska

August, 1888

New Era

October, 1888

Enterprise

Albatross

Two weeks later, with deep daytime fog prevailing over the Manitous and as far south as Pointe aux Bec Scies, doubtless putting numerous ships in difficult circumstances, the lumber steamer *Alaska* went aground four miles south of the North Manitou station. One of her crew hiked to the station to inform the surfmen of their trouble. They quickly launched the surfboat and headed to the site, where the keeper boarded and took charge of shifting the vessel's cargo sternward while his crewmen sought unsuccessfully to heave her off. They then dropped the vessel's main anchors and chains in an effort to further lighten her bow. By heaving on a kedge anchor they had placed farther offshore and working her engines, they managed to free the steamer, saving her large cargo of general merchandise and crew of twenty-four men.

On that same August day, the lumber-loaded steamer *New Era* stranded in the fog a mile north of the Pointe aux Bec Scies station. The surfmen tried to free her, but with their efforts failing, they sent for a tug. The men shifted her cargo, enabling the vessel's own engines to pull her bow off the bottom with only slight damage. She resumed her way after the surfmen had repositioned the cargo.

About two months later, the island's Keeper Olsen dutifully wrote that early in the morning "the watch at the station saw a steamer's head light come into view on the south side of South Point. 5 minutes later it appeared to stop and the watch immediately reported the fact to the Keeper who ordered out the surfboat and proceeded to the point. After a sharp pull of 40 minutes, we arrived alongside the stranded steamer *Enterprise* and her towed consort schooner, the *Albatross*, both heavily laden with corn."

In extraordinarily clear penmanship (a trait future researchers would much appreciate!), Olsen's account continues:

> As the Sch. did not appear to be on very hard we stretched the tow line from the bow of the Sch. to the stern of the Str. and with the assistance of a steam winch set a heavy strain on it but were unable to move her more than a few inches. Not successful in getting her off, we hoisted colors on board the sch. and sounded four 'blasts' aboard the Str. for the surfmen at the station to come down to the vessels with the supply boat as the Capt. of the Str. wished to send a dispatch for a tug. As soon as she arrived I sent two men...with the dispatch out to a passing Steam barge with orders to ask them if they would take it, which they did. As soon as they returned an anchor was carried out abreast of the Sch. and a heavy hawser bent to it and run to the stern of the Str. as we hoped that as she would not come off by the

head maybe we would move her by the stern but after working for two hrs. we were unable to get her off. We then went over to the Str. and assisted to shovel corn overboard to lighten her. After laboring for about two hours the Str. backed off. All hands then manned the surfboat and the heavy line was carried out to her to the bow of the Str. At the first jerk the line parted. But it was...spliced and this time the Str. successfully pulled her off. We then hove the anchor home and with many thanks from the Capt. returned to the Station and arrived at 4 P.M.

Later that fall, the North Manitou crew responded to a distress signal from the schooner *David Stewart* from Detroit, anchored about a mile and a half northeast of the station in the face of south-westerly gale-force winds. The already leaking vessel was rolling such that her rigging was in danger of being destroyed.

November, 1888

David Stewart

After the keeper advised the anxious captain that his ship would be better off at another nearby site, the vessel's eight-man crew managed to work her to safety, where the lifesavers helped to pump her out. Two days later, the weather having moderated, the station's men piloted the schooner to open water. She then resumed her course from Buffalo to Chicago, where she was to deliver her cargo of coal.

The service's 1889 report renewed its leaders' compensation concerns, in this instance calling for pensions to be available to the officers and other personnel, as well as to widows and children of crewmen lost in the line of duty. The appeal added that an appropriate "simple and inexpensive" uniform requirement had been imposed upon the stations' personnel, but no appropriation had been enacted to cover this expense; hence, the men might regard that as a tax, and as yet another "good reason" for an increase in their compensation.

At Pointe aux Bec Scies, Keeper Miller, whose boat handling skills were highly recognized within the Great Lakes district, had his crew practicing with the station's self-righting Dobbins surf-boat on June 18, and lamented in his daily report that the men had capsized her twice and that she had failed both times to right herself. "It was about as hard to right her as it was to turn her over," he reported, but promised to try again when the weather improved. A week later, he reported another failing of the model, writing that "she would not right today until we rolled her over on her beam ends. My men are all disappointed in the Boat as well as myself, for we supposed we had a Self-righting Boat."

July, 1889

Rochester

On July 27, 1889, North Manitou's Keeper Olsen wrote another of his typically detailed reports, this one of a rescue undertaken by his crew that morning after a beach patrolman heard the "heavy working of a steam engine on the south point about five miles" from the station in thick fog. The surfman returned to the station immediately and informed the keeper of his discovery. The station's surfboat was launched and "all possible haste made" to reach the steamer, which proved to be the *Rochester* of Buffalo, bound for Chicago loaded with general merchandise.

Keeper Olsen reported that his crew found the vessel aground despite attempts by the helpful crew of a nearby steamer, the *Chemany*, to pull her off. Several hard pulls having resulted in a torn hawser, Olsen's crew worked to retrieve the parted line, recognizing that additional pulls would not succeed unless some of the *Rochester's* cargo was first removed. For two and a half hours, the surfmen shifted cargo to the other steamer. The *Rochester* was then able to back off from the shallows into deeper water. As Olsen summed up the event, "all saved, we returned to the station with many thanks from the Capt. and arrived at station at 3 p.m."

August, 1889

Charlie Crawford

Just over a month later, he wrote that at 4:00 a.m. on September 5, the watchman at the station saw a schooner, the *Charlie Crawford*, displaying distress signals. He alerted the keeper, and the surfboat was launched. When the crew came alongside, they found that she was in dangerous condition, with about sixty fathoms (360 feet) of chain out and listing two feet. The keeper and crew assisted in weighing her anchor and as the line was strained, the windlass's brake broke in two. The lifesavers quickly pulled for the shore and retrieved the broken part. They went aboard the vessel again, repairing the windlass, and then were able to heave up the anchor, enabling the schooner to depart for Chicago. The surfmen returned to the station just before noon, having received the captain's many thanks.

October, 1889

Enterprise

Albatross

In early morning darkness that October 7, both the steamer *Enterprise* and schooner *Albatross* under her tow ran aground five miles south of the North Manitou station. The surfman on watch had seen the steamer's lights approach the shore, then stop, and he had promptly reported the incident to the keeper. Leaving one of the crew to man the station, the surfmen headed to the scene in the surfboat, where they found the two vessels, both from St. Catherine's, Ontario, carrying full loads of corn from Chicago for delivery to Buffalo. Fifteen crewmen were aboard the steamer, and five aboard the schooner.

The lifesavers first made two unsuccessful attempts to free the schooner using a deeply anchored line, then returned to the steamer to aid her crew in lightening the vessel by tossing corn overboard. Keeping the engines going while they did this work for over two hours, they then were able to back off the shoal. The surfmen then ran a hawser between the vessels, so the steamer could try to free the schooner. The hawser broke under the strain, but the men were able to splice it together and refloat the schooner.

That fall, as work was underway to enhance the protection of the Pointe aux Bec Scies Lighthouse, the lifesaving station keeper noticed that laborers were trying to pole a scow off the beach to where a waiting tug would take over. He realized, however, that in the face of a strong southerly wind and high seas, the men would be unable to reach the tug. He put his surfmen to work, and by towing from their surfboat and continuing poling by the six workmen on the scow, they managed to move the craft off the beach and to where the tug could reach it. Without the assistance, the scow likely would have broken up.

A couple of weeks later, the lifesavers again came to the aid of the lighthouse repairmen, helping to get a scow out to the tug. And at yet another occasion during the lighthouse project, the lifesavers spent three days unloading a stone-filled scow when no other help was available—one service again aiding the other.

On an 1889 December day, when Pointe aux Bec Scies' Keeper Miller's young daughters were walking the log- and stone-strewn beach to Frankfort, they were startled to come upon a man's body. The coroner was informed, but the body could not be identified.

Point Betsie Tower and Lighthouse entrance, ca. 1900. During the 1890's the site's name would evolve from the French Pointe aux Bec Scies to the English Point Betsey, then Point Betsie.

Author's collection.

Challenges Mount in the Nineties

Shortly after the station's April opening for the 1890 season, when Keeper Miller was away from the station working on the south patrol post, a small sloop was observed washing ashore at about 7:00 p.m. Two men, having been unable to manage her in a stiff wind, were aboard. The station was not yet fully staffed for the season, but one of the surfmen was close by, and he and the keeper soon were able to save the boat and its two sailors, caring for them overnight until sea conditions had improved.

Early that spring, the Point Betsie station, having been equipped recently with a telephone, received a call from the Manitou Passage's settlement at Otter Creek, about fourteen miles north-east of their station. A steamer loaded with timber had severed her moorings during a storm, drifted away from shore, and was sinking. It took two hours for the lifesavers to reach the scene in the keeper's fishing boat, which had been equipped with sails. A tug had been called to bring a pump to the ship, but the cargo on her deck had to be removed before the equipment could be effectively used. Working together for several hours, the lifesavers and the ship's crew got the job done. She then surfaced, enabling her to be safely docked.

In late April, the North Manitou station's watch discovered a large buoy drifting in a fresh north wind and heavy sea. With the lookout keeping the elusive, potentially hazardous navigational aid in sight, the surfboat was immediately launched and headed to the buoy, which they identified as having come from South Fox Island, where it marked a dangerous reef. The surfmen towed the heavy buoy to the station, and the district lighthouse inspector was notified of its recovery. Within a few days, the lighthouse service's *Dahlia* stopped at the station and took the buoy for resetting.

Near the end of May, the island's crew took the surfboat about a mile out to the steamer *Charlevoix*, which was displaying a signal for a boat, and ferried four passengers to shore. In early June, the men responded to a signal of distress coming from a steamer whose captain had lost his reckoning amid dense fog. The keeper piloted the vessel away from the island's dangerous south point and put her on a safe course.

That mid-June, the eight-manned schooner *North Cape*, heading home to Chicago with a load of cedar ties, grounded in thick morning fog at North Manitou Island's northwest point. Alerted by a fisherman to the accident, the lifesavers rowed to her in the surfboat and carried an anchor and line from the ship to about four hundred yards offshore. Using the windlass, they managed to draw the ship free and undamaged, after about six hours' hard work.

June, 1890
North Cape

Also, late that spring the men aided the steamer *St. Louis*, which had run aground on the southwest point of the island, about nine miles from the station. The vessel was lightened by throwing off about one thousand bushels of grain and tons of coal while her engines kept running, and she then floated off the bottom without significant damage. A captain's main goal being to save his ship, such were the risks growers and merchants faced in sending their products to distant markets.

June, 1890
St. Louis

Two weeks after the opening of the Point Betsie station for the spring of 1891, a woman came to notify the keeper that the tug *Campbell* had run aground about seven miles north of there in heavy fog. The crew went to the wreck by surfboat, finding her full of water. The surfmen began pumping and bailing her with pails for several hours, but could not free her. Keeper Miller sent a man to Edgewater, a small settlement about three miles farther north on the Platte River, where he could telegraph Manistee for another tug and a more powerful pump. Shortly after arriving at about 2:00 a.m., she pulled the wreckage free of the bottom. Doubtless assisted by Point Betsie's beacon, the crew was back to the station two hours later, "tired and hungry."

June, 1891
Campbell

Several weeks after the opening of the North Manitou station for the season, a steamer and the schooner *John T. Mott,* with three barges in tow, headed for Racine, Wisconsin, from Buffalo with a huge load of coal, anchored south of the station where the wind was "blowing stiff from the southwest with a heavy sea." Olsen wrote that at 2:00 a.m., the steamer and schooner began to drag until they were three miles northeast of the station, where they both reanchored in water sixty fathoms deep.

June, 1891
John T. Mott

That afternoon, the captain of the schooner came ashore by a small craft and asked for a blacksmith to fix his windlass. Keeper

Olsen requested a surfman to repair the windlass parts that the captain had brought to shore. After having done so, more difficulties were encountered with the device, and the captain requested that the anchor chain be cut. With the appreciation of the captain, the station crew cut the schooner free from its buried anchor, thereby enabling her to get underway.

At about this time, with passenger ships increasingly offering cruises up and down Lake Michigan, the lifesavers were frequently asked to provide water taxi service to the ships, such as one day when the *City of Charlevoix* blew six whistles to alert the North Manitou station that she could not land at the island's wharf due to excessive wind and rain, where she was to pick up nine persons. The surfmen took the stranded passengers and their baggage out to the steamer.

Two months later, when the island keeper and some of his crew had gone to Leland for supplies, they were informed by a relative of one of the surfmen that the father of a surfman was seriously ill. Asked if he could stay with his father when the group headed back to the island, the keeper kindly gave his permission.

On July 12, 1891, an unnamed small sloop with three inexperienced men came to Point Betsie during a gale, but their boat remained exposed to the battering waves. The surfmen were able to beach the boat and provide its men overnight lodging.

In a squall later that month, the north island crew came to the aid of a disabled schooner and discovered that two of her crew were injured. The surfmen trimmed the boat's deck load, pumped her out, and got her underway. In November, the steamer *Clyde* went aground near North Manitou. The lifesavers responded by trimming her cargo and running out anchors, then freed her by using her engines to pull her off the bottom. Early the next month, a fisherman came to the station, saying that he had found a man's body floating in the water about three and a half miles from the station. The keeper and three surfmen headed out to recover the body and bring it to the station for examination. The victim was an island resident named Anderson.

In the cold of November 27, the Point Betsie crew went to aid a waterlogged schooner, the *Ebenezer*, whose five crewmen, having endured thirty-six hours of exposure to the cold without food, had abandoned their ship in a small boat that was likely to overturn in the big breakers. The lifesavers rescued them and took them to the station, where they received food and clothing, and those suffering

June, 1891
City of Charlevoix

July, 1891
Clyde

November, 1891
Ebenezer

from frostbite were given medical treatment. Two surfmen went to assist the schooner, and a tug soon towed her into Frankfort.

The service's 1891 annual report again cited the general superintendent's concern that many excellent keepers and surfmen were giving up lifesaving on account of finding employment opportunities that were better paying and less demanding and risky. The report emphasized, in particular, trying circumstances at Great Lakes stations where about 30 percent of the experienced surfmen were being lured away by the substantially greater compensation commercial marine firms were offering. The service urged that the pay "of these gallant men be fixed at such rates as will place them above the allurements which constantly beset them to engage in other pursuits, where, with a higher scale of compensation, there is less hardship to be encountered and comparatively no risk to life or limb."

In its next annual report, the service acknowledged that the US Congress had responded to its persistent calls for pay increases for surfmen. The administrators anticipated that the new rates "will undoubtedly materially check the exodus of the trained veterans whose experience and valor have so conspicuously ennobled the Service and honored the Government, and make it easier to obtain in the future recruits of the highest qualifications, while the hardships and perils of the Service will be cheerfully accepted and a healthier *esprit de corps* be established and maintained."

A year later, while reiterating its gratitude, the service made note of one curious caveat: the rise in surfmen's pay from fifty to sixty-five dollars per month applied specifically to men working no more than eight months of the year. If a man worked even a single day more than that, his rate fell to sixty dollars, a limitation which seamen serving on the Great Lakes found to be unfair. Lifesaving stations were required to be open to serve mariners until the close of the navigation season, which often was a few days shorter on Lake Superior than on longer ice-free Lakes Michigan, Huron, and Ontario. Furthermore, seeking to maximize profits, companies commonly tried to continue shipping as long as weather conditions would permit, and so their customers' inventories would meet their needs until whenever spring arrived.

Because there was no way to know well in advance when navigation would cease, this differential in pay not only troubled the surfmen on the more southerly lakes, it raised havoc for the service's accounting staff. Given the appropriations process, about a year passed before this penalty was addressed, but the service in 1893 advised Congress that while the enacted provisions initially had helped to reduce the number of men who had been choosing not to reenlist, the seasonal inequity threatened to cause the same adverse effect on the lakes.

Irrespective of that situation, as the surfmen were generally employed by the service for only eight months, they were required to save for the remaining four months' living expenses or to find temporary employment elsewhere. Not until 1908, a decade and a half later, would there be another increase in compensation; by legislation enacted in that year, keepers' pay went up from $800 to $1,000, and that of a station's most valuable assistant, its no. 1 man, went up by five dollars, to seventy dollars a month. There was one other benefit: the statute granted keepers and all surfmen a single daily ration, valued at about thirty cents, while leaving the men on their own for other meals.

In the wee hours of June 2, 1892, the North Manitou surfman making the south patrol sighted a steamer in the darkness dangerously close to shore. He quickly exhibited his Coston flare, to which the vessel's crew promptly reacted, the steamer immediately sheering off to a safe distance from shore. Such reports became more frequent as steamers gradually replaced the lake's commercial schooner fleet, steamers being able to respond more rapidly to patrollers' warnings and alter course with only a quick turn of the wheel, while not having also to man the sails to avoid a frequently destructive stranding.

Keeper Olsen reported that month that he had sailed to Leland to pick up the station's life car, but was unable to immediately return on account of lack of wind. The following day he was back at the station, having towed the wallowing car fourteen miles across the passage.

In late June 1892, when the schooner *Fleetwing* ran aground near Point Betsie, the station's surfmen went to her in the surfboat and brought the three crewmen to shore after trying without success to heave her off the shoal with a deep-set anchor. Two days later they landed her cargo of perishable goods and shipped it to the destination, and thereafter pumped out the schooner and carried lines between her and a tug that pulled her free. However, the schooner was leaking badly, so three surfmen went aboard her to man pumps while the tug towed her to Frankfort.

The Point Betsie lifesavers provided yeoman's service on July 19,

June, 1892
Fleetwing

1892, in responding to a boat with two fishermen aboard, one of whom was seriously bleeding from the lungs. At the request of his companion, the crew placed the ill man in the surfboat and rowed him home to South Frankfort.

There were days when things didn't go as well as might have been expected, particularly if the public happened to be aware of them. Such was the case at Point Betsie on July 24, 1892, when fifteen persons were visiting the station. Captain Miller wrote that because the visitors had never seen the beach apparatus in operation, he decided to run a practice for them. "Powder used 2 oz., elevation 18 degrees, range of shot 168 yards, distance from sand anchor to drill pole 75 yards. [But] when the [breeches] buoy was about ¼ of the way in, the sand anchor gave way, not having been buried deep enough to hold.... It made a bad exhibit for the spectators. I reprimanded the men for their carelessness in burying the anchor; I don't think it will happen again with us."

About a month later, Captain Morency of the new Frankfort lifesaving station took out the self-righting lifeboat, with the wind blowing quite fresh from the southwest. He made a tack to the northward, and when about abreast of the Point Betsie station, he came about, heading back toward Frankfort. He made two more tacks but gained no headway; the Betsie crew ultimately saw him take the sail down and put out the oars, but in the wind and the high sea his men were unable to hold the boat on course. When it became clear that they were heading for the beach, Captain Miller sent his men with tackles and other gear to help with the boat as it came to shore. He recorded that if his crew had not been there, the boat likely would have been badly damaged. Quipping that he was aware that the Frankfort keeper had vowed to show those "[Betsie] Boys" how to sail, Miller observed that he would not be following his town colleague's example.

The North Manitou crew went to the aid of the schooner *Lottie Mason* several days later, after she had dragged her moorings in gale-force winds. They got her underway and sought to get into the harbor, but when her foresail split, they anchored her safely until the storm had passed.

An August day presented an emergency which called for rather drastic service by Keeper Olsen. About 11:00 a.m., the schooner *Rosa Belle* of Sheboygan anchored in the bay about a half mile south of his station. The vessel's captain came ashore to tell the station's crew that one of his men had been hurt badly; he had two large

July, 1892
Lottie Mason

August, 1892
Rosa Belle

cuts on his chin, and his upper lip was split from the right corner of his mouth up to his nose. He was in agony, and as no medical assistance was available within fourteen miles of the station, Keeper Olsen decided to "perform the operation." He sewed up the poor man's lip and bandaged the cut on his chin, making him as comfortable as he could; a keeper leading an isolated station would have expected the need to be a jack of all trades.

On August 25, 1892, Olsen recorded that the crew had practiced with the surfboat in high sea as well as in loading and unloading the boat directly from its wagon. That same day, Olsen and one of his surfmen observed a small skiff that had capsized due to the boatman's "mismanagement." Olsen and his crewmen saved both the occupant and his craft.

In September, they were back to providing taxi service, bringing nine passengers from the steamer *Lawrence* to shore amidst high wind and heavy seas.

October, 1892

Simpson

In early October, the schooner *Simpson* sought assistance in anchoring in the lee of North Manitou to ride out a gale. Her captain being unfamiliar with the vicinity, the lifesavers boarded the schooner and guided her to safer anchorage.

That October 9, the island crew took the widowed Mrs. Anderson, whose husband's drowning was said to have left her in "destitute circumstances," to Leland in the station's supply boat, along with her children and their personal effects. Due to rough weather, the crew had cared for the family for four days prior to being able to ferry them safely to the mainland. Once again, the surfmen had served compassionately on land as well as water.

On October 28, 1892, while the schooner *Maggie Thompson* was being loaded with tanbark on North Manitou for delivery across the lake to Milwaukee, she was overtaken with heavy weather and forced to anchor in an exposed position, from which she was in danger of being driven ashore. The crew boarded the schooner to be of assistance, and then discovered that another schooner, the *Waukesha*, was dragging toward her. The lifesavers assisted both ships' crews, and stood by them throughout the night. In the morning they brought the station's beach apparatus in case it might be needed for a rescue, but both ships managed to ride out the storm.

October, 1892

Maggie Thompson

Waukesha

W. H. Gilcher

Ostrich

Also during that October gale-filled night, the steel steamer *W.H. Gilcher* disappeared near the Manitous, with the loss of her entire twenty-one-member crew, having possibly collided with the *Ostrich*, a schooner known to have gone down with all hands at that time. Built in Cleveland only a year before her tragic demise, the 302-foot-long, forty-one-foot-wide steamer is memorialized in these (summarized) chantey verses:

> On October twenty-eight,
>   Oh, how the wind did scream!
> The last time the Gilcher
>   And crew was ever seen.
> Of death these jolly lads
>   Never once did dream
> As routed for Milwaukee,
>   They from Port Huron steamed.
>
> It was a fearful night,
>   The Gilcher should turned-to,
> But she held to her course
>   'Till off the Manitous.
> Says a sailor's hurried note
>   That later came to light,
> They were breasting mounta'n'us seas
>   At nine o'clock that night.
> Lost in Lake Michigan,
>   They did not reach the shore,
> Never once did dream,
>   As routed for Milwaukee,
> They from Port Huron steamed.
>
> Lost in Lake Michigan,
>   They did not reach the shore,
> The gallant ship and crew
>   Will sail the Lakes no more!

But life on the lake must go on. About ten days later, the North Manitou station's morning lookout spotted what was initially thought to be the hull of a dismasted schooner about ten miles north of the station. Manning the surfboat, the keeper and his crew pulled to the hulk and determined it was actually a large, apparently very new, unmanned dump scow whose line to her tug had broken about twenty miles off Sturgeon Bay in gale-force south winds, casting her free to drift across the lake. They notified the owners, who sent a tug to retrieve her. In a letter of acknowledgement sent to the service's district superintendent, the grateful captain said the station's rescue had saved his company about $5,000 (about $143,000 in current value).

And on another late fall day, the captain of the schooner *Simpson*, who was unfamiliar with these waters, wished to gain the protection of the island as he confronted gale-force winds. The keeper boarded the vessel and anchored her safely.

That same month, a schooner under close-reefed sail appeared off the station during high winds. The keeper suspected she was in difficulty, so the crew pulled out to her. The vessel's captain sought guidance to an anchorage, so Keeper Olsen piloted her to safety, where she remained until the gale subsided, and then the vessel, loaded with lumber and shingles, resumed course for Chicago.

November's reputation for particularly fearful weather was surely borne out that year. The Buffalo-based schooner *Annie Vought*, headed for Milwaukee with a cargo of coal, was driven aground on South Manitou Island, about ten miles from the North Manitou lifesaving station, in a severe late-November snow squall.

Happening to spot the wreck, the crew of the US revenue cutter *Andrew Johnson* informed Keeper Olsen of the impending disastrous breakup. The island crew's first task was to load all the equipment for breeches buoy rescues into the surfboat and row to the cutter, which stood by offshore. It took an hour and a half for the surfmen to disassemble the beach cart, put it into the surfboat, and pull to the cutter, which then towed the surfboat and beach apparatus to the wreck. With the lifesavers aboard, the cutter steamed to South Manitou, and the apparatus was rowed to shore and readied again for service.

Many persons, some of them from other vessels that were riding out the severe gale, quickly lent their hands to the rescue effort. The cart was hauled to the wreck site over driftwood-covered sand. The rescuers could see that the schooner had already broken in two, with her starboard side "stove-in." More ominously, they could see members of the schooner's crew huddled together on the deck's forecastle, which gave them a little protection, but they were nonetheless in grave danger of being washed off the vessel by deck-sweeping, ice-cold waves.

Having mounted the breeches buoy apparatus on the shore, the lifesavers fired their Lyle gun toward the schooner, their first shot falling directly across the mast's crosstrees, toward which a

November, 1892

Annie Vought

November, 1892

Andrew Johnson

crewman could be seen making his way across the slippery surface to try to grab the line. However, the huge running seas made it impossible for the men on deck to haul in the line, which kept drifting away. The frustrating circumstances led the lifesavers to retrieve it and prepare for a second shot which also hit its target, this time a man being able to fasten it about twenty feet up the mast.

When the hawser was finally in place for rescue, a sailor was seen to be hesitant about getting into the shorts-like carrier. The keeper could be heard hollering from shore, encouraging him. After the sailor finally found the courage to begin his ride, it surely wasn't a pleasant experience for him, as slackness in the hawser caused him to be dragged through the breaking waves. Exhausted when finally reaching shore, he was given a drink of brandy by the captain of another steamer at Keeper Olsen's order, and taken to a fisherman's cottage to recover.

Six other men and the one woman were rescued in the same fashion, she so badly frozen on reaching shore that she had difficulty walking to a house whose residents would care for her. The seventy-seven-year-old schooner captain had suffered terribly from the cold, and he, too, was unable to walk. He and the other men were given brandy (apparently not the woman), and when the mate, the last man, reached shore, he grabbed Keeper Olsen's hand and cried out, "Thank you, gentleman, you have saved my life."

Unable to find dry clothing, the lifesavers still confronted the challenge of getting their frozen equipment into the surfboat, and then completing their journey back to the North Manitou station on the revenue cutter.

The agency's national commanders reported on the June 30 end of fiscal 1893 that "the fears expressed in former reports of threatened decadence of the Service on account of the frequent resignations of many of the best surfmen have been dispelled by the recent increase in their pay granted by Congress." The report also stressed, "This enactment, together with the continued observance of the law requiring that appointments 'shall be made solely with reference to fitness and without reference to political or party affiliations' now enables the Service to obtain the best qualified men, whenever recruits are needed."

The North Manitou crew was called upon on July 8, 1893, to assist the schooner *Frank W. Gifford*, which faced a challenge off the island's shore after having paid out 150 fathoms of anchor while

July, 1893
Frank W. Gifford

riding out a gale. Her crew could not bring in the heavy anchors, so the lifesavers boarded the vessel and worked seven hours to free her. Upon her master's request, they then supplied the vessel with provisions to meet her crew's needs until reaching their port.

In mid-September, the Point Betsie lifesavers went to the aid of the dismasted schooner *Three Bells*, anchored three miles offshore and eighteen miles north of the station with her rudder also broken. A team was hired to pull the equipment to the site, which they reached in the dark. Launching the surfboat, they rescued five persons. The next day a tug came and towed the schooner to Frankfort, with the surfmen cleaning up the wreckage and assisting in weighing her anchor.

Just a few days later, the island's crew came to the aid of the schooner *C.L. Fick*, which grounded on rocks nine miles from the station, her crew having abandoned her under the presumption she would be considered a total loss. The rescuers were not so easily discouraged; they boarded her, and managed to refloat and sail her to the station.

Her captain had been severely injured by falling into the hold when she had stranded. The lifesavers attended to his needs with remedies from the medicine chest, then carried him aboard and put him to bed and helped the crew get their ship underway on a course to Frankfort. The *C.L. Fick's* master subsequently wrote General Superintendent Kimball to express his appreciation for the North Manitou Island lifesavers' "gallant services" in saving his vessel from destruction.

The weather during the late summer and early fall of 1893 must have been especially troublesome in the passage, as the North Manitou lifesavers were called upon nearly daily to deliver passengers to and from steamships that could not reach the pier. As passenger business continued to rapidly expand on the Great Lakes, the steamers *City of Charlevoix* and *Puritan* were among vessels whose captains frequently sought the lifesavers' assistance for their customers in rough passage seas.

On September 24, the Point Betsie crew went to the aid of the dismasted sloop *Two Brothers*, which had anchored about fourteen miles from the station. The lifesavers headed to her in the surfboat, arriving just after two seamen had been taken off by a fishing boat. A new mast was made for her, but because of the sea conditions her own crew could not raise it themselves or get the sloop to shore. Before departing at 1:15 a.m. for the long trip back to the

September, 1893
Three Bells

September, 1893
C. L. Flick

September, 1893
Two Brothers

North Manitou
Island Station,
ca. 1893.

US National Archives.

station, Keeper Miller directed two of his crew to stay behind and help repair the vessel and get her underway. The surfmen reached home in the surfboat about five hours later, and the other two men arrived the following morning, having declined the sloop captain's offer to pay them for their essential assistance. Meanwhile, the station was a bit shorthanded, but under Keeper Miller's leadership, surely prepared to handle an emergency.

On November 19, 1893, the schooner *Iris* sought the protection of North Manitou's lee during a western gale, but dragged her anchors and drifted dangerously toward the mainland. The vessel was heavily coated with ice, and her crewmen were exhausted from their continuous work and exposure to three days of bitter weather. With the ship's windlass having broken, its crew was unable to bring up the anchors and seventy-five fathoms of chain, so the lifesavers did the task with tackle, then worked the ship to a safer spot and pumped her out.

Winter passed, and the new active season arrived. On June 15, 1894, the schooner *Restless* of Milwaukee was about four miles off the North Manitou station when she encountered a squall that carried away her forebooms, jibbooms, and bowsprit, rendering her virtually uncontrollable. The lifesavers boarded the schooner and helped clean up the wreckage and get her to a safe anchorage. They

November, 1893
Iris

June, 1894
Restless

returned the next day with a length of timber from which to fashion new spars, making all the essential repairs to enable the schooner to resume her voyage. Lifesavers could sometimes be valued carpenters as well as welders, innkeepers, and deliverymen!

The schooner *H.D. Moore*, which had anchored that August in shallows off the town of Leland, began to pound the bottom severely, and a distress signal was heard from her. The island's keeper and a surfman, who happened to have gone to Leland together for supplies in a small boat, responded to the vessel's plight by boarding her and assisting in manning the windlass as waves swept across the decks, forcing the two crews to stop their work. But after six hours of hard work, they were able to heave the schooner to deeper water. As the old vessel was already in leaking condition, had the lifesavers not happened to be at the site, poised to help, the schooner likely would have been destroyed.

On a night in early August, the schooner *Anna P. Grover* stranded in fog and high seas on North Manitou's southeast coast, about four miles from the station. Discovering her the next day, the surfmen went to her and found her too high on the beach to be movable. They took her master to Leland to secure a tug, returning late that night, and after housing the master, took him to his vessel the next morning.

After running lines to help prevent her from pounding to pieces, the surfmen took the master to Good Harbor Bay to arrange for a second tug. The next day they brought him and his wife to the station because of harsh weather, where they stayed for three days, when the ship was finally freed. That was one more skill—bed and breakfast providers!

On August 9, the Point Betsie crew assisted the "wet-through and worn-out" crew of the waterlogged lumber schooner *Magdalena*, which was exhibiting a distress signal after rounding the point several miles north of the station, her men having been pumping for many hours without food or rest. Several surfmen were put on board to help man the ship, while Keeper Miller and his other crewmen started rowing to Frankfort to procure a tug. They got there just as the tug, having been alerted by the harbor's station to the need of assistance, was already underway to the site. Doubtless frustrated, Miller wrote in the journal, "This is another case when [a] telephone would have come in good use," meaning that had he been kept apprised, his crew's efforts could have been reduced.

August, 1894
H. D. Moore

August, 1894
Anna P. Grover

August, 1894
Magdalena

Three weeks later, a passing steamer alerted the station that another steamer had stranded on the passage's mainland Pyramid Point, fourteen miles north, in thick and smoky weather occasioned by nearby forest fires. The crew immediately started for the vessel, the *Florida,* and worked through the night, attempting without success to lighten her. The crew then rowed eight miles to and from Glen Haven for a tug. Managing to free the ship the following day, the crew returned to Point Betsie after working for almost forty-eight hours in this rescue effort.

The schooner *Maggie M. Avery,* her sails having blown away, was sighted dragging offshore from her anchorage a mile off the Point Betsie station on September 3. Managing to catch her several miles farther up the lake and finding her "down by the head," the surfmen shifted some of her lumber cargo and dumped it overboard, and then were able to get her to a safe anchorage. A surfman then went to Frankfort to arrange for a tug to haul her to town for repairs.

In October 1894, a North Manitou surfman came to Keeper Olsen, saying he was ill, unable to work, and was going to see a surgeon. Describing him as a sickly and weak man, Olsen reported to his superiors that whenever the crew was called to a wreck, this man had to be left behind. "He is no good for this service," Olsen opined, but several days later he apparently relented, allowing the doubtless ashamed man to rejoin the crew for the remaining season, possibly because finding a replacement when the fishing was good could be difficult.

On a morning in early May 1895, the steamer *A.A. Parker* was found to have stranded the previous night on an exposed place, two miles offshore and seven miles from the station. Upon her discovery, the North Manitou station keeper engaged twenty-nine men and assisted in throwing cargo overboard. The next morning a tug arrived, the crew taking soundings and running lines, but still more lightening was required. After twenty-five thousand bushels of wheat had been jettisoned, the tug worked the steamer free and sent her on her way.

Later that month, the steamer *Alva* was found stranded on a reef eight miles from the North Manitou station. Upon boarding, the crew realized that a tug would be needed. They tried to reach mainland Leland, but could not land there on account of rough sea. They returned to their station for the night, then reached the mainland where the mate sent dispatches for a tug.

August, 1894

Florida

September, 1894

Maggie M. Avery

May, 1895

A. A. Parker

May, 1895

Alva

May, 1895
Ingeborg M. Forrest

The lifesavers put an insurance man on the stranded ship, having traveled sixteen miles for this purpose, then worked with a party of wreckers, ferrying them to and from the ship and assisting in the operations for thirty-three hours. However, the lifesavers had more work to do, having discovered a waterlogged schooner, the *Ingeborg M. Forrest*, near the shore. They boarded her and manned pumps throughout a long day, then helped to get her underway and into the more protected waters of South Manitou's harbor.

While some days were quietly boring for lifesavers, other days tested their strength, endurance, and creativity. The Point Betsie crew was busy overhauling their lake-service utility boat and painting her outsides in late July. While doing so, they found a bad split in her keel that previously had been filled with cotton and putty. Miller reported that he repaired it with cotton and white lead, then attached a copper strip over it. The crew also found openings in the bulkheads which Miller believed were letting water into the boat. They would make repairs, then roll her back over and try her again.

Apparently, she didn't pass the test, as the next month the keeper reported having pumped the boat full of water to trace a very bad leak which he opined should be repaired by her builders. The need was urgent, he insisted, with the busy fall season fast approaching and the boat being useless until fixed. In late September, after the repairs apparently had been made (by whom is unclear) he tested her and reported that she would "be tight as a bottle after being in the water a few times." She had been in the boathouse so long some of her seams were open, but he was confident that the hidden sources of her trouble had been identified and repaired.

July, 1895
Presto

The North Manitou station was called to action at 2:30 a.m. on July 30, 1895, when the patrolman spotted a distress offshore. The keeper and crew immediately manned the surfboat, pulling for over two miles in rough seas, where they found the schooner *Presto*, anchored with only a woman and three children aboard, leaking rapidly and in real danger of sinking. They managed to get the vessel underway to a lee-protected anchorage, then brought the family to shore, all of whom they determined to be sick and in need of clothing and medications. The lifesavers manned the schooner's pumps through the night to keep her afloat until daylight, then spent two days working on her leaking seams while the family sheltered at the station. Five days after the discovery, the ship was again seaworthy, so the family was put back on board, and *Presto* departed for her destination.

On August 3, 1895, the steam yacht *Nellie D.* stranded about six miles north of the Point Betsie station near the Platte River mouth, her boiler feed pipe having become blocked. One of her passengers got to land and hiked to the station to report the incident. The keeper sent a surfman to Frankfort to obtain services of a tug, the crew then running lines between the two vessels. The tug was able to pull the yacht free and tow her to Frankfort for repair.

On August 11, 1895, an event occurred which brought together the services of the Frankfort and Point Betsie lifesavers. The steamer *Milwaukee* stranded about halfway between the two stations at 2:00 a.m. in thick fog. A surfman patrolling the beach heard her whistle and awakened the Frankfort station crew, who accompanied a tug to the scene, where they found that another large steamer was standing by to await lifesavers' arrival. Lines were run to the tug, and the men began to throw her cargo of flour overboard. Having also come to the scene, upon the request of the *Milwaukee* captain, the Point Betsie crew took charge of the cargo being pitched. The steamer was soon released undamaged, and several days later the two crews worked together in helping to recover the jettisoned barrels. That said, a significant amount of the jetsam, presumably short-lived given its exposure to the elements, was not worth returning to its owners, and reportedly wound up in local residents' baked goods.

In early 1896, when the North Manitou station opened for the season on April 6, William L. Andres had replaced Keeper Peter Olsen, who had transferred to the new Wisconsin lifesaving station at Bailey's Harbor. In the same year, his brother Ingar was named keeper of the new station at Plum Island, Wisconsin, which would primarily serve Portes des Morts Passage, their appointments giving the brothers the unusual opportunity of leading closely situated stations.

The new North Manitou keeper put his crew through a full day's tasks, making all the equipment ready for action, drilling with the station's Long Branch surfboat, and conducting a beach patrol that night. The following day the crew took out the station's Beebe surfboat, the keeper reporting that she leaked quite badly, requiring substantial bailing.

At the federal level, by order of President Grover Cleveland, that year the lifesaving service became subject to the nation's civil

August, 1895
Nellie D.

August, 1895
Milwaukee

service requirements, including specific employment classifications from which a number of federal agencies had previously been exempt. One effect of the change was a requirement that new hires could only be at the surfman grade, and have to work their way to station leadership.

The lifesaving service's annual report for fiscal 1896 offers an illuminating view of the importance of its Lake Michigan operations in the service's Eleventh District, in which twenty-eight stations were situated. By way of comparison, the Tenth District, covering Lakes Huron and Superior, had sixteen stations at the time. During that year, there were 104 recorded disasters on Lake Michigan to which the stations responded, a higher total than in any other district in the country; Lakes Huron and Superior together had seventy-five.

The economic value of those events, including both vessels and cargo, totaled almost $1.5 million. More importantly, there were 1,184 persons aboard the vessels on Lake Michigan, not a single one of whom was lost. Forty persons were cared for in various stations, over a total of forty-five days. Six of the disasters resulted in the total loss of the ships, off of which property worth $1.3 million was saved, and only about $127,000 lost.

May, 1896
Selwyn Eddy

May, 1896
Sea Gull

May, 1896
Stella

Meanwhile, routine functions continued at the stations. On May 21, 1896, the lookout notified Keeper Andres of twice hearing four long blasts of a steam whistle. The North Manitou crew immediately went to the assistance of the steamer *Selwyn Eddy* ashore at the island's south point, providing "all possible assistance," the keeper duly reported, including running hawsers to another steamship, the *Colonial*, which had been standing by the distressed vessel, and ferrying messages between the two ships. Having helped to raise the *Eddy's* anchors, and employing the power of the *Colonial*, the men soon had the two ships in safe water without apparent damage to either vessel.

Two days later, the sloop *Sea Gull* was towed near the island station by a passing steamer, leaking badly and partially waterlogged. The crew took charge of the sloop, bringing her to shore and removing her nets to dry them. They took the appreciative fisherman to the station, where he was given "a change of clothing, a good meal, and a warm bed."

Another sloop, the *Stella*, which had been anchored off the station during thick fog, was observed at 3:30 a.m. to have parted her cable during a heavy squall and to be drifting away. The awakened lifesavers quickly launched the surfboat and caught up with the sloop after a hard pull, towing her to the station and securing her properly.

On a foggy morning in July 1896, the beach patrolman discovered the schooner *Grace M. Filer* stranded about two miles north of the station. The lifesavers were quickly aboard, where they unloaded an estimated thirty thousand feet of lumber off the deck, forming it into a raft. They then carried her anchors off the stern, leading hawsers back to her windlass, and by also using the schooner's sails effectively, they were able to refloat her. They then reloaded her cargo so she could resume her delivery.

On August 3 of that year, the waterlogged schooner *Wallis* anchored about eleven miles north of the Point Betsie station and sixteen miles north of the Frankfort station, enabling both crews to promptly respond to a call for men to relieve sailors worn out from continuous pumping. The surfmen kept her afloat as she was being towed to Frankfort Harbor, where she grounded upon entering, but was raised and repaired, then able to resume her course.

Later that month, the schooner *Delos De Wolf* dragged anchor and was being driven offshore of the North Manitou Island. The keeper discovered that the schooner's own crew had paid out forty-five fathoms (270 feet) of chain and was preparing to bend on an old hawser to extend the anchor line, a tactic which the keeper immediately recognized as destined to fail and thus to allow the ship to drift off without her anchor and chain. He took charge, raised her sails, and brought her to a safe anchorage.

In the middle of a cold night the following April, a man later described officially as demented came to the Point Betsie station suffering from exposure, having thrown away his coat. The station took care of him through the night, and in the morning the keeper took him by surfboat to Frankfort, from which he had gotten away from his caregivers.

During a southerly gale on September 21, 1897, the schooner *Chicago Board of Trade* was observed coming around the North Manitou's south point, laboring heavily and flying a distress signal. The surfmen went to her and found her waterlogged. At the master's request, they took charge of the ship, shortened sail, put all spare hands to the pumps, and turned for the island, bringing her to a safe anchorage in North Manitou Bay.

Less than a month later, the steamer *Majestic* stranded on a reef seven miles from the North Manitou station late at night, in smoky

July, 1896
Grace M. Filer

August, 1896
Wallis

August, 1896
Delos De Wolf

September, 1896
Chicago Board of Trade

October, 1896
Majestic

weather. At five thirty the following morning, when the lookout heard the ship's fog whistle sounding, the surfboat was launched and reached the steamer two hours later. The master having decided that lightening the vessel was required, the men jettisoned sixty tons of iron ore. Soon thereafter another steamer, the *Ira H. Owen*, was sighted and alerted to come to the scene. The lifesavers ran a hawser to her, and she was able to free the *Majestic* after three hours of pulling.

In mid-November, a neighbor of Point Betsie came to the station. His horse had fallen into a well, and he hoped he could obtain help in trying to extricate the animal. The crew responded to this rather unique request with shovels and tackle, and after extensive digging were able to release the presumably petrified horse.

On November 25, a resident of North Manitou's west side came across the island to alert the lifesavers that a large steamship, the *Gogebic*, had gone ashore in a blinding snowstorm and was stuck on a rock. The ship's master had sent four of his men to the mainland to telegraph for a wrecker that might free his vessel. Recognizing that it would be impossible under these icy conditions to reach the *Gogebic* by surfboat, the keeper decided his crew would haul the surfboat across the island. Upon completing this arduous task of five miles or more, the keeper determined that there was nothing his crew could do until a powerful ship arrived. However, the master asked the keeper to stay in the event the ship, which was pounding heavily on the rocks and incurring major bottom damage, got into more trouble that would require getting her crew to land.

November, 1897
Gogebic

After arriving, the wrecking tug *Favorite* went to mainland Glen Haven to pick up the four *Gogebic* crewmen. It was decided that the steamer's crew should spend the night on board the tug, lying in South Manitou Island's harbor in poor weather. With their services no longer required at the wreck site, the surfmen returned to their station. With only a few days left in the station's active season, the no.1 surfman took temporary charge, and the keeper was taken to the mainland by the *Favorite* for a thirty-day, seasonal leave of absence at his home.

On the second day of 1898, the ferry *Ann Arbor No. 1* became stranded in thick fog, a mile and a half south of the Point Betsie lifesaving station. The surfmen ran a towline between the *No.1* and the *Ann Arbor No. 2*, which had come to the site and, in a not unusual challenge, was able to pull her free of the bottom without

January, 1898
Ann Arbor No. 1 and No. 2

any damage. This was likely a time when Lake Michigan's level was cyclically low, as two weeks previously the Point Betsie lifesavers had been busy lowering their utility boat's launch ramp.

In its fiscal 1898 report, the lifesaving service addressed a practical problem posed by a new civil service requirement for employment. Pointing out that the chief qualification for the position of surfman is "surfmanship," General Superintendent Kimball, likely having heard from numerous station keepers, asserted that "some difficulty was experienced in devising a plan for applying the principle of competitive examination to the ascertainment of the comparative qualifications of candidates." He continued, "Were it practicable, the most accurate and satisfactory test would unquestionably be by actual trial in the surf," but such a test "would entail much expense to the candidates and the Government, and would be extremely dangerous."

Kimball further explained that numerous boards of examiners would have to be organized, one at least for each district, and in some districts, two or three. A place of trial having been set, a majority of both boards and candidates would have to travel great distances to reach it, and when assembled, in nine cases out of ten, they would be obliged to wait several days for a suitable surf. Once this surf was present, "boatload after boatload of candidates of all degrees of skill and experience, unaccustomed to work together, and used to different words of command for the same maneuver or action, would be called upon to exploit their proficiency. Loss of life would be the inevitable result."

As he summed up the situation, "The danger alone of attending a test of surfing skill by actual trial in the surf puts such a method entirely out of the question." He added, "In considering whether any practicable means of testing qualification in surfmanship by competitive examination could be devised, the idea of making experience the criterion suggested itself."

In his report, the general superintendent noted that the Civil Service Commission had approved of this solution. Based upon a foundation of relevant experience, a plan had been worked out that clearly defined the qualifications for the position of surfman, as well as for promotion from that role to the position of station keeper.

The district superintendents overseeing the service's Great Lakes operations were generally satisfied with the results of the new recruitment procedures, the principal goal of which was to officially eliminate any political or personal influences in the selection and promotion of the service's personnel. This was a basic commitment within the civil service, and a goal that Kimball insisted upon throughout his tenure.

August, 1898
Rouse Simmons

August 20, 1898, found one of the Great Lakes' most famous schooners, the *Rouse Simmons*, known for later generations as the "Christmas Tree Ship" for her annual holiday deliveries from the north woods to Chicago, was observed by the North Manitou lookout to be heavily laboring as she came around the island's southeast point. Her cargo had shifted to starboard, causing her to list badly and take on water. Spotted by the station lookout, the surfboat was quickly launched and the vessel was soon boarded. The lifesavers found four feet of water in her hold, and with so much water coming in, her crew would not have been able to keep her afloat for long.

Keeper Andres urged that she be anchored, and the lifesavers then rigged her booms to portside, causing the vessel to somewhat right herself. All hands then manned the pumps, and after four hours' work she was on an even keel. After shifting her cargo, she was determined to be in safe enough condition to continue on her way, and the lifesavers returned to the station. (Saved from that potential disaster, the three-master, widely loved for her seasonal missions, sank in a violent 1912 storm off Two Rivers, Wisconsin, sadly taking all hands.)

On August 28, 1898, the schooner *F. Fitch* collided with a steam barge several miles southwest of Point Betsie at two o'clock in the morning. The station lookout saw a torch and a weak red light out on the lake. He reported this to Keeper Miller, who awakened the crew and launched the surfboat. Heading southwest for about a mile, they heard a cry for help coming from a small scow, within which they found the captain and his son, who had come from the schooner. Having only one oar, their efforts to reach the land would have been futile.

August, 1898
F. Fitch

The captain told the lifesavers of the collision that had occurred about twenty minutes previously. He said that because their vessel was rapidly taking on water, with only the two of them aboard, they had climbed into the scow after burning the torch signal. The lifesavers soon found the schooner, with her cargo of fruit floating about the wreck. They climbed aboard, set her anchor so as to hold her until a tug could be summoned, and sent a surfman to Frankfort to secure a tug's services.

The lifesavers reached the Point Betsie station in the surfboat at about 3:30 a.m. Having lost all their clothes on the schooner, the captain and son were given what they needed from the Women's National Relief Association's allotment to the station. At daylight, the wreck appeared to be about five miles out from Point Betsie, but she rolled over and sank in the morning, the tug arriving too late to be of assistance. After the gale winds and high seas that arose during the wee hours had subsided, the captain and some surfmen went to look for the schooner, but she could not be found.

November 25, 1898, brought powerful winds and heavy snow to northeastern Lake Michigan, impacting both North Manitou Island and the mainland's Point Betsie. The steamer *John Mitchell* stranded about two miles southwest of the North Manitou lighthouse. Upon hearing the vessel's distress whistle, the surfmen loaded their boat on a sleigh and used a horse to take it to the island's south shore. They were able to launch their surfboat there and pull out to the ship in a strong gale. They dropped anchor to head the boat into the wind, and when the surf began to diminish they went aboard to jettison its cargo of corn. As the *John Mitchell* lifted off the bottom, her master was able to signal another steamer, the *Desmond*, which drew close and hauled her off, towing her to safety in South Manitou Bay's harbor.

November, 1898
John Mitchell

The St. Lawrence *Wreck and Rescue*

1898

St. Lawrence

A coincidental situation at nearby mainland Point Betsie proved more dire. The corn-filled steamer *St. Lawrence*, northbound from Chicago to Prescott, Ontario, on the St. Lawrence River, was storm-driven off course into shallow water, two miles south of Point Betsie, where she stranded an estimated 350 yards offshore. Her captain began sounding the steam whistle repeatedly, the blasts being heard at the lifesaving station, but since they were not in the pattern of a distress signal, the crew thought that they probably came from an Ann Arbor ferry. Realizing that the ferry could be getting too close to shore in the blinding storm, Keeper Miller sent Surfman Bedford down the beach to warn her off with a Coston flare.

Unable to see the ferry's lights amidst the snow until he was opposite her, he then fired two flares, but hearing no response, he hustled to the station and alerted the crew to the apparent grounding. Miller sent one surfman to procure a team of horses from a nearby farm, and the rest of the crew readied the surfboat wagon to be pulled to the wreck site. Upon the boat's arrival, he and his men immediately tried to go to the steamer, but when a breaking wave dashed upon the surfboat, almost swamping it as it crossed the second bar, he immediately returned to the beach and sent the crew back to the station with the horses to haul the beach apparatus. The conditions were simply too dangerous for a rescue by surfboat.

Two cart trips proved necessary on account of the storm, obstructions that were encountered on the beach, and the weight of the cart and its equipment. On the second trip, Surfman Jeffs, stopping to light a lantern, saw a man staggering toward him, "wet, weak and scarcely able to stand." In a feeble whisper telling the surfman that he and four others had left the steamer in a yawl boat which had capsized, he then told Jeffs to leave him and search for his shipmates.

Jeffs soon found three men, and, after removing the beach

apparatus from the cart, used it to convey the exhausted sailors, fortunate to have survived their experience, to the station where they would receive the care of the lifesavers' spouses, who would nurse, cook, and otherwise assist them without compensation.

Soon thereafter, Miller found another man from the steamer, lying on the water's edge. He dragged him higher on the beach and began the service's "procedure for the restoration of the apparently drowned," but in the light of a lantern, it quickly became clear that the victim's resuscitation was impossible. Based upon his ghastly wounds, he had likely been battered to death by the overturned boat, a victim of his mate's having claimed on ship that he would reach shore in the small boat without wetting his feet. His companions barely survived after washing up on the beach, where they were found by the patrol, taken to the station in the beach cart and placed under the care of the lifesavers' spouses, who would nurse, cook and otherwise care for them, without compensation.

As riveting as is this initial account, the story of one of the most heroic rescues in Great Lakes history then begins, made possible by an amazingly accurate Lyle gun shot from the beach in terrible weather, more than twenty inches of windblown snow falling that night. Unable in the storm to see the results of their first or second shots, the lifesavers were retrieving the line for yet another try when they realized that with each pull from shore, the vessel's whistle blew. Their shot line had draped over the ship's whistle cord, causing piercing blasts which alerted the ship's crew that a rescue effort was underway. A connection to the ship had been established in this extraordinary undertaking, and subsequently strengthened with a hawser so that the breeches buoy presumably would be deployed, but the conditions were too dangerous for use of that rescue device. A courageous alternative had to be pursued.

It came under Captain Miller's inventive direction, with the lifesavers bringing the remaining seamen to shore in the service's surfboat by pulling hand over hand on the hawser to the steamer, and back to shore, in several harrowing trips. The survivors later described the surfmen's rescue work in such frightening weather and sea conditions as "simply one of the most heroic acts that any of them ever saw." And as for the man who had lost his life, Miller also said he would never understand how anyone would try to reach shore in a small boat in such conditions. (The extraordinary *St. Lawrence* rescue is now vividly portrayed in the museum at Point Betsie Light Station.)

A Century Draws to a Close and Another Begins

1899
Waverly

In the early spring of 1899, the steamer *Waverly* became stranded on the southwest corner of South Manitou Point in heavy fog, about twenty-three miles northeast of the Point Betsie lifesaving station. Learning of the wreck from the master of a fishing tug, the surfmen departed the station in their surfboat, being towed to the scene by a tugboat. The surfmen worked through the night, setting out lines and shifting cargo, but the tug was unable to move the steamer. A repair to the tug being needed, she headed in the morning for Frankfort while the lifesavers remained on-site.

When increasing wind and seas concerned the station's keeper, he advised everyone to go to shore in the surfboat while it was possible to do so. Thirteen people, including three women, were cared for by island residents. Upon returning to the steamer when the conditions had improved, the captain found the vessel full of water. Two tugs hauling steam-operated pumps came to the vessel from Frankfort. The water being quickly pumped out, the steamer, though seriously damaged, was saved.

District officials and Keeper Andres conducted an annual inspection of the island's station in mid-June, observing all buildings, grounds, apparatus, and boats, then put the crew through its drills. They found a considerable number of pieces of equipment to be worn out, and authorized Andres to purchase two hundred feet of good lumber with which to fix the station's Long Branch surfboat. As was typical, the station crews would make the repairs.

1899
Miztec

On August 2, 1899, the schooner *Miztec* stranded on the mainland's Sleeping Bear Point while under tow of the steamer *Toltec*. The North Manitou lifesavers boarded her and moved seventy-five thousand feet of her deck's lumber load onto a barge, then ran a line to a tug which succeeded in hauling the schooner off the lake's bottom. With the vessel apparently uninjured, the surfmen then reloaded the cargo and she resumed her trip.

About a week later, Keeper Andres and his no. 1 went to the aid of the island's mail carrier, who had fouled his gasoline launch's propeller with a line. Only a couple of weeks later, presumably embarrassingly, the mail carrier's launch fouled its anchor and was observed drifting out into the lake, causing Andres and his crew to again spring into action to uphold the mantra "the mail must go through."

These late summer days found the crew frequently assisting passengers to and from lake steamers that were unable to reach the wharf on account of high seas.

In late October 1899, the Point Betsie crew went to the aid of a steamer, the *G.R. Green*, a steam pipe having burst about ten miles north of the station. Spotting the rising steam, the men started for the scene but soon came upon a tug which towed them swiftly to the steamer. The men ran a hawser between the tug and the steamer so the incapacitated vessel could be towed to Frankfort.

October, 1899
G. R. Green

The schooner *William H. Dunham* went aground at Otter Creek early in November. In mid-month, a tug hauled her off, but while trying to tow her to Frankfort, her waterlogged hull could not be controlled. The Point Betsie keeper went to assist, transferring the captain back to his schooner and providing a surfman to assist in steering the schooner during the tow.

November, 1899
William H. Dunham

On December 6, 1899, command of the North Manitou Island crew passed to Canadian-born veteran keeper Telesford St. Peter (St. Pierre, more formally), succeeding William L. Andres. Having spent four years in the Civil War, St. Peter had a thirty-six-year lifesaving career at several stations, including twenty-two years as captain of the Chicago station.

Early in his Chicago service, when he saw a harbor crib structure drifting away in a sixty-five-miles per hour northeast wind, he had sailed a boat out to save four men who were clinging to a piling. Highly respected, this veteran keeper, described in one news story as a "typical Life Saver, being bold, skillful, strong, and vigilant," captained the North Manitou crew for over a dozen years until 1913, when he transferred to the mainland station at Pentwater, Michigan, for his final assignment.

Reporting on its July 1, 1898–June 30, 1899, year of operations on the Great Lakes, the service noted with understandable pride that in the months of October and November alone, when "disastrous tempests" had occurred throughout the lakes in which twenty-eight vessels and 162 persons were involved, not a single life had been lost.

In 1899, the service began actively investigating the practicality of gasoline-powered rescue boats. The weight added by a motor, tanks, and fuel, as well as the loss of space in the boat that otherwise could be available to put rescued persons posed an important trade-off at that time, considering the greater speed with which rescues likely could be mounted by powerboat. Keeper Henry Cleary of the Marquette, Michigan station in particular, drew attention for his extensive investigations of the suitability and reliability of a motorized lifeboat.

April, 1900
Onoko

In April 1900, the steamer *Onoko* stranded two hours after midnight in foggy weather about seven miles from the North Manitou station. She signaled for assistance at daylight with four long whistle blasts, which the lighthouse fog whistle repeated, and the lifesavers pulled to her. They ferried the master to the nearby steamer *George T. Hope*. After the lifesavers had sounded for the best depth, the rescuing steamer attempted for more than two hours to pull her free, but finally gave up and departed. Having returned the captain to the stranded vessel, the lifesavers then shoveled overboard about twelve thousand pounds of corn, at which point she floated off the bar and resumed course, sans corn.

On another April day, with Lake Michigan still covered with ice, the North Manitou lightkeeper came to the lifesavers with a set of international signal flags which he had received, asking for instructions on their use. Keeper St. Peter wrote, "I took half of the crew with me to a pole while the rest of the crew went with the lightkeeper to another pole about 1/4 mile [distant]. Opened communications and made several signals back and forth without a break."

In mid-September, the Point Betsie crew went to aid a yacht that had come to shore a mile north of the station, finding it filled with water. The six persons aboard were taken to the station and given food and lodging for the night. The surfmen bailed her out and repaired her rudder.

May, 1901
Emily B. Maxwell

Two sailors from the schooner *Emily B. Maxwell* came to the north island station on May 30, 1901, and reported that their ship had gone ashore at 3:00 a.m., about a mile to the south. Keeper St. Peter wrote that the schooner had gone off-course and stranded in a thick fog under full sail. The vessel's crew had worked for two hours trying unsuccessfully to heave her off the bottom. Giving up, the schooner's yawl was lowered, and two men pulled to shore and reported to the lifesaving station.

The keeper and his men took the surfboat to the vessel and proceeded to shove overboard about twenty thousand feet of lumber, forming the logs into two rafts. The crewmen were then able to heave the ship off the ground with a long-practiced strategy: working from the grounded vessel, pulling a strong line that had been laid between their ship to an anchor they had set in deeper water. While the crew was concentrating on refloating the schooner, one of the lumber rafts got free of the vessel, but the life-savers were able to retrieve it and bring it back to the schooner. All the lumber was returned aboard the vessel. As St. Peter concluded his log entry, "The captain said he could never get the vessel off without our assistance, for which he was very thankful." St. Peter added that the ship's cargo was "all saved—good."

Bearing mention in this chronological account is a relevant, historically significant lifesaving feat that occurred about seventy-five miles south of the passage at the entrance to Ludington Harbor, four days before Christmas, 1901. The car ferry *Pere Marquette 16* had become stranded while attempting to enter the port, the shock of the ship's grounding causing the rupture of a steam pipe, killing one crewman and injuring others.

Particularly noteworthy, in retrospect, is the fact that over thirty ferry crewmen, as well as the body of their deceased colleague, and last of all the captain, were taken off the vessel. Breeches buoy operations were conducted by a group of men who were quickly summoned to respond to this crisis, the lifesaving station having been closed for the winter. The rescue was a heroic reminder of the vital role that the breeches buoy procedure played through many decades.

Two New Lifesaving Stations Provide Expanded Passage Service

With respect to its Manitou Passage operations, the service reported at the end of fiscal 1901 that after years of unheeded requests, funds had been appropriated and construction was underway for two additional stations, one on South Manitou Island near the lighthouse, and the other on the mainland at Sleeping Bear Point, west of Glen Arbor. The last stations the service built on Lake Michigan raised the total number of lifesaving stations on its coasts to thirty-one. Before the new stations would become operational in the late summer of 1902, however, the North Manitou and Point Betsie stations continued to cover the busy passage waterway themselves.

August, 1902

Eloise L. Hackley

On the evening of August 2, 1902, Surfman Anderson of the North Manitou station heard a distress whistle from the small steamer *Eloise L. Hackley*, bound from Leland to the island with four men aboard. She was adrift some three miles offshore, with a squall in sight. Promptly launching the surfboat and pulling to the vessel, the crew found that the vessel's propeller shaft had broken, leaving her "helpless in the trough of the sea," as Keeper St. Peter recorded. The surfmen took her in tow, and "after three and a half hours of hard pulling brought her to anchorage in six fathoms of water." At four o'clock the next morning, the keeper and the no. 7 surfman went to Leland in the station's sailboat with a dispatch to summon a tug, which then towed the vessel north to the Charlevoix harbor for repairs.

In late August 1902, the long-anticipated South Manitou Island and Sleeping Bear Point stations were finally ready to serve mariners of the passage. Each station included six surfmen during an initial partial season of August 20 through November 30, 1902, and from April 5 through the end of the fiscal year on June 30, 1903.

However, preparations had been underway at the new stations prior to their official openings. Both new stations were to be assigned thirty-four-foot lifeboats, equipped for pulling and sailing, constructed by Frederick Beebe, of Greenport, New York, and delivered to the Glen Haven dock. In that first year of operation, they were also assigned two pulling surfboats, one of them a Monomoy model and the other a Beebe-McClellan. The new keepers helped each other handle the shipments. William Walker of Sleeping Bear Point aided Gus Lofberg in sailing the boats to South Manitou. Lofberg in turn helped Walker get the point's boats to his mainland station and, in the nautical sense of the term, helped "heave them into the boathouse."

Walker, who was born and raised in Grand Haven, Michigan, where the lifesaving service (in its later years) located its Lake Michigan district's headquarters, took charge at Sleeping Bear Point on February 21, 1902. Prior to his promotion to lead the new station, he had been a longtime surfman at Grand Haven's lifesaving station, to which he ultimately returned in 1910, serving as its last keeper under the US Life-Saving Service. On South Manitou, Gus B. Lofberg relieved Patrick McCauley, who had temporarily cared for the station.

At the time the two stations were constructed, having been recommended for decades, the frequency of disasters on the lake was diminishing, owing to several factors. The famed wooden, two-masted and larger schooners and ships employing other sailing rigs being dependent upon favorable winds and seas were losing market share to proliferating steamships.

Numerous wooden ships were converted to barges to be towed by steamers until they were fully worn out, leaving many of them on the lake bottom or against a riverbank or shoreline, where they were picked over by wreckers and gradually succumbed to nature's destructive forces. A hundred years later, those timbers occasionally wash up on Lake Michigan's storm-pounded beaches. The lake fleet was consisting of larger, stronger, and faster vessels that not only offered more efficient service to shippers, but whose seamen had the aid of more effective navigational and communications gear, the support of more informative weather forecasts, and, with those developments, the ability to better maintain schedules and profitable operations.

Irrespective of the changing fleet, the two long-awaited lifesaving stations were enthusiastically welcomed by islanders, area residents, and passage travelers, and by the crews on North Manitou and at Point Betsie. Historical records tell of the many circumstances when rescues or other assistance were sought from one or more of the four US Life-Saving Service crews, who would be the passage and its environs' emergency responders for more than a dozen subsequent years.

Keepers Walker and Lofberg were soon recording their respective preparations for the stations' operations. Their early entries related to receipt of requests from the district superintendent that they determine the cost of locally acquiring wood and kerosene for their stations, as well as the posts on which their patrol clocks were to be mounted. Under General Superintendent Kimball's disciplined leadership of the service, no proposed expense was too trivial to be incurred without the approval of a district's headquarters. Supplies for the South Manitou station were brought to the island by ship or small boat, whereas goods for the Sleeping Bear station typically would be loaded from a dock into wagons and hauled to the point by horses.

Later that winter, Keeper Lofberg wrote that he had sailed to Glen Haven to obtain his mail; because of unfavorable spring weather, no delivery had been made to the island for nearly a week—a reality of island life.

In early May, Lofberg reported that he had posted bid requests at two places for the furnishing of wood and oil for his South Manitou station, and mailed a copy to one potential source in mainland Glen Haven. On May 10, under the instructions he had received from the district, he opened the bids and accepted the lowest ones: from H. Haas of South Manitou Island for twelve cords of wood at three dollars per cord, and for oil at twelve cents per gallon from D.H. Day.

Several days later, he sailed to Glen Haven to pick up a barrel of kerosene from Mr. Day for the station's use, and soon thereafter reported that he had received the requested twelve cords of wood. He also informed the district that he had received word from the agent for the Northern Michigan Transportation Company that freight for the station's use had been landed on the dock in Glen Haven, for which there was a charge pending of $6.09. He said he had written to the superintendent of construction for guidance on how to handle the freight charge.

Keepers being responsible for all supplies delivered to their stations, Keeper Lofberg recorded on May 30 his receipt by schooner of nearly fifty items for his station, some of them as minor as a box of soap. The quantities of each item were dutifully recorded,

Ancient flotsam continues to wash ashore.
Author's 2021 photo.

along with his payment to the captain of twenty-two dollars for the shipment.

The first record of rescue activity attributed to the South Manitou station occurred on April 6, 1902, when the steamer *M.C. Neff* had stranded about two hundred yards from it during a thick snowstorm. No crew having yet been appointed, Keeper Lofberg reported that he had launched the South Manitou lighthouse's supply boat and boarded the vessel with Lightkeeper Thomas Armstrong to offer their assistance—another cooperative endeavor.

The following morning they helped the crew to shift some of the cargo, and that night Lofberg used the lighthouse's boat to take the ship's captain to Glen Arbor, from where he could send messages. In the course of landing in rough sea, the captain fell overboard, but Lofberg managed to pull him safely back into the boat. After changing clothes and sending the message for a tug, they started back to the island, arriving at midnight. By the next morning, the water level had risen and the vessel was able to work her way off the bottom and resume her voyage.

The first account of a crisis confronting the Sleeping Bear Point's keeper came at seven thirty in the morning on a foggy July 9, when the steamer *Charles R. Van Hise*, bound from Two Harbors, Minnesota to Chicago with a cargo of iron ore, came dangerously

April, 1902
M. C. Neff

July, 1900
Charles R. Van Hise

close to shore. Keeper Walker tried to warn the vessel off by using his megaphone, but the crew on the ship could not understand his message. Thinking the sound was coming from a schooner, the *Charles R. Van Hise* kept to her course and stranded south of the station.

Not yet having a crew to assist him, Walker launched a small skiff and went to the vessel to see if he could be of any assistance. Two steamers came later that day and pulled all afternoon, to no avail. On the following afternoon, however, she was able to get underway without incurring damage from the grounding.

On North Manitou, the surfmen responded to another unusual emergency involving a horse on July 17, 1902, when the horse, pulling a wagon, broke through the pier. The men were able to free the animal and to report the saving of that valuable property.

In late July, Keeper Lofberg received word that he would be instructed to go to the Bailey's Harbor station across Lake Michigan to pick up a Mackinaw sailboat for his South Manitou station's use. About two weeks later, he heard that the Mackinaw was ready for the trip, and in early September he went to Wisconsin on the *Ann Arbor* ferry to pick up the Mackinaw boat, a beach cart, and other equipment.

On August 2, the North Manitou Island's lookout heard a distress signal from the small steamer *Eric C. Hackley*, headed from Leland to the island with ten men aboard, but adrift several miles offshore, a broken propeller shaft having left her helpless in the trough of the sea. It took several hours of hard rowing, towing the little steamer by surfboat, to get her to a safe anchorage close to the beach. A call was then made to Leland for a tug, which came and towed the vessel to Charlevoix for repairs.

In mid-August, Sleeping Bear Point's Keeper Walker had his first crew to command, including George W. Mastain, Robert E. Smith, Jessie L. Bell, Herman W. Allers, Charles Robinson, and John Dwiggins, the latter two, like their keeper, being from Grand Haven.

At about the same time, Keeper Lofberg was told he could finally select South Manitou's first surfmen from a group of eight whose eligibility for service had been certified. He had informed the men of their selection and asked them to advise him of whether or not they would accept the position.

Anticipating the beginning of the station's beach patrols, he reported on August 12 that he had set out a key post, where a

U. S. Life Saving Crew drilling in the Harbor at Frankfort, Mich.

Lifesavers demonstrating surfboat re-righting in Frankfort.

Author's collection.

patrolman would mark completion of his trek. Given the ground conditions in this vicinity, the post was about two and one-quarter miles southwest of the station. Several days later, he recorded having set the north key post on the beach, about the same distance from the station.

When the patrol reached the post, he would use a key kept there to mark the time on the paper dial of the clock he carried, thus proving that he had completed the required trek. To further ensure the reliability of the system, the clocks and keys were stored by the keeper when not in use, the keeper frequently rotated them (informing the district superintendent of the switches), and the dial papers were sent to the district superintendents for his review. Failure to mark the clock was a serious offense.

In the same log entry, Keeper Lofberg recorded the visit of the service's construction officials to determine a site for the building of a boathouse for the station's lifeboat.

An important day for the South Manitou Island community came on August 20, 1902, when Lofberg recorded having officially opened the station for active service at midnight, with three regular surfmen along with three temporary hires, the latter an indication that securing a crew on the island was not an easy task. As was his duty, the keeper also reported the identity of a surfman who, while undertaking his first beach patrol in the darkness between two and four o'clock in the morning, had failed to find the post where he was to mark fulfillment of his duty.

Several days later, Lofberg reported that a surfman had failed to make an impression at a lookout station's clock at 11:30 p.m. The keeper wrote that he had excused the failure on grounds that the man had proven he was not asleep on duty; being new to the service, he had simply overlooked the requirement.

Two days later, however, Lofberg reported that the same man had told him he "desired to leave the station at midnight...as his feet [were] very sore and he [could not] continue to make the patrols any longer." Lofberg said he had accepted the man's resignation, and that a replacement had reported to the station that day with a certificate showing him to be "physically sound"; he would begin service at midnight.

As of August 28, the South Manitou station had four regularly signed surfmen, arranged as follows for their respective roles in surfboat pulling and other essential tasks: Edgar Phelps, no. 1; John Hanneson, no. 2; Jacob Jacobson, no. 3; and Alexander Egeland, no. 4. Afterward, Nelson, the new replacement, would become no. 5.

The no. 1 would take over for the keeper on the steering oar and other duties in the event of the latter's absence or incapacity, such as during Lofberg's round trip to Wisconsin. Upon his return, the crew was immediately engaged in fitting out the sailboat.

The Sleeping Bear Point crew's first recorded rescue work came on August 31, 1902, when the surfmen assisted the schooner *Rob Roy*, which had dragged anchor during strong southwest winds on Sleeping Bear Bay. The surfmen rowed about four and a half miles to reach her, and upon boarding found her leaking and in danger of wrecking on the beach. A tug happened by and towed her to a safe anchorage, where the surfmen pumped water from her holds and assisted with her anchors.

Just days later, the point's crew again went into action, at about 3:00 a.m., when the schooner *Alice M. Beers* was anchored about four miles from the station. A shift of a strong wind out of the

August, 1902
Rob Roy

September, 1902
Alice M. Beers

northwest had caused the vessel to break anchor and come along-side the pier. Her sailors jumped from the ship to the pier, and she went on the beach with a big hole in her bow. Although the station's lifesavers had been patrolling the beach, they could not see that she was ashore on account of hard-blowing sand. At the schooner captain's request, two surfmen went aboard and assisted him in taking gear off the vessel to protect it from further damage.

Soon thereafter, a steam barge passing the South Manitou station sounded four quick whistle blasts, to which the crew responded by heading out to her in the Monomoy surfboat. The steamer's captain handed them a telegram addressed to one of the men who were constructing the station's boathouse, and requested that it be delivered to him at once. Keeper Lofberg carried the tele-gram ashore and passed the note, thus informing the workman as promptly as possible of the death of his mother. Later that month, having obtained prior approval, Lofberg and his crew sailed a phy-sician over to North Manitou Island to assist a seriously ill female resident.

In early October, Lofberg took his crew to assist the men of the schooner *William Jones* in heaving up her anchor and getting underway. And on the twenty-first of that month, he informed the service's construction office that the shoreline where crews were erecting the boathouse had completely collapsed. The surfmen were doing what they could to stabilize the bank, but the situation amounted, in his service's terms, to a "disaster."

Later that month, the schooner *Swan* dragged anchor during the night and was discovered early the next morning to be abreast of the Point Betsie station and inside a dangerous sandbar. Her mainmast had come down during her heaving about on the rough sea, and that had taken down the fore topmast as well. Keeper Miller saw that the vessel would soon be driven onto the beach unless the crew reached her and gave her anchor more chain so she would not pitch so vigorously. The crew went to her in their Beebe-McClellan surfboat but had a tough time getting aboard without damaging their own craft, as the sea was breaking over the schooner's deck and the mast was dangling off her side.

After several surfmen got aboard and started pumping, a tug arrived for which the *Swan's* captain had requested. The surfmen assisted in connecting lines, then accompanied the vessels toward the Frankfort harbor. With the schooner having more than a foot of water in her hold, the towline parted several times, the surfmen

October, 1902
Swan

repeatedly restoring the link. The schooner finally reached safety about noon. The crew made it back to their station in the early afternoon, "wet, cold, and hungry," as Keeper Miller wrote. The next day they were out again, retrieving the *Swan's* anchor and chain and getting their rescue boats ready for new business.

In early November, the steamer *Pueblo* stranded on the south island's southwest point during thick fog. She sounded a distress signal heard by the South Manitou beach patrolman, who immediately ignited a Coston flare to assure the vessel's crew that their plight was known, and then hastened back to the station to inform the keeper. The crew went by surfboat to the vessel, and upon request took the master to Glen Haven, where he could call for a tug. The lifesaving crew then undertook to lighten the vessel, ultimately taking off twelve thousand bushels of her cargo, which enabled the tug to free the *Pueblo* two days later and tow her into the harbor, where divers could make temporary repairs.

As the station's active season wound down in late November, the South Manitou men spent a day cutting firewood for the station's use, and were called upon to aid the schooner *Mary A. Gregory* in leaving the harbor. Her sailors had been unable to raise canvas and get underway promptly to take advantage of favorable winds. The lifesavers then spent the last days of the month cleaning the station and preparing it for the seasonal shutdown on the thirtieth. The end of the "active season," however, did not relieve a keeper of his responsibilities, he being in charge of the station throughout the year.

On January 3, 1903, Second Mate Fredricksen and Wheelsman Smith of an Ann Arbor ferry came to report that their vessel was ashore on South Manitou's north side. The station being closed for the winter, Keeper Lofberg recruited a volunteer surfman, and they took the two men to Glen Haven to place a call for help. Upon returning to the station, they learned from Lightkeeper Armstrong that the ferry had managed to free herself and resume her course to Frankfort. The station housed the ferry's two crewmen overnight, and they departed the next day aboard a tug that had been sent to pick them up.

When a fire threatened to destroy a dwelling at Sleeping Bear Point on February 9, 1903, the seasonally inactive station's surfmen extinguished the flames. Doubtless, Surfman Allers was especially appreciative as it was his own house, located about three hundred feet from the station, whose roof was ablaze.

November, 1902
Pueblo

November, 1902
Mary A. Gregory

During that spring, a much anticipated underwater telephone cable providing a direct connection between the island and the mainland was scheduled to be installed. In mid-March, South Manitou's Keeper Lofberg received an order from General Superintendent Kimball to construct a telephone line to the station from the spot where the cable from Sleeping Bear Point would reach the island.

In preparation for the coming season, Lofberg wrote that he had received authorization from the district superintendent to purchase two hundred feet of lumber for the construction of a temporary lookout at the station. And on March 29, he noted receipt of an order announcing that his station would open for active service on April 5, 1903. He had notified his crew and forwarded certificates for their medical examinations.

Anticipating April's start of the active season at the South Manitou station, in late February he had recorded his selection of William O. Cribbs from the list of certified eligible men to fill the only vacancy on his crew.

But just days before the station's opening, amidst very dense morning fog, Lofberg heard a steamer sounding signals of distress on South Manitou's west side. He recorded in the log that with the aid of the lighthouse keeper, he had launched the Monomoy surfboat and sailed around to the side of the island opposite the station to ascertain if a steamer was, in fact, ashore. When he reached the place from which he believed the sound had come, he spotted the steamer several miles off the shore, appropriately repeating its customary warning for operating in fog. He thought the ship likely had been aground, but in the meantime had managed to work herself off.

On the fourth of April, he sailed to Glen Haven to pick up his crew, learning that only three of the men had arrived there. Two others arrived on the fifth, but one other crewman informed him only that day that, having purchased a farm, he would rather manage it than serve the station. On the sixth, Lofberg had arranged the crew by the numbers, with Edgar Phelps, no. 1; John Hanneson, no. 2; Jacob Jacobson, no. 3; Alexander Egeland, no. 4; and newly appointed William Cribbs as no. 5. Spending the day doing general work around the station, they were ready when duty called.

As only two ships, both steamers, had passed the station that day and just two schooners the next, the men anticipated a gradual increase in lake traffic through the spring. Meanwhile, they could contemplate many days of drilling and caring for the station's structures and grounds.

One early spring day when only three steamers had passed, Lofberg led his crew through the beach apparatus routine, reporting it took the men five minutes and twenty seconds to mount and complete the firing of two ounces of powder, which successfully propelled a line sixty yards to the drill pole that simulated a ship's mast. This was the mandatory, time-sensitive on-beach practice repeatedly performed at every station in preparation for a crew's suddenly being called upon to mount such a lifesaving rescue of persons from a vessel stranded in surf, perhaps hundreds of yards offshore where conditions precluded a rescue by boat. The men filled the rest of that day by scrubbing the station's supply boat. The next day's drill was devoted to the procedures for attempting to resuscitate the apparently drowned, another vital surfman's skill for which a need could quickly arise.

On April 12, Keeper Lofberg logged delivery off the schooner *Wells* of the following articles: two boxes of hardware; one box of soap; six chairs and a table; six oars; six brooms; one mop stick; one anvil; and one ship's bell. He postponed the crew's surfboat drill on the fourteenth, "as the surf and weather [were] very unfavorable for launching a boat." Instead, the men were engaged in doing "general work" at the station. A day later, amidst a fresh north wind, they drilled with the International and General Service Codes of Signals.

In mid-month, Lofberg reported that a sailboat had left the island on the previous day, headed for Glen Haven to bring a doctor to assist a very sick woman. Realizing that the boat had not returned by ten o'clock the following morning, he sailed the station's Monomoy surfboat to Glen Haven to see what had become of this mission. Finding the sailboat at the wharf, he wrote that it was "waiting for the doctor who did not want to go over as long as the stormy weather continued." Lofberg added, "I took some medicine that the doctor prescribed for the woman and sailed back [the weather would not deter him], arriving at the station at 4 p.m.," and the other sailboat brought the doctor several hours later.

A week later, Lofberg was again off to Glen Haven in a Mackinaw sailboat, with two surfmen also aboard. Such a trip, by which he brought some telephone equipment and a signal tower to the island, consumed a full day.

Traffic in the passage continued to mount; on May 8, twenty-five steamers and six schooners were recorded as passing the South Manitou station. Two days later, the keeper reported that his men were scraping the Mackinaw boat in preparation for its painting.

The Sleeping Bear Point crew was also characteristically busy that spring with the mandatory drills and duties, Keeper Walker reporting that his men had secured the cable for a telephone connection to South Manitou station. He also told superiors that a surfman had failed to mark the dial in the lookout at seven thirty that morning, his excuse being that he had been watching a schooner very near to the end of South Manitou Island. His offense having been forgiven, he continued to serve the station.

In mid-May, the sloop *Kaayoshk* out of Traverse City stranded on a Platte Bay reef between the Point Betsie and the Sleeping Bear Point stations. Calling for a tug's services, the point's crew rowed to the vessel, finding her full of water with her keel having been largely torn off, hanging by a single bolt. The surfmen bailed and pumped her out, and then cut away the keel, thereby enabling the sloop to float free of the reef. A tug could then get a line to the sloop and tow her to safety for repair in Frankfort Harbor.

May, 1903
Kaayoshk

The Sleeping Bear Point crew provided another form of service on a hazy, mid-June morning when the lookout observed a small yacht with its canvas lowered and flying an unclear sort of flag. The surfmen launched their boat and rowed out to her, finding that because there was no wind at the time, the boat was trying to attract a tug's assistance and be towed to Frankfort Harbor. Two weeks later, during another quiet night on the lake, the schooner *L.B. Coates*, headed for Glen Arbor from Milwaukee, became becalmed close to shore at Sleeping Bear and was drifting slowly toward the shallows. Working over most of the day, the surfmen launched the surfboat, got to her, and pulled the schooner into deep, safe water.

June, 1903
L. B. Coates

A farmhouse fire called the North Manitou crew into action in mid-July, the crew working hard to put out the blaze. The keeper reported that without their help, the house would have been totally destroyed.

Recording in late July that a South Manitou man had been seriously hurt during a stabbing fight, Keeper Lofberg wrote that he had been asked by the manager of the island's sawmill to go to the mainland and bring a physician to the island to dress the victim's wounds. He sailed the Mackinaw to Glen Arbor and brought back a doctor who provided the necessary treatment, after which Lofberg then took him back to the town.

At the close of fiscal 1903, the US Life-Saving Service had finally achieved its full strength on the Great Lakes, maintaining sixty-one stations in three districts. The thirty-one stations on Lake Michigan's shores reflected the potential dangers that the lengthy lake, with its widely separated, sometimes difficult to access ports, posed to mariners, especially in the days of aging sailing ships working on borrowed time.

As reported at the close of the next year's operations, the North Manitou and Point Betsie stations had seven surfmen from July 1 to December 5, 1903, and from April 1 to June 30, 1904. The South Manitou and Sleeping Bear Point stations both had six surfmen from July 1 to November 30, 1903, and seven from April 1 to June 30, 1904. As was the case at US lifesaving stations that operated seasonally, however, it was the service's policy that all keepers were not only caring for their stations' properties throughout the year, they were also expected to respond to needs that arose on the lake, gathering a crew if necessary.

As an example of the significance of the services of the Lake Michigan district's stations overall, 120 "disasters" were reported that year (second only to the Massachusetts coast's 181), with seven vessels classified as total losses. The value of the vessels and cargo involved in the lake's disasters was over $650,000. Just six of the 405 persons aboard those vessels were lost, and fifty-seven were succored at the stations, which amounted to 234 days' care for victims. The lake's lifesaving stations were reported to have saved property valued at slightly more than $514,000, with property losses tallying $137,000 (sums roughly equivalent, respectively, to $43 million and $4 million today).

A crew of lifesavers often had to devise what they needed for their tasks, as illustrated at the point where the men devoted a July 1903 day to making a sink where they could wash after cutting brush on their drill grounds. And at South Manitou, the crew was described as spending a day constructing a dock in front of the station, a job likely to be revisited a number of times, owing to changing lake levels and surf conditions.

Rescues reported by two of the stations' keepers suggests the likelihood that events may have involved the same boat. On July 25, the South Manitou crew was busy cleaning the house when a gasoline launch came into the harbor with a broken rudder and requested help in repairing it. Using tackle and a capstan from the station, they "hove the boat out of water," Keeper Lofberg wrote, and unshipped its rudder to make the repairs. However, eight evenings later, a gas launch with two persons aboard cruising the lake about twelve miles north of Point Betsie lost her rudder and drifted helplessly in the midst of strong winds and a rough sea.

The boat was spied at 11:40 p.m. by the Point Betsie lookout, who alerted his crewmates to the crisis. The surfboat immediately went to the disabled launch, where the crewmen used oars to rig a temporary rudder, then lashed the surfboat to the launch so as to obtain better steering. The two boats together proceeded under the launch's power to Frankfort, where more substantial repairs could be accomplished. Without the rescue, the launch and her occupants likely would have been lost.

Serious squalls in early August 1903 brought challenges to lifesavers all along the eastern Lake Michigan shore. On North Manitou, a gas launch broke free of its mooring and stranded where breakers were pounding her. The surfmen were able to haul her clear of danger. On South Manitou, the schooner *Mary Ludwig* dragged her anchors and drifted broadside to the breaking sea about a mile from the station. The crew quickly responded by surfboat to an appeal for help, running a line from the ship to a dock so they could heave the vessel's bow further offshore. When the wind then shifted from easterly to southward, they raised sail and were able to reach a better anchorage in the bay. The vessel's rudder had become unusable during the grounding, so the crew rigged tackle and hoisted it off the bottom to enable a surfman to dive below and guide the rudder into its step, where it could function properly.

August, 1903
Mary Ludwig

Because communications had been improved, Keeper Walker reported that month receiving a telephone message from Glen Haven that a tug hauling a loaded raft from Glen Arbor to South Manitou had lost its connection and needed help. With their surfboat quickly towed to the raft by the tug, the point's crew retrieved and saved the load, towing the raft into still water.

A resident of South Manitou came to the keeper in late August to report that his wife, who had seemed to be acting in a confused way, had wandered from their home. The keeper started a search and succeeded in finding the woman on the ground in the woods. "I carried her to the station and administered restoratives," he reported.

By chance, a government vessel had come within sight of the island station, enabling Lofberg to communicate, by flag signals, the need of a doctor. The vessel's surgeon promptly came to the station by skiff and diagnosed the woman's symptoms as acute hysteria. He left medicines and recommended that a physician immediately be called to care for her. A gas-powered boat was sent to Glen Haven and returned with a doctor, this account being another instance in which lifesavers served as valued forerunners of emergency medical technicians.

Before the end of August, Lofberg received word from the district superintendent that the transfer of a Long Branch surfboat from the Point Betsie station to the island had been authorized. Lofberg took advantage of the first favorable weather to bring the boat to its new home.

The South Manitou crew soon went into action in response to a signal for help observed by Surfman Cribbs at 1:30 a.m., while on watch. It came from the schooner *Mary A. Gregory*, which had dragged anchor to within one hundred feet of the shore. Surfman Cribbs fired a Coston flare to signal his awareness of the ship's plight, then the keeper and crew launched the surfboat, went to the schooner, and ran out an anchor with which they hauled her offshore. Also finding the ship's mainsail torn, they assisted in mending it and then helped in sailing her to a safer anchorage.

No one else was available, so in mid-September the South Manitou crew took a physician in the station's sailboat to North Manitou to treat a seriously ill woman. Late that month, the steam tug *Maggie Lutz* moored to a dock about a mile north of the South Manitou station, carried her lines away, and drifted onto the beach. The lifesavers pulled to her in the Monomoy, but before they arrived the tug's crew had managed to free her with her own power.

It was the Sleeping Bear Point crew's turn to assist struggling sailors on October 1, 1903, when the schooner *George W. Westcott* was unable to get away from the harbor at nearby Glen Haven, and her skipper asked for help. They carried out an anchor and heaved her away from shore, then made sail and worked her to a good anchorage.

Two days later, the point's crew experienced the tragic death of an on-duty surfman, an experience that must have been traumatic for all of them. A storm had been brewing throughout the day, with winds and seas converging to the extent that there was serious concern for the safety of sailors whose ships were in the vicinity. Surfman John Dwiggins punched the clock at 7:30 p.m. for

August, 1903
Mary A. Gregory

September, 1903
Maggie Lutz

October, 1903
George W. Westcott

night duty, then headed to the lookout tower, situated for watch purposes on a hill about 150 feet above the station, from which he could train his eyes over vast Lake Michigan.

The following morning his companion Charles Robinson, also from Grand Haven, entered the tower to assume watch duty and immediately sensed that something was wrong. Thinking he smelled gas, he then noticed two distinctively smooth holes in the roof, which he later said looked "as if they had been burned in by a hot iron." And then he saw Surfman John Dwiggins's badly burned body lying on the floor. An investigation concluded that while Dwiggins had been bolting the lookout's door shut, the fastener had been struck by lightning.

A footnote to the Dwiggins tragedy is what happened later that year to his widowed wife and father-in-law. She was traveling with her father in a horse-drawn sleigh in Grand Rapids on John's birthdate, when he would have turned thirty-five years of age. A street vehicle hit the sleigh, throwing her some twenty feet and breaking her neck, killing both passengers.

Early that October, South Manitou's Keeper Lofberg received notice from the US Weather Bureau that a bad storm was approaching South Manitou Island from the southeast. Aware that several vessels had come into the harbor, and concerned that the schooner *Harry Ransom* was anchored dangerously close to shore, he immediately boarded her and alerted her master, who then hired a tug to haul her to an appropriate anchorage.

October, 1903
Harry Ransom

On October 17, the body of an unknown seaman was found on the beach at Sleeping Bear Point, near that station. The crew made a coffin and temporarily buried the body until authorities took charge.

The fall of 1903 proved to be no exception to the tradition that November typically posed potentially dangerous conditions on Lake Michigan, with large temperature differentials between water and sky fomenting stormy seas.

For example, on November 4, both the South Manitou and Sleeping Bear Point stations were called to action. While Surfman George Haas was on patrol, the crew at the station heard the sound of a steamer's whistle signaling distress amidst thick afternoon fog. With Haas off the premises, there were only five surfmen at the station, so Lofberg recruited a volunteer, and the crew launched its Beebe-McClellan surfboat and started for the scene

November, 1903

Walter L. Frost

of an impending disaster. They found the steamer *Walter L. Frost*, heading from Chicago to Ogdensburg, New York, stranded on the southwest coast.

The crew located Haas as they made their way to the wreck, and at the steamer's request a surfman was instructed to return to the station to telegraph for a tug as the others began lightening her cargo. The steamer's condition deteriorated, however, when wind from the northwest caused the vessel to pound, creating a leak toward the bow. At the order of the ship's master, the crew scuttled her (sank her intentionally) to keep her from smashing to pieces against the lake bottom.

When the tug arrived at 1:30 a.m. on the second day of the crisis, the lifesavers returned to the station at 4:00 a.m. At 8:00 a.m., the keeper and four surfmen went back to the ship in the Monomoy surfboat, having left two surfmen to respond should another need of assistance arise. They helped jettison the steamer's cargo, staying there until midafternoon of the following day, when the seas had risen so much that the tug had to seek protection in the harbor. A bit later, the lifesavers launched the Beebe-McLellan surfboat and sailed to the steamer, two tugs having declined to tow them to the vessel. They took seven of the ship's crewmen to the station.

A day later, the lifesavers took the last seven crewmen from the ship to the station, arriving at 1:30 a.m., seven others having reached the beach in the ship's own boat. The rescued men were treated and given dry clothing, sheltered, and fed for about ten days.

With the steamer a total loss despite the efforts to save her, the surfmen helped her men retrieve some of their valuables and recovered the ship's anchors and chains. Meanwhile, the keeper had learned that a waterlogged schooner, the *Robert Howlett*, had anchored in the bay and that her yawl boat had gone onto the island's beach. The lifesavers pulled the small boat off the beach and went to assist the schooner's crew, pumping her out over several days.

November, 1903

Robert Howlett

Events at Sleeping Bear Point on November 4 had been less dramatic but nonetheless, the men were dutiful; a gas-powered launch had broken her moorings and become stranded toward the beach. The station's men employed tackles to haul her onto the beach, protecting her from the high seas.

At Sleeping Bear Point and the two island stations, surfmen were also busy securing everything properly for the winter closure.

Storm damage
at North Manitou Wharf.

*Leelanau Historical
Society Museum.*

The South Manitou's crew repaired the boathouse to prevent snow from getting through the rooftop. Soon the station was under the temporary leadership of the no. 1 surfman, because Keeper Lofberg had been ordered transferred across Lake Michigan to lead the Racine, Wisconsin station, south of Milwaukee, where he had previously served. A few days later, the crew helped him pack his furniture and get his goods to the dock where he would catch a boat to Chicago.

Lofberg had a distinguished career with the lifesaving service, serving first as a surfman at the Racine station and later as its long-time keeper following his brief island command, and thereafter as the superintendent of the service's Lake Michigan district. Surely worthy of note, his son, Gus B. Lofberg, Jr., who was born on April 6, 1903, while his father was serving on South Manitou, had a distinguished naval career, perhaps inspired by his childhood experiences on Lake Michigan. He rose to be the commanding officer, at age thirty-nine, of the USS *Little*, a high-speed transport vessel (formerly a destroyer), which was attacked and sunk by Japanese surface forces near Guadalcanal in 1942, with Lofberg losing his life in the battle. A destroyer was later named for him.

The North Manitou crew had one more challenge to face that season. The *Charles Stewart Parnell* had steamed around the north

November, 1903

Charles Stewart Parnell

end of the island, seeking shelter from fresh snowfall, but then stranded about two hundred yards off Vessel Point. The lifesavers quickly pulled to her in the surfboat, sounded for nearby water depths, boarded her, and stood by in the event of a more serious crisis. The vessel's crew began throwing overboard her cargo of grain, but stopped soon because water was washing over the deck and flowing down her open hatches.

The lifesavers took the master ashore the next morning, and returned for her crew that afternoon. Ten men were taken to the station for shelter, but five others insisted on remaining aboard the vessel. A day later, No. 2 was dispatched to Leland to wire for help, which arrived the next morning. The keeper and other surfmen continued to unload cargo and provide other assistance, taking the captain to a nearby steamer that was waiting to assist the grounded *Parnell.*

When yet another attempt to maneuver the ship off the bottom had failed, the surfmen put her crew back aboard to continue unloading the vessel, while their no. 1 went to Leland with several men to send for help. Ultimately, using the power of a wrecking tug, the lightened ship was pulled free.

Justifying the simultaneous presence of three lifesaving stations situated within the passage itself, together with the Point Betsie station's significant supportive role, was the number of strandings there between mid-1893 and mid-1903. Stranding was the most common risk that lake vessels experienced, and without a competent response, vessels would likely be destroyed and numerous lives lost. Over that decade, there were eleven recorded strandings at Sleeping Bear Point, thirteen at South Manitou Island, and sixteen at North Manitou Island, tallies notably high when measured against those for the entire Lake Michigan shoreline.

The figures doubtless would have been far higher had not so many ships been warned off shallow waters and beaches through long nights and foggy days, often in horrendous weather, when faithful Manitou Passage beach patrolmen ignited their Coston signals or otherwise alerted the endangered ships.

Passage Experiences During the Service's Final Decade

Initially, things were relatively quiet after the stations' respective openings for the active season in April 1904. On South Manitou, new keeper Jacob Van Weelden recorded opening the station at midnight on the fourth of the month, as floating ice had prevented him from bringing a crew to the island for April 1 as scheduled. He organized his men by the numbers, and within a few days the crew was engaged in laying a cement walk on the premises. The crew was again doing construction work in early June, building a pier in front of the boathouse and then fashioning an incline from the boathouse to the water.

About ten days into its active season, the Sleeping Bear Point's crew responded to a call from Glen Haven for help in recovering two circular saws that had fallen off a pier—a task not exactly in their job description, but they were always ready to give assistance.

The South Manitou station received a more typical request for help on June 22 when the schooner *Elida* anchored there, with two feet of water aboard and her crew totally exhausted from pumping to keep her afloat. The lifesavers came aboard and pumped her out, then helped her crew to stop the leak, raise canvas, and get underway again.

On a foggy July 9, the steamer *Black Rock*, headed from Buffalo to Chicago with a cargo of hard coal, stranded on the beach about one thousand feet west of the Sleeping Bear Point station. The lifesavers launched the surfboat and went to her aid, running lines, taking soundings around the stricken vessel, and sending dispatches. Later that day, with the added power of a passing steamer and the Frankfort tug *Holden*, the ship was freed from the shore and able to continue her voyage.

Keepers St. Peter of North Manitou and William Walker of Sleeping Bear Point recorded inspection visits of General Superintendent Sumner Kimball and Captain Charles McLellan,

June, 1904
Elida

July, 1904
Black Rock

its chief inspector, on July 14. Arriving on the revenue cutter *Tuscarora*, as was customary during midsummer cruises by the commanders, they inspected the premises and apparatus, and put the crew through the drills before continuing on their route, also visiting the South Manitou and Point Betsie stations and others along the shore.

The North Manitou keeper called the crew to fire quarters later that month, entering in the logbook that they produced a water stream in thirty-two seconds. The crew was also busy assisting in laying telephone cable on the island. Keeper St. Peter's logs also show how rapidly steam-powered vessels were replacing schooners in the Lake Michigan commercial fleet; on the second of that month, in the middle of the navigation season, only six schooners, but twenty steamers, passed the island.

On the twenty-first of July, St. Peter's crew drilled with the life car, shooting a line to the dock and running the car to it, where crewman no. 7 put five persons into the rescue capsule. The crew also intentionally capsized their service boat and recovered it. Four days later, the North Manitou crew drilled with the beach apparatus, completing the simulated recovery of a shipwreck victim in three minutes, five seconds. During the remainder of the day, the crew was busy painting the inside of their supply boat and catching a rowboat that had washed off the beach and drifted away in a strong wind.

At Point Betsie, Keeper Miller recorded on September 1 that "the men broke up the old Dobbins boat and burnt her to save the old iron," a fate that awaited numerous well-worn wooden surfboats through the years. A week later, the journal entry bore the signature of the "keeper pro tem"—no. 1, Edwin Bedford—who would eventually succeed the legendary Miller, who was ill and under a doctor's care at the time.

In early September, an assistant inspector arrived to evaluate the North Manitou station and its equipment, then drilled the crew in signaling and in the resuscitation of an apparently drowned person. During that month, preparations were being made by the crew, including the building of a wall around ground that had been filled in as a possible site to relocate the station building.

At 2:00 a.m. on September 16, South Manitou's Keeper Van Weelden sent a surfman to the northwest end of the island to see if a vessel might be in distress. About a mile from the station, the surfman spotted a tug anchored in the bay. He found a skiff, went aboard the tug, and learned that the vessel, the *Duncan City*, was headed to Petoskey from its home port of Sturgeon Bay, Wisconsin, with two scows loaded with stone that had become disconnected from the tug several miles from the west end of the island.

The crewmen on the leaking tug had failed in an effort to pass another line to the scows, which were also slowly sinking. Later in the morning, the tug's captain asked for help in finding the scows that were no longer visible, but after the crews' searching the area's waters for miles around, they were given up for lost.

About a week later, the North Manitou crew was told that a large scow was ashore on the island's west side, with holes in its bottom and stern. The men were unable to do anything to save the scow, which possibly could have been one of those lost the previous week.

On the night of September 24, the two assistant Point Betsie lightkeepers were returning to the light station from Frankfort in a boat loaded with supplies when the craft rolled over as it crossed a bar. Four surfmen who were on the beach rushed into the water and righted the boat, bringing it and the two men ashore, but most of the supplies were lost.

A drill with the life car conducted in late September by the North Manitou crew illustrated once again that such exercises did not always end as intended. The crew had very successfully fired a line from their Lyle gun 132 yards to a moored skiff, with the station's no. 7 man aboard. After he had been safely brought to shore in the rescue car, it became caught in lines and capsized. The keeper acknowledged that it had to be pulled to shore "bottom up."

That fall, the South Manitou crew received a call from the post office reporting that a steamer at a dock, loaded with lumber, was engulfed in flames. Her captain requested that Van Weelden's crew try to tow her away from the dock and scuttle her, which they succeeded in doing. Working all through the night, the crew manned the pumps, trying to save her and the cargo, some of which they were able to off-load, but the steamer sank the following morning, a total loss. At the request of the captain of another steamer whose anchor and chain had been lost during the night while he had sought to get his own ship away from the fire, the lifesavers successfully searched for his mooring equipment.

Soon thereafter, two crewmen from the steamer *Allie E. Shipman* came to the South Manitou station, saying that she had dragged her anchor and stranded at 1:30 a.m. Upon their request, they were given beds for the night, and two surfmen went to maintain watch

October, 1904

Allie E. Shipman

of the ship and run lines to her to keep her steady until the sea subsided. Keeper Van Weelden telegraphed for a tug, which arrived from Frankfort two days later, and the station's surfmen assisted in getting the ship underway.

In mid-November 1904, North Manitou's Keeper St. Peter recorded having sailed to South Manitou with two surfmen to obtain eggs and hay. On another day that month, he reported that the station's lookout had observed a boat seemingly dead in the water, displaying the American ensign at half-mast. Upon pulling out to the craft, the lifesavers found that she was the *Bessie*, the island's mail boat, which had run out of gasoline after traveling only a few miles of its run to Leland. Until being rescued, she was "at the mercy of the wind and sea." The men towed her back to the shore, where she took on gasoline and started off again to deliver the islanders' mail to the post office.

Not long after that, when the North Manitou crew was busy preparing the station for winter closure, the *Bessie* broke her mooring chain in a southeastern sleet storm and was driven onto the island beach. The lookout reported the incident and the crew used heavy tackle to haul her from the seas' crashing reach.

That same windstorm caused a problem at Sleeping Bear Point when the crew saw two steamers trying to gain the protection of the bay in the dark of night. Realizing that the shore's outline could not be spotted from the vessels, a surfman was sent from the station to burn a Coston flare. On seeing his light, the two boats, whose identities were unknown, headed out into the bay.

On the morning of November 20, 1904, the Point Betsie lifesavers immediately headed for Platte River Point, about nine miles north of the station, to assist the steamer *Jesse Spalding*, as word of her stranding at 1:00 a.m. did not reach the station until 9:00 a.m. Procuring a team of horses to pull the rescue boat much of the way up the shore, they then launched the boat and rowed a half-mile to the steamer. Rough seas prevented the men from coming alongside the vessel, but they were able to use a lifeline to take off two seamen, who then went to Frankfort with the lifesavers to hire a tug, which arrived shortly before noon on the twenty-first. After the lifesavers and steamer's crew had succeeded in lightening her by off-loading a portion of her cargo of iron ore, with the surfmen ferrying tools and equipment back and forth and running lines, the vessel was pulled free of the bottom on the evening of the twenty-second.

November, 1904
Bessie

November, 1904
Jesse Spalding

On November 28, the mailboat *Bessie* was yet again a concern, this time for having parted her chains in high winds, and wound up on the beach. Mail service being coveted by the island's isolated residents, the station's crew used heavy tackle to haul her farther onto shore for safety, and then relaunched her the next day.

November, 1904
Bessie

The service annually informed its funding sources of the many people assisted by its surfmen who otherwise likely would have lost their lives. With the experiences of the Manitou Passage stations showing they were no exception, the 1904 report listed 103 such examples service-wide, reminding readers of the perils that individuals might face in the opening years of the twentieth century, and of the public's dependence on the service's timely response:

> *Eighteen had fallen from wharves, piers, bridges, etc.; 12 were bathers in imminent danger of drowning; 20 were cut off from the land by water; 12 were in a burning building; 22 were in buildings endangered by sea and storm; 8 were in danger upon drawbridges; 3 were intoxicated; 1 had broken through ice; 1 was attacked by a ruffian; 1 was deranged and was lost among the hills; 1 was adrift upon some wreckage; 1 had fallen unconscious from neuralgia of the heart; 1 had descended into the water in an airship; 1 was an electrician who had come in contact with a live wire and was suspended, unconscious, from the cross arm of a telegraph pole; and 1 lay insensible, having been thrown from a buggy.*

Throughout that year, US stations reported the rescue use of the surfboat 867 times, making about 1,100 trips, and stations' lifeboats, then mostly self-righting and self-bailing models, used sixty-one times, making 104 trips. The breeches buoy was employed on twelve occasions, landing 147 persons. Wreck guns were used on nineteen instances, firing forty-five shots.

Having closed the North Manitou station for the season at the end of November, Keeper St. Peter logged on January 20, 1905, that he "availed myself of fine weather and opened the doors of the boathouse to air the inside," thereby affirming that a keeper was always responsible for his station, even when closed for the winter season.

After opening the following spring, South Manitou Island's Keeper Van Weelden recorded that George Kelderhouse had reported to the station and would commence duty at midnight on April 23, 1905. He also reported receipt of a letter from the general superintendent's office, ordering him to care for the telephone line connecting his station with the North Manitou and Sleeping Bear Point stations.

Building upon demonstrations which the Marquette, Michigan station had initiated about a half-dozen years previously to evaluate the benefits of installing gasoline-powered motors in lifeboats, the service began to slowly place motorized boats at locations where they could be speedily launched, such as the Manitou Passage stations. Among other benefits, powered boats would gradually eliminate the procuring of horses to pull heavy beach rescue equipment substantial distances from lifesaving stations to wreck sites.

About a week after opening the South Manitou station for the 1905 season, Van Weelden made special note that on a foggy day he had ordered an extra lifesaving patrol and launched the Beebe-McClellan surfboat to look for the lighthouse keeper, who was reported to be trying to reach the island in a sailboat without lights, and that the barometer's low reading warning meant even more foul weather. Unable to find him that night, the men were doubtless relieved when they received a telephone call the next day in which the lightkeeper said he had turned back shortly after starting his trip across the passage, sailing instead to the mainland town of Empire.

In retrospect, it was certainly helpful that the telephone connection was functioning. And given the friendly rivalry that commonly characterized relations between keepers of lighthouses and lifesaving stations, one would assume that this episode was not quickly forgotten by either of the men.

Early in May 1905, Keeper Van Weelden reported that his lookout had seen a small sailboat leaving its anchorage and heading for a pier somewhat north of the station. Watching its progress, he saw that they had lost the use of the bowsprit and were drifting toward the beach. The crew headed to the site in the Beebe-McClellan boat and tried to pull her off, but she began to pound on the bottom. They secured her with lines and the keeper left a man to observe her.

The following morning, they took anchor and tackle to the sailboat and were able to pull her off the beach. After they repaired the damage, she resumed her trip to Manistee, and the crew then drilled with the beach rescue apparatus and cleaned and dried the Beebe-McClellan boat. The South Manitou crew's next home maintenance task was to plaster the station's sitting room, and to clean their house.

Soon thereafter, Keeper Van Weelden sailed to Glen Arbor to post advertisements for materials to repair the boathouse's incline. While he was away on that mission, his crewmen cut firewood for the station's use and serviced the lifeboats. Then, after routinely performing the capsize drill, they were engaged in building a wooden sidewalk to the station's outhouse.

On North Manitou, crewmen were tasked that spring with making cement walkways around the station and repairing the dock when sea conditions permitted.

At month's end, the keeper reported visiting the south patrol post, where he changed the key for recording a surfman's completion of his patrol, removing key no. 8 and substituting no. 5. These records would be routinely examined by district supervisors to be certain that stations' patrols were being properly completed. If not, the offending surfman would be penalized and typically terminated in the event of repeated offenses.

On May 10, 1905, the sloop *Togo* collided with a pier on South Manitou Island and wound up on the beach. Strong winds and a heavy sea prevented the lifesavers from refloating her, so they carried lines from her masthead to the pier and caused her to list (lean to a side) so as to prevent her from swamping. When the weather improved, they succeeded in repairing and floating her.

At North Manitou on June 4, the steamer *Simon J. Murphy* stranded in thick fog. In another act of interagency cooperation, the island's lightkeeper had seen the accident and alerted the lifesaving station, whose men stayed by the vessel through the night in the event they were needed. The next morning, they sounded surrounding depths and the vessel was able to free herself and thus be on her way.

About a month later, a log reported that the North Manitou lifesavers crew put out a house fire after nearly an hour's struggle against the flames. A week thereafter, the keeper on South Manitou went for a doctor to treat an islander who had been seriously stabbed. Several days later, Van Weelden received notice of the transfer of one of his surfmen to the mainland Sleeping Bear Point station, illustrating once again the challenges island stations' keepers faced in recruiting and retaining reliable surfmen.

On August 13, the Sleeping Bear Point crew was called to distant duty by a phone call from Empire, reporting the drowning of two men in Empire Bay, about seven miles southwest of the station and beyond sighting distance. The crew reached the area about an

May, 1905
Togo

June, 1905
Simon J. Murphy

hour later, having been informed of the situation by an intoxicated man who, along with another man, had reached shore safely. The four men had been sailing together when the boat capsized. One of the four had been unable to hold onto the overturned craft and the other had attempted to help him, but both were lost as the hull, with the two survivors, drifted to shore.

The survivors pointed to the spot where their boat had turned over, but they were unable to provide any precise information. The crew dragged the bottom for two hours with grappling hooks, but with a strong undertow, a fresh northeast wind, and the uncertainty of the bodies' locations, recovery efforts were unsuccessful, and the disheartened crew returned to their station.

In October, the south island's crew had another medical call to action, being asked to accompany a fish tug to Glen Haven to bring a physician to the island on the condition that the lifesavers would also make the trip, presumably to reassure the doctor of his safety. After treating a dangerously ill woman who had given birth, the doctor was returned to the mainland by the crew.

As was customary, the three passage stations were then preparing for the season's closure at midnight on November 30. Irrespective of his station's shuttering, Keeper Van Weelden recorded the weather conditions and barometer readings at South Manitou at sunrise, noon, and sunset each day throughout the long winter.

The active season of 1906 began on April 1, with Keeper Walker at Sleeping Bear Point and Charles Robinson as his no. 1 surfman. On the evening of April 6, the North Manitou station received a telephone message from Leland reporting that two boats were at the edge of ice on the lake and needing assistance. Keeper St. Peter ordered the surfboat to the scene, as well as a gas-powered boat he had hired, loaded with blankets and provisions.

While underway, they met one of the stranded boats coming to the north island, having maneuvered herself free of the ice. Continuing on their mission, the lifesavers came to the gasoline-powered fish launch *Morning Dip,* which had broken her propeller in the ice. Finding the occupants in poor condition from cold and exposure, the crew passed the men blankets and food, and towed the launch and surfboat back to the island. St. Peter wrote that "they would have perished but for the assistance as they were thoroughly exhausted, having worked in the ice for many

April, 1906
Morning Dip

hours without anything to eat." The station's lifesaving efforts had consumed seven hours.

On May 1, 1906, the Sleeping Bear Point's lookout saw that a schooner, the *Fearless* (appropriately named?) had run onto the beach about two thousand feet from the station. The crew took the surfboat to the scene, put out an anchor to steady her, and began to unload several cords of wooden edging. With the use of the foresail to back the vessel, they then were able to swing her around toward deep water, enabling her to be soon underway with no significant damage having been done.

On May 7, 1906, both the South Manitou Island and Sleeping Bear Point station crews became involved in a rescue of the gas-powered launch *Reliance*, whose engine had failed in the passage about four miles north of the point, with seven passengers and the US mail on board. The Sleeping Bear crew took four of the occupants by surfboat to South Manitou, where they secured another powerboat, then returned to the disabled launch where they met the arriving South Manitou crew. The launch was towed to South Manitou by the two crews for repair.

The next day, the Sleeping Bear Point crew was alerted by telephone from Glen Haven that an unnamed sloop with a man, woman, and three children aboard was on the verge of pounding to pieces against a pier during a fresh wind. Carrying tackles and lines, the crew traveled overland to the site, where they hove her to safety and a good anchorage.

About ten days later, those lifesavers were responding to a crisis facing the schooner *Stafford*, which too was being smashed against a pier. Working in similar fashion, they brought her to a safe anchorage.

Soon thereafter, under the watchful eyes of visiting inspectors, the point's crew performed mandatory surfboat, beach apparatus, and fire drills, as well as drills for the treatment of apparently drowned persons or those suffering from frostbite. Employing another skill later that month, a surfman burned a Coston flare to successfully warn off a schooner that had come too close to the Sleeping Bear shore. Some of the flame got to his eye, fortunately without serious injury. Another such near grounding occurred at the point in early June, causing a surfman to resort to the megaphone to warn the vessel off, as it was too light for the Coston signal to be effective.

In early August, the Sleeping Bear watchman saw a fire in what

May, 1905
Fearless

May, 1906
Reliance

appeared to be the middle of the passage between their own station and South Manitou's. The crew launched the surfboat and pulled more than eight miles in the direction of the fire, only to notice their own lookout signaling them by flare to return to the station. He had received a phone call informing him that what his crew had been concerned about was merely an island-beach bonfire.

Another episode involving the two stations occurred that August when the Sleeping Bear lookout spotted a small launch about seven miles north of the station. The crew had sailed about four miles when they discovered that the boat was in tow by the South Manitou crew, so they returned to their own station, knowing they would have to repair their cart's wheel, which had broken during that unnecessary boat launching.

In mid-October 1906, the mail boat *Bessie* again needed attention when an early morning watchman on South Manitou reported her sunk at her moorings. The keeper ordered his crew to quick action; they ran a strong line between the wreck and the pier and managed to haul her to shallows, where they undertook to bail her out. The boat's cabin had washed away, but the crew found it and returned it to the private owner.

The south island's crew had a memorable day in November, beginning with a flag signal drill, then sawing wood and making ballast bags for use in sailing their Mackinaw boat. At 9:40 p.m., Keeper Van Weelden visited the station's lookout tower and found the surfman on duty was asleep on the floor. The keeper wrote, "I watched him for thirteen minutes then woke him up and suspended him for neglect of watch duty." The keeper fortunately was able to immediately employ a temporary surfman, who went on duty at midnight. In early December, there came what the sleepy surfman had probably anticipated—a notice of termination from General Superintendent Kimball. A surfman must not fall asleep on watch duty!

Two days later, at 11:30 p.m., the schooner *Margaret Dall* dragged anchor and drifted toward the shore. Going to her in the surfboat, Van Weelden's South Manitou men "found her high and dry upon the beach and the crew had walked ashore and found shelter at the South Manitou Post Office." A day later, the island's post office called to say that another schooner was dragging her anchor and getting close to shore. Van Weelden and some of his crew ran down the beach and stood by to be ready to assist if needed, but by morning a wind shift had moved her out of danger.

October, 1906
Bessie

November, 1906
Margaret Dall

Nearly three weeks after the December 1, 1906, seasonal closing, Keeper Van Weelden heard distress signals east of the station. He gathered two of his own crew, another surfman who was on the island at the time but had served that year at the Charlevoix station, and also two volunteering brothers, and they launched the Monomoy surfboat and pulled to the island's point, where they found the tug *Potawatomi* stranded just offshore.

The captain requested that they send a telegraph dispatch to Frankfort for another tug. The keeper wrote that he and his men returned to the station and sent that message, then returned to the stranded vessel and took soundings, finding deep water ahead. They then ran an anchor to hold her bow away from shore. "The tug worked ahead, and in two hours she was released off the bar," he later reported, the men having returned to the station late that night.

Before the start of the next season, the South Manitou Island Lifesaving Station experienced its second leadership change: Jacob Van Weelden, who was born in Grand Haven, Michigan, was transferred to the nearby Holland station as its keeper, leaving his no. 1 in charge until his replacement, Eli E. Pugh, arrived in late January, after being delayed by thick Lake Michigan ice.

One of Pugh's early actions was to request that physical examinations, usually conducted by a surgeon of the Marine Hospital Service, be performed by a local physician, owing to the lengthy and costly journey that would otherwise have been involved. The permission was received and the station's surfmen were examined and approved for retention.

The Sleeping Bear Point lifesavers spent three successive days preparing for the station's mid-April 1907 opening, but had a change of activity at daylight on the seventeenth, when the lookout discovered a capsized schooner, the *Eliza Day*, about five miles northeast of the station, her lights having not been visible from the station in the dark, snowy weather. The lifesavers quickly launched the surfboat and started toward the wreck, but when they had traveled about two miles they saw the ship's crew coming down the beach; the four men had landed near Glen Arbor in their yawl boat, and the waterlogged schooner, which capsized at about 3:00 a.m., drifted toward Pyramid Point, and stranded. While returning to the station and landing in the surf, the surfboat hit a cobblestone which damaged its bottom. The lifesavers made the necessary repairs to the boat and sheltered the schooner's crew at the

December, 1906
Potawatomi

April, 1907
Eliza Day

station for a day. They went to the wreck by surfboat the following day, and after working nine hours with the crew, they managed to right the schooner. The next day, after working ten more hours, the lifesavers got her pumped out and into a safe anchorage.

One day in early May, Keeper St. Peter logged that his north island crew had planted fruit trees on the property, that he had drilled the crew with its beach apparatus, and that he had gone to the south patrol post to switch its key.

May, 1907
Oneida

And one late May night, the schooner *Oneida* sprung a bad leak in gale-force winds with late-season snow and sought the north island's protection, but stranded when she got too close to the shore. The lookout spotted her and the surfboat was dispatched to her aid, the crew pumping for many hours to no avail, more water coming aboard than they could pump out. Several days later, a steam tug came to the scene, but the ship's master decided to wait for a more powerful tug, which arrived after two more days.

The lifesavers were engaged again in pumping her, and after working three and a half hours, the tug was able to pull the schooner free. Deciding to try to get her across the lake to the dry dock at Sturgeon Bay, the master asked the keeper if he would send two surfmen to pump if necessary, while the schooner was under tow. Surfmen nos. 1 and 7 were sent, and returned to the station about a week later.

In mid-June, the Sleeping Bear Point crew was called into action, quickly extinguishing a fire that had started in a nearby shop. On South Manitou, while on the 4:00 a.m. beach patrol, the surfman warned off a dangerously close steamer in thick fog by pounding on a dry hardwood plank with a rock.

Later that month, Keeper Pugh granted three days' leave of absence to Surfman Kelderhouse to enable him to care for his sick wife. Pugh was able to engage a member of his own family as the substitute. Three days later, Pugh granted extended leave to Kelderhouse, who was under diphtheria quarantine with his family. Two weeks passed before he could resume his duties.

July, 1907
Henry Phipps

On July 7, 1907, North Manitou's Keeper St. Peter was routinely inspecting his crew's quarters and lockers when he learned of a steamer's stranding in deep fog at 4:00 a.m. off Pyramid Point. The men quickly headed to the scene in the surfboat, towed by the mail boat. Arriving at 2:30 p.m., they found that both the Sleeping Bear Point and South Manitou Island crews were already at the site of the steamer *Henry Phipps*. A south island surfman had discovered the steamer when fog there had lifted, and his crew had rowed eight miles to the scene, where they had run a hawser and attended the vessel until her release from the shallows that evening by two passing steamers. There being nothing more for the lifesavers to do, the crews stood by until the ship was underway on her own power.

Early that July, the Sleeping Bear Point lookout discovered smoke rising above the fog layer, apparently rising from close to shore off nearby Pyramid Point. Pulling to the site for an hour and a half, the crew found a "big steel steamer which had run on a reef. As there [were] two big steamers working on her, we stayed by until she was off." As required, Keeper Walker dutifully reported in the day's log that the normal 8:00 p.m. patrol had been omitted due to the emergency.

The north island mail boat, *Manitou*, became disabled on August 5 while heading for distant Leland, and was seen drifting in the wind a mile north of the station. Keeper St. Peter hired a power-boat to catch her and tow her back, then secured her to a mooring.

On August 15, while the schooner *Petrel* was anchored north-ward of the South Manitou station, she was run into by the schooner *Rosa Belle*, which forced the *Petrel* toward the beach. The station crew went to the accident scene by surfboat and separated the vessels. After hauling the *Petrel* off the shallows so she wouldn't strand, it was discovered that she was leaking. They pumped her out and made temporary repairs, then further prepared her for a tow to Milwaukee. Because the schooner was still leaking and undermanned, a surfman was directed to accompany the vessel.

The *Petrel's* master later wrote to thank the service for the assistance, saying that after the collision, "we were in pretty bad shape" and that the lifesaving crew under Captain Pugh "had rendered us very necessary assistance." Lauding Pugh's competence and willingness, he gratefully noted that the island crew not only had cleared the two schooners of the wreckage, but spent three days, morning and afternoon, pumping his vessel.

On September 10, 1907, the South Manitou crew responded to an appeal for help from the schooner *Melitta*, which was having difficulty in getting underway. And later that day, the schooner *H.D. Moore* stranded at 10:45 p.m. on the island's northeast point, a mile and a half north of the station, while trying to enter the harbor in a severe thunderstorm. The lifesavers reached her by surfboat and took her four crewmen to the station. On the next day, the

August, 1907
Manitou

August, 1907
Petrel
Rosa Belle

September, 1907
Mellitta
H. D. Moore

September, 1907

Reliance

September, 1907

R. H. Becker

September, 1907

Rouse Simmons

October, 1907

Beatrice

schooner crew's clothing and valuables were retrieved, and thereafter the lifesavers and vessel's crewmen were able to save forty-five thousand feet of lumber and shelter her crew, but the ship and remainder of her cargo were a total loss.

In mid-September, the Sleeping Bear Point surfmen were alerted that the gas launch *Reliance* broke her mooring chain and had drifted into the shallows at nearby Glen Haven. It was too rough to pull the launch into deeper water, so the crew hauled her onto the beach where she would be protected. Two days later, after more than two hours of heaving, they managed to work her off the beach undamaged.

Late that month, both islands' crews were called into action when the schooner scow *R.H. Becker* broke her centerboard on a reef while tacking in gale-force winds and became uncontrollable. The vessel dropped anchor two miles south of the North Manitou lighthouse and displayed distress signals that were seen by lookouts at both islands' lifesaving stations, whose crews promptly responded.

The crews returned to their stations when they had determined that the vessel was not in immediate danger and that they, working alone, could not free her. They notified the vessel's owner and arranged for a tug to tow her into South Manitou's harbor. The lifesavers assisted there in fixing and reinstalling the old centerboard, much to the vessel master's appreciation. His ship being able to continue the voyage, he wrote his thanks to the service, saying that each of the two stations had performed gallantly.

Near the end of September 1907, the three-masted schooner *Rouse Simmons* displayed a signal for assistance in getting away from the South Manitou harbor. The surfmen helped heave up her anchor and get her underway.

About the same time, the north island's mail boat once again broke her moorings. The surfmen caught up with her and moored her safely, doubtless much to the gratitude of the isolated islanders. Only a few weeks later, the Sleeping Bear Point crew was alerted that the gas-powered mail launch *Beatrice* was pounding the bottom near Glen Haven in heavy surf. They hauled her out onto the beach to protect her, then relaunched her the following day.

A schooner captain came to the South Manitou station in September and asked that the keeper help to put a sick sailor aboard a Chicago-bound steamer about to depart the harbor, thus enabling the ill man to soon get to his home.

In mid-November, the Sleeping Bear Point station received a phone message from Glen Haven that a small boat with four men in it was adrift in the bay. Arriving at the craft by surfboat, they found it belonged to a steamer that had anchored while the crew went ashore to send a message. Upon returning to the skiff and starting for their ship, they had broken two oars and were drifting away. The surfmen took them in tow and saved the men from a very perilous cold night.

On November 20, the steamer *Kearsarge* anchored in Sleeping Bear Bay and her crewmen went to the station in her lifeboat to send messages. While trying to get back to their ship in a southeast gale, they broke two oars. To stop being blown out to sea, they anchored and were spotted by someone in Glen Haven, who notified the point's lifesaving station. The surfmen went to her by surfboat and attempted to tow the lifeboat, but after pulling for an hour and a half, were unable to make much headway. They beached the lifeboat safely and sheltered her occupants overnight. The next morning the winds had died, and her crew made it out to their vessel.

November, 1907

Kearsarge

Late that month, the two island crews were again working together in an attempt to save a vessel from complete destruction and the loss of her contents. The schooner *Josephine Dresden*, loaded with lumber for a sawmill and other island structures, was anchored on the west side of North Manitou Island to off-load cargo when a sudden wind shift quickly caused her to become stranded.

The island's lifesavers and four volunteers pulled the surfboat across the island's high and steep hills to get to the wreck. Keeper St. Peter arrived more quickly, finding the vessel on the beach, to which her crew had jumped. With the lifesavers and volunteers exhausted from dragging the surfboat to the scene, the team stayed by the vessel under the direction of the no. 1, returning to the station by surfboat the following day. A few days later, the surfmen worked with a tug's crew in an attempt to free her, but even with the help of a second tug, they could not get her off the beach. When the owner concluded that the ship's situation was hopeless, the crews helped him save her valuable items.

November, 1907

Josephine Dresden

As was customary for keepers of lifesaving stations who had end-of-year breaks between two active seasons, Eli Pugh returned to the South Manitou station from his leave on January 30, 1908. He recorded that day having received treasury department checks for his four surfmen who had voluntarily served in the *Dresden* schooner rescue during four days of the officially inactive month of December.

In April, Keeper Pugh reported having informed the captain of the revenue cutter *Tuscarora* of the location of the sunken hull of the schooner *Margaret Dall,* which could obstruct navigation within South Manitou's harbor.

Keeper St. Peter reported from the North Manitou station on May 1 that a fifty-six-year-old male island resident, "while under the influence of liquor undertook to carry a bag of feed from the dock to the shore when he stumbled and fell into the lake." No.1, having seen the man fall, ran to him and pulled him out. "But for the prompt assistance of No. 1 the man might have drowned," the keeper recorded.

On July 3, Pugh wrote that upon his refusal to grant his no. 7's request for a leave of absence, the surfman had deserted and left the station. He appointed Walter Pugh to temporarily fill that slot, and a few days later appointed another family member, Wilbur Pugh, to replace himself when he took a lifeboat to Frankfort so it could be shipped to New Jersey, likely for preparation for reassignment. The three members of the Pugh family served the station extensively.

When the gas launch *Beatrice* failed in mid-August heat, leaving her drifting "helplessly," the South Manitou surfmen towed her to the station and replaced her dead batteries. Later that fall, when the *Beatrice* parted her moorings in a powerful sea and landed on the beach, the crew again rescued her, mooring her more securely.

Soon thereafter, a gas launch bearing a party of visitors ran broadside onto the Point Betsie beach. The nearby surfmen came to the passengers' aid and bailed her out. At Point Betsie later that month, a boy came to the station from a resort on nearby Crystal Lake to report that "the woods were all afire around the cottages and that they needed help." Edwin Bedford, the former no. 1 under Keeper Harrison Miller, whom he had succeeded as the station's keeper, wrote that he took several surfmen to the scene and helped to extinguish the blaze.

In early September 1908, the gas launch *Willow H.* became disabled about two miles southwest of the South Manitou station, whose lookout spotted a torch being burned. The surfboat was soon underway and headed to the disabled craft, where it was learned that the two occupants wanted a tug to tow them into Frankfort. A surfman went to shore and walked the four and a half miles to the

August, 1908

Beatrice

September, 1908

Willow H.

town to arrange for a tug, while the station's surfboat towed the launch to smoother water until the help arrived.

That fall, after Keeper Bedford had completed the Point Betsie station's surfboat drill, the station received a telephone call that the steamer *Robert Wente* was aground on Platte River reef, about nine miles northeast of the station. The crew went to the site and set a kedge anchor for them in deeper water, using it in an attempt to pull her off the bottom, but to no avail. Soon the tug *E. Holton* came from Frankfort, as well as the Frankfort station's surfmen, and the two lifesaving crews ran a towline between the tug and the steamer and then threw huge quantities of lumber and shingles overboard before she lifted off the bottom. The crews were able to return to their respective stations that night.

One September day, Keeper Pugh reported that his surfman in the South Manitou watch tower "prevented a schooner from stranding on the harbor's southeast pier by shouting through the megaphone, 'Ship ahoy, hard aport!' The warning was quickly heeded and stranding avoided."

And late that month, while the South Manitou crew had been conducting the surfboat drill by rowing three miles to the southwest patrol post, the steamer *Charles A. Eddy* appeared in sight through dense smoke. The men pulled hard and met the steamer, informing the master as to the danger. The ship immediately backed away into safe water, turned to a new course, and disappeared into the offshore murk.

The same threat arose at Sleeping Bear Point that week, but at night, a surfman swung his lantern to alert the ship, which quickly "stood out" into deep water. It happened there once again the next evening, a surfman preventing a disaster by use of his Coston flare. The number of such imminent wrecks that were avoided by lifesavers' warnings to vessels very close to shore can hardly be overstated, nor can their value and that of their contents be disregarded.

On the eighth of October, when the schooner *Emily and Elizabeth* stranded a half-mile northwest of the South Manitou station at 3:30 a.m., the lifesavers carried out a kedge anchor, led a cable to the ship's windlass, and hove the vessel off the beach. They followed up by getting her to a safe anchorage, pumping her out, and getting her underway and back to sea.

Later that month, when the *Ann Arbor No. 3* entered Frankfort Harbor, her captain told the Frankfort lifesaving station's keeper that a vessel had sprung a leak and capsized about ten miles off

September, 1908
Robert Wente

September, 1908
Charles A. Eddy

October, 1908
Emily and Elizabeth

Point Betsie. Keeper Morency telephoned a store closer to Point Betsie and asked them to notify the station that there was a wreck about ten miles out, and that six men were coming to shore in the ship's yawl, and to look for them. The men from the schooner were soon found in a farmhouse, all well. They were from the lumber schooner *Ida*, which ultimately drifted ashore south of Point Betsie. In his journal entry, Keeper Bedford noted that if his station had been equipped with a telephone, its response could have been more useful.

North Manitou's Keeper St. Peter received a postcard in mid-November, asking him if he had received a letter in which the writer had expressed his admiration of the lifesavers' "noble work" and wishing the recipient "a pleasant winter to you and a safe return in the spring." The North Carolinian writer added that he had sent such letters to all the US keepers and had heard back from 140 of them, five of which were from keepers in the Lake Michigan district. "I want the men of the service to know me as their friend," he explained.

In 1908, the service noted that nationwide, a total of 246 more disasters were referenced that year than in the previous report, owing primarily "to the installation of power in the service lifeboats [which] has greatly extended the scope of rescue and salvage operations, making it possible to render assistance to a larger number of vessels."

By that time, submarine sweeps, conducted by a steamer's dragging a heavy copper wire underwater through a channel, were being used to alert observers to any obstruction's presence. In sweeping the Manitou Passage near Sleeping Bear Point, an uncharted seventeen-and-a-half-foot deep boulder was located that had previously seriously damaged a vessel. The Lake Carriers Association, made up of commercial lake-shipping companies, had closed the passage until the boulder had been found and navigation charts changed to mark the danger, and the discovery also led to marking a new course through the passage.

Consistent with the powerboating trends, the service's nationwide effort to equip its stations with self-righting and self-bailing powerboats continued, with gasoline motors having been placed in forty-four of the thirty-four-foot lifeboats that were in stations' use. Six new thirty-six-foot powerboats were also commissioned, bringing the fleet's total number of powered rescue and salvage craft to fifty.

In another headquarters initiative, likely inspired by the decades-long program benefiting lighthouse keepers, Congress authorized the secretary of the treasury to transfer books from the departmental library that were no longer needed by the department's employees. More than four thousand such books were transferred, including more than 1,100 volumes of fiction, over seven-hundred volumes of history, a similar number of biographies, and also travel books, art reproductions, and other works. With an average of sixteen books being sent to each lifesaving station, the service hoped that these contributions would appeal not only to the crewmen, but to victims of shipwrecks, etc., who could be sheltered at stations for substantial periods.

On November 11, the Sleeping Bear Point crew, their surfboat towed by the lighthouse service's tender *Dahlia*, responded to the loaded schooner *Seaman*, which stranded near the pier at Empire. With the wind coming directly toward the pier, she could not get underway and be clear of a nearby sandbar.

Two days later they were back at Empire, running lines to her and attempting to heave her off the bar with the use of a kedge anchor, but they eventually had to give up, opting instead to secure her to the wharf and await more favorable weather or the assistance of a steamer. The steamship *J.S. Crouse* was hired for the task but instead of heading toward Empire, put into South Manitou Harbor due to a heavy snowstorm. The next day, when the lifesavers headed for Empire a third time, they had gone about halfway when they spotted the *Seaman* finally underway. Their services no longer needed, the surfmen returned to the station.

With the end of the active season drawing near, the three crews were preparing their stations and equipment for closure. At South Manitou, the men were busy hauling and servicing the Mackinaw supply boat for winter. Their dutiful keeper recorded receipt of "twenty-six transcript envelopes and twenty No. 7 and 9 envelopes" that would be ready for the season to come. A few days later, the men were cleaning the station's floors, woodwork, and windows.

The patrols continued until closure. When a surfman reported that the patrol clock didn't work properly, Keeper Pugh examined it and found that a screw had gotten loose and jammed up the winding apparatus. Repairing the clock and being satisfied that the surfman had faithfully completed the patrol, he noted that the occurrence was not the patrol's fault.

November, 1908
Seaman

As it had done previously, near the end of the first decade of the twentieth century, the service appealed in its annual reports for retirement benefits for incapacitated lifesaving station crewmen. This objective was described as so essential that "it is regarded as a duty to continue to revert to the matter until the relief desired is secured."

As the service elaborated:

Wreck duty requires vigorous men, and in order to keep the personnel of the establishment up to a normal state of efficiency its administrative officers are compelled to ignore sentiment and drop from the rolls those members of the station crews who become infirm through age or incur disability serious enough permanently to incapacitate them for duty. The very fidelity and heroism of these men in the face of the hardships and dangers to which they are subjected operate to their ultimate undoing, often resulting [in] injury or disease which must finally, if not immediately, end their activities and leave them incapable of making a living in any pursuit.

The numerous tasks of the Manitou stations continued, some more dramatic than others, but all came in the course of duty, and with an awareness of the risks that surfmen might confront at any time.

On December 3, when the schooner *Alice* dragged her anchors to an unsafe place, North Manitou's St. Peter summoned a volunteer's aid since the station was closed for the season. They went on board, raised sail, and got her to safety. A few days later, South Manitou's Pugh reported receipt of a notice of shipment and bill of lading for a thirty-four-foot power lifeboat for his station, along with instructions for operating its motor. A week later, Pugh recorded leaving the station for Frankfort, having been notified of the lifeboat's arrival. Two days later, the powered craft was at South Manitou, with the station's crew presumably looking forward to its use the next season.

On December 6, a week after the North Manitou station had closed for the winter, the schooner *Alice* dropped anchor a half-mile southeast of it and then dragged the anchor to an unsafe location. One of the station's surfmen informed the master, who in turn asked if the crew could help in heaving the anchor. Keeper St. Peter collected six of his crew, who boarded the schooner, heaving up her anchor and hoisting her canvas to get her to a safe anchorage.

December, 1908
Alice

In early February 1909, Sleeping Bear Point's Keeper Walker obtained fifty gallons of kerosene oil from local businessman D.H. Day in Glen Haven while the station was still closed for the winter. As ordered, he opened the station on April 1 at midnight, with No. 1 Charles Robinson taking the 2:00 a.m. east patrol and another man going west.

On the third of that month, the Sleeping Bear Point station received a telephone message at 8:30 a.m. saying that a sick woman on North Manitou was requesting a doctor, but the island station had been unable to reach the operator. Walker sent a man to Glen Haven to wake up the operator so a doctor could be sought. The next day the station had another call, this one from the south island where a crewman had suddenly taken ill. When that station was also unable to raise the Glen Haven operator, Keeper Walker again sent a man to the mainland town to get the operator's attention!

South Manitou station was without the leadership of No. 1 Surfman Martin Furst starting on April 5, when he was absent on account of illness. A physician found him to have meningitis and declared him unfit for duty. He was off for almost two weeks, returning to work on the seventeenth of the month, when he completed the midnight to 2:00 a.m. patrol and stood the two-hour 6:00 p.m. watch.

In mid-April, a South Manitou surfman burned a Coston signal to again warn the schooner *Emily and Eliza* of her closeness to the beach, but before she had changed course enough to avoid impact, she stranded on the harbor's southeast point. The lifesavers were able to board and work her off to a safe anchorage.

April, 1909
Emily and Eliza

In mid-June, the South Manitou lighthouse's assistant keeper fell thirty-five feet while working on the tower, surviving but injuring himself badly. Keeper Pugh sent a surfman for a doctor, and later had him return the doctor to the mainland.

With some of a keeper's caretaker responsibilities being targeted at the grounds of their station, Keeper St. Peter that month had a man cultivating the soil around the trees in order to enhance the North Manitou station's appearance. A week later, the crew was engaged in putting up a windmill.

Later that month, Pugh reported that the motor in the south island station's powerboat had overheated to the extent that the crankshaft bearings had melted, prompting an order from the district superintendent that Pugh should get the job done by a local machinist. About two weeks later, he reported that the task had been performed and that the boat was again in good working condition.

In late July, fire broke out in the South Manitou station's wood house, caused by spontaneous combustion in some painting clothes that had been hanging there. The men were able to put the fire out without damage to the building. Within a day or so of that close call, a three-year-old child fell off the South Manitou pier. Hearing the mother's screams, the surfmen rushed to the water and saved the child from likely drowning.

July, 1909
Little Georgy

When the schooner *Little Georgy* showed distress signals some four miles southeast of the South Manitou station on July 23, the surfmen responded in their surfboat and found her to be leaking badly, her forward boom broken and her canvas torn, her pump also failing. The men assisted in sailing her into the harbor, where the station repaired the pump and reinstalled it, pumped her out, plugged the leak's source, and repaired the boom and sails.

The schooner was able to resume course the following day, but she didn't stay seaworthy for very long, as her captain sailed her into the Holland harbor the following month. The old ship was again leaking badly, and her two-man crew was totally exhausted. Surfmen there reportedly spent several hours working her pumps until additional repairs were made, once again attempting to extend the life of the aging schooner.

Keeper St. Peter reported on September 27, 1909, that a man apparently under the influence of liquor had fallen off the dock into the water. Having rescued him, he was given a pair of drawers, a pair of socks, and a shirt from the station's Women's National Relief Association inventory.

Sadly, however, not everyone could be saved; almost two months later, in cold November, a fifteen-year-old boy had fallen out of a rowboat four miles south of the station. He was brought to the station and given resuscitation for three and a half hours before being pronounced dead by a doctor.

On October 1, the north island no. 1 surfman's nearby house was discovered by the lookout to be on fire. Responding with buckets and an extinguisher, the crew managed to get the blaze out without serious damage.

In late December, the North Manitou lighthouse keeper telephoned the station to report that the gas-powered fishing boat *Morning Dip* was once again in distress off Lighthouse Point. The lifesaving station had already closed for the season and Keeper

St. Peter was on leave, but the person he had left in charge of the facility called someone who owned a gasoline boat, and the two men brought the disabled craft to the station.

The service's fiscal 1909 report made clear that although the addition of powered boats to the rescue stations was enabling them to operate more effectively, the number of casualties was also rapidly increasing nationwide, due to the huge increase in the use of gasoline-powered small craft for pleasure boating. About forty percent of all the marine casualties that were serious enough to be attended by the lifesaving crews involved such boats. Unmentioned, however, was the lessening susceptibility of the commercial lake fleet to be in peril, given better weather forecasting, stronger hulls, chart and navigation improvements, and enhanced communication capabilities.

That trend didn't prevent the steamer *Binghampton* from running aground in 1910 during thick fog on the west side of South Manitou, four miles distant from the station. The surfmen carried messages, ferried ship's officers and workers to and from shore, and used their power lifeboat to take off cargo and run hawsers. Three days later, with the help of the revenue cutter *Tuscarora* and a wrecking tug, the vessel was floating and able to be towed to the island's harbor.

1910
Binghampton

Two days later, following the transfer of Sleeping Bear Point's William Walker to the station in his hometown of Grand Haven, the point's crew had a new keeper, Frank Partridge.

One June day when the South Manitou crew was working the surfboat, they heard a woman screaming and pulled to where she was on the beach. Her three-year-old son had fallen overboard from a skiff about a hundred yards offshore, into twenty-foot-deep water. Her husband had jumped overboard to rescue the child and she had seen the two of them swimming toward shore, struggling a bit, then disappearing. The skiff meanwhile had drifted to shore, so she had jumped into it, rowed to where they were last seen, and managed to pull the child into the boat and get him to shore.

Upon arriving at the scene, two of the lifesavers immediately began resuscitation efforts on the child, while two others grappled for his father. After twenty minutes of work, the child was restored to normal breathing. But after the surfmen had found his father, brought him to the beach, and performed respiration for an hour and twenty minutes, a physician then arrived and pronounced him deceased from a burst blood vessel.

Frankfort's busy harbor, ca. 1908.

Author's collection.

Early in the afternoon of June 14, the surfman stationed in the Point Betsie lookout tower reported that a gas-powered fishing boat had "broke down" and her crewmen were waving a flag of distress. The crew went to them in the Monomoy surfboat and towed the boat to shore. Finding that the boat's batteries had worn out, Keeper Bedford gave them three replacements, and the engine then started, enabling the fishermen to continue on to Frankfort.

Mid-August saw the start of a musical-chairs reassignment process. Keeper Eli E. Pugh was transferred from South Manitou to Charlevoix's station as its keeper, being succeeded on the island by Allen A. Kent, who had been Charlevoix station's keeper; in essence, they switched jobs. Pugh would serve at Charlevoix until 1913, when he became keeper at the Ludington station, and Frank Partridge, captain of the Sleeping Bear Point station from 1910 to 1913, then took command at Charlevoix.

One noteworthy change brought to South Manitou through Kent's appointment was that he was the first of its keepers to use a typewriter to write wreck reports and other documents rather than writing by hand, an innovation his superior officers (and this historian!) surely appreciated.

Late that month, South Manitou's crew had a telephone message that a passenger launch was holed on the rocks in Good Harbor Bay. The crew went to the scene in the power lifeboat with the surfboat in tow, but found that about twenty farmers and fishermen had already gotten to her and had her in the tow of a small power-boat toward Glen Arbor.

Early on the night of September 1, the south island's lookout burned a Coston signal to warn off a forty-foot boat that was sailing directly for the beach. The sailor immediately corrected course, then later came into the harbor and walked a mile to the station just to thank the crew for the red light's display, which he attributed to keeping him from running fast onto the shore.

Later that month at Point Betsie, the crew was preparing to enlarge the station's boathouse to accommodate a new surfboat. Bedford's journal entry, reporting on his purchase of materials from a Frankfort lumber yard, is an indication of the project's size: thirty-five 2 x 4s, ten feet long; thirty 2 x 6s, sixteen feet long; forty 2 x 4s, fourteen feet long; thirty-two 1 x 12s, sixteen feet long, six hundred feet of maple flooring, etc., as well as seven thousand shingles, more than 160 pounds of a variety of nails, and eight pairs of strap hinges. Clearly, this would not be a small job.

That same day, the lookout reported to the Point Betsie's no. 1 that a small powerboat had quit operating about a mile and a half south of the station and close to shore. Its sole occupant hoisted a flag of distress. Reaching him to tow the boat to the station, they found that they were rescuing Roy Grant, the first assistant keeper of their station's lighthouse.

In September, the 150-ton schooner *J.B. Newland* became stranded at North Manitou's southwest point. Both islands' life-saving crews responded by boat, the north's surfboat towed to the site by a hired gasoline-powered craft. It was immediately clear to both crews that they could not save the schooner without the help of a powerful vessel to pull her off. Keeper St. Peter's men then returned to their station and telegraphed for the assistance of the steamer *Tuscarora*.

Meanwhile, the South Manitou crew stayed at the site, trying to offer assistance, but that night there was a wind shift that caused them to leave the wreck. They landed six men, with their personal effects, off the stricken schooner, then hid the items in the woods and walked about five miles to the north island lighthouse. They arrived wet and cold, the wind still blowing a gale from the north, at about 11:30 p.m., and camped for the night in the fog signal building and on the station's floor.

Though the two lifesaving crews had been unable to free the vessel, their prompt response to the emergency and their

September, 1910

J. B. Newland

availability in case of a greater crisis had been much appreciated. The next morning, the crews stripped the vessel of her sails and running gear. Several days later, the lifesavers were again at the wreck site, and at the captain's request were pumping her out, but that didn't do any good. The battle continued the next day, when they pumped four feet of water out of her hold before the *Tuscarora* reached the scene and took over the rescue.

On September 23, the South Manitou station had an early morning call from Keeper Partridge of Sleeping Bear Point, who said he could see what appeared from the mainland to be a four-masted schooner off the west side of South Manitou Island. Keeper Kent sent one of his men to the top of the lighthouse tower to search from that elevation. Before he returned, however, the mate and ten sailors from the package freight steamer *Bethlehem*, carrying a mixed cargo including over two thousand tons of flour, arrived at the lifesaving station. They reported that it was their vessel that was aground on the island's southwest shore, and asked to send a message to the ship's owner in Buffalo for instructions as to what to do.

The company replied that the crew should get people to help off-load cargo in order to lighten the vessel. With a gale blowing and rough sea, the lifesavers stood by the wreck in case they were needed before morning. Fifty men were recruited to undertake the lightening, but the wind initially was too strong. Provisions were obtained to provide three hundred meals for the workers. Two days later, the lifesavers had made many trips between the station and the wreck to deliver messages and take an official to Glen Haven, where telephone contact with the company could be established.

Four to five days into the disaster, the surfmen were asked to look out for the crew, as Keeper Kent was reporting that there were "many thieves around trying to get cargo." The lifesavers were at the wreck all night, returning to the station at 11:00 a.m., where the surfmen slept until 4:00 p.m. The wrecking personnel who had been sent to the scene called at 7:00 p.m. and asked the station to keep an eye out, as they had two men aboard the stricken ship who were to display a red light "if anything happened."

Keeper Kent next recorded that officials from the *Bethlehem's* owner, the Lehigh Valley Railroad, happened to be traveling from Chicago to Buffalo on the steamer *Saranac* and had come by to take a look at the wreck. They wanted the lifesavers to take them closer

September, 1910
Bethlehem

to the scene by boat so they could get a photograph of it. Kent tried to discourage them on the grounds they would be unable to keep their camera dry with so much water flying around. A senior official then persuaded Kent to take the men on a short ride to see what it was like to ride in a lifeboat.

As Kent recounted that experience:

I took them out with lifeboat under sail and power, got outside of the lee of island...seas begin to board us pretty regular, all was wet as drowned rats, still no one proposed to go back, finally a big one came along and boarded us right when we came out of it...there was one of them setting down in the bottom of the boat in water up to their hips...all wanted to go back...then, arriving at the Saranac at about 3 p.m. where they left us, they threw a box of cigars into the boat as we left for the station, thanking us, saying it was the best time they ever had.

A week following the accident, Kent wrote that he and the captain of the *Bethlehem* had hiked across the island to assess the wreck's situation. He also reported that the *Saranac* had left that afternoon with all the cargo that had been saved, which was apparently about one-third of the total load. "The rest is up to the insurance company to pay for," he added, saying that the insurance man "had told us to take whatever flour we wanted and put it on the ground to dry. There would be lots of good flour," he assured them.

Of one day in this saga, Kent reported taking ten men off the wreck. "One of the worst nights I ever put in," he wrote; they had "burnt much gasoline," and about 3:00 a.m. there was "some complaining among the men, they were wet and cold getting all they wanted of it ... so was I [and] three men sick, [who] turned in until 4 p.m., as we were tired out."

A full ten days after the accident, the ship was pulled free and taken into the harbor by a wrecking company. Despite having been battered by powerful Lake Michigan seas for days, there were no fatalities and the *Bethlehem* apparently survived, later being repaired, sold for use on the Atlantic, and finally scrapped in 1923. After this exhausting experience, it is noteworthy that when Keeper Kent closed the South Manitou station on November 30, he wrote that all his surfmen had said they would be back to serve in the spring.

To put the *Bethlehem's* experience in a useful context, in an accounting of vessel strandings in Lake Michigan over ten prior years, the service's 1910 report tallied three such incidents at Sleeping Bear Point, six at North Manitou, and nineteen at South Manitou (second only to Milwaukee's twenty-one). Four years later, both the Milwaukee and South Manitou stations reported eighteen strandings, again the highest total on Lake Michigan.

Given that strandings in the midst of powerful seas often resulted in the vessels being pounded to pieces and the loss of both lives and valuable cargo, the above numbers are testimony to the care with which sailors needed to navigate through the shoals of the Manitou Passage, particularly those working aged schooners, finding their way through dense fog without the benefit of reliable weather forecasting or much in the way of technological aids.

This time saw a continued growth in the lifesaving service's motorized national fleet, its annual 1910 report emphasizing that this trend "continued to excite general admiration and comment, owing to the extended facilities which their speed and power afford for the prosecution of rescue and salvage work." The new thirty-six-foot lifeboats were being equipped with thirty-five-to-forty-horsepower motors, and eight-horsepower engines were being installed in a few surfboats.

On March 15, 1911, two weeks before the Manitou Passage stations were to open, South Manitou's Keeper Kent wrote, "When I got up this morning at 7 a.m., [I] found the lookout tower and storm warning tower had disappeared; where they were is now very deep water." Investigating the situation, he discovered that about two hundred feet of shore had slipped into the lake for at least a thousand feet, and the telegraph pole, which had been set well back from shore, was instead about fifty feet offshore, with only its top foot above the water and the connecting wires still attached to it. Communications with the north island and the mainland were clearly going be interrupted for a considerable period of time.

Keeper Kent's discovery that early spring morning was neither the first such occurrence on Lake Michigan's shores, nor would it be the last, as the caretakers of Point Betsie Lighthouse and owners of residences situated on coastal dunes over the succeeding century would attest. In reality, the big lake knows no bounds; the shorelines of its mainland and few northern islands move inward and reach farther out as its level rises and falls over decades, while nature's unending forces carve its distinctive dunes.

Upon opening the North Manitou station for the 1911 season, Keeper St. Peter noted that one member of his previous crew was no longer serving, having resigned in 1910 to be a fisherman. As fishing Lake Michigan continued to provide a more enticing financial opportunity than surfmen experienced, this posed a challenge with which keepers had to contend in seeking to maintain an experienced, reliable crew.

On May 1, the south island's crew began the day by conducting the wigwam (waving) signal-flag communications drill. That afternoon, they went by their Beebe-McLellan surfboat to the aid of the schooner *Petral* that had gone ashore about a quarter of a mile northwest of the station. After an hour's "hard pull," the lifesavers managed to take three men off the stranded vessel to the station, where they were provided lodging and meals. Due to heavily iced sails, the schooner's crew had been unable to control their ship, which was carrying one hundred cords of wood edgings to Manitowoc, Wisconsin.

The surfmen worked at the wreck all the next day, but in Keeper Kent's words, "without accomplishing anything." However, the steamer *Crouse* came alongside the schooner a little before midnight, and all the men began shifting cargo to the steamer. He added a note expressing the frustrating challenge before them: "Wreck leaking bad. Two timbers torn off her keel. Rudder unshipped and broken. Talk of abandoning her. Captain discouraged, no money to get her off."

On May 3, the unloading continued until about 5:00 a.m., when the lifesavers returned to their station. They were back at the wreck in two hours and the *Petral* was pulled off the beach and towed alongside the pier, the surfmen using their boat to run lines between the vessels. At about 10:00 p.m., the wreck was taken in tow by the *Crouse*, the goal being to get the schooner into a dry-dock in Manitowoc. Kent sent two surfmen aboard the *Petral* to pump while the two ships made the trip across Lake Michigan; the men would be returned to the island by the steamer. Meanwhile, the lifesaving crew would be shorthanded, but personnel from the lighthouse and fog signal pledged to assist if they were needed. According to the logs, the surfmen returned to the station as scheduled.

Several days later, the surfboat went to a tug that was to bring a telephone linesman to the station to repair a broken cable, for which the crew had been dragging. However, it turned out that about two thousand feet of it was buried too deeply to be recovered, so it was decided that the cable would have to be cut and new pieces inserted. That necessitated a trip to Glen Haven, where the

May, 1911
Petral

linesman wired for more cable as well as for instructions from Washington. Cable arrived at Glen Haven after several days, but the crew found it badly kinked and damaged from being dragged off a scow onto the dock.

With help from the lighthouse crew and surfmen from the Sleeping Bear station, they finally had about 1,700 feet of usable cable, hauling it to the island. Within a few days of hard work, communications between the passage stations had been restored.

In early May, a man who had fallen off the dock at North Manitou was rescued by the station's crew and given necessary clothing—a suit of underwear, one shirt, and one pair of stockings—donations from the Women's National Relief Association's program to aid victims of disasters on the seas.

On July 1, a gasoline boat with eight persons aboard ran out of fuel and drifted north of the North Manitou station. Not yet having a powerboat at the station, St. Peter and his men went in one belonging to a crewman, and towed the troubled boat to safety.

July, 1911

Lottie A. Burton

Paisley

Amazonas

Later that month, the schooner *Lottie A. Burton* was anchored in an exposed place and hoisted a flag to signal the steamer *Tuscarora* that assistance was needed. Aware of the schooner's vulnerability, the north island crew went to her, but on arrival learned that the *Tuscarora* already had a line to her. Towing her to South Manitou proved impossible in the stormy weather, so she was towed under the protective lee of North Manitou, where the lifesavers pumped her for almost ten hours.

That same day, the Sleeping Bear Point station received a telephone call from Glen Arbor, informing them that a barge, the *Paisley*, was flying a distress signal. The crew went to her, finding that she was dragging anchor near the beach. In the high winds and surf, they couldn't immediately aid her but stood by until the barge was no longer in jeopardy. Returning to the station, they learned that the steamer *Amazonas* was in trouble about five miles east of the station. As the Sleeping Bear Point lifesavers were unable to row to her against the high wind and seas, Keeper Partridge called the South Manitou crew, who started for the steamer in their power lifeboat.

About halfway to the wreck, the island boat's engine stopped and the surfmen had to put up their canvas and sail to Glen Haven, where they anchored and began repairing the motor. They were unable to get it restarted until the next morning, when they proceeded to Glen Arbor, where they found the wrecked steamer and learned that her crew had already been brought safely to shore.

Sleeping Bear Point's Keeper Partridge's log provides a detailed record of how his station had completed the rescue: "At about 5:40 P.M., the steamer lost her anchors and started for the beach. Telephoned for two teams of horses…loaded up the Beach Apparatus and was soon on the way to the wreck…we went on beach about 4 and ½ miles S.E. of station. We hurried to the wreck, got there in about 50 minutes, got the apparatus in position, shot the line, put up the gear and took off with breeches buoy 2 women and 15 men, total 17. Got the apparatus together and returned to the station at 10:00 P.M."

The South Manitou crew, meanwhile, had headed back to their island, detouring briefly upon hearing a whistle from a nearby steamer, the *Venezuela*, whose captain wanted to be taken to shore so he could send messages.

Several days later, the south island's no. 1, Martin Furst, had taken over the duties of Keeper Kent, who had seriously sprained his ankle earlier in the month. Furst reported a telephone message from the point's Keeper Partridge, asking him to bring his crew to a wrecked barge at Glen Arbor. Arriving, they learned their job was to use their lifeboat to dredge a three-foot channel alongside the stranded barge so the *Venezuela* would be able to pull her free. After several days' work by the two lifesaving crews, the steamer and her barge had both survived their perils.

A week into September, during a thick fog, the large schooner *J.B. Newland* with a crew of six men went off-course and stranded about five miles northeast of the South Manitou station, where she was observed at 7:00 a.m. by North Manitou's lightkeeper, who informed both islands' lifesaving stations by telephone. The two crews went to the vessel but were unable at first to provide any assistance, owing to the "dangerous position in which she lay and to the state of the sea." When conditions moderated about noon, they were able to get to her, where they set a 1,200-pound anchor on which they pulled until late at night in an unsuccessful effort to free her. She was eventually saved by the revenue cutter *Tuscarora*, after which the north island crew spent two days retrieving anchors the schooner had deployed during the mishap.

On September 27, 1911, the surfman on watch at South Manitou Island reported that the small steamer *Three Brothers*, which was carrying hardwood from Boyne City, Michigan to Chicago, appeared

September, 1911
J. B. Newland

September, 1911
Three Brothers

waterlogged and headed for land. Rising water in the ship's hold and her coal bunkers forced the use of kerosene instead of coal to keep her going, and her captain decided the best thing to do was to try to land on the beach near the lifesaving station. Upon impact, however, her bow split open and her pilothouse tore loose. The bow was in about fifteen feet of water, but her stern was in much deeper water. The lifesavers went immediately to the vessel by surf-boat and landed the thirteen-member crew, the steamer sinking after an attempt to pull her free was unsuccessful. Her crew was provided meals and lodging for the night.

Three days later, the crew recovered a lifeboat from the *Three Brothers*. Furst also reported that after her crew had left for Chicago, the hulk had risen to the surface during the night. Soon thereafter, her master sent instructions to the lifesavers, asking them to remove the steering gear and care for it at the station. Two days later, after the surfmen had fulfilled his request, the hull sank, no longer having salvage value.

At Sleeping Bear Point, November began in somewhat typical fashion, the crew practicing signaling drills, cleaning paint brushes, and somewhat unusually for the first of the month, shoveling snow off the station's walks. But things were about to change. As Keeper Partridge elaborated in his log entry, at 1:00 p.m., "Got a terrific wind and snow storm from the [northeast]. D.H. Day telephoned the station that the schooner *Geo W. Westcott* was tied to the Glen Haven dock and in great danger of being smashed to pieces."

Partridge took five men to the schooner, whose captain wanted to move her to the end of the dock where he could attempt to raise his anchor. Three of them went aboard the schooner to operate the windlass, while two stayed on the dock to handle her lines. The keeper's account continues:

> *After several hours hard work crew heaved her [the schooner] out to the anchor; by that time the sea was high and there was danger of the schooner going to pieces. She was too far from the dock for the crew to get off (about 30 yards). I got a team of horses, took the beach apparatus to the end of the dock, fired a line over the schooner, took the three surfmen and the captain off [by breeches buoy]. The three sailors refused to go ashore. Shortly after, the lines to the dock parted, schooner dragged her anchor for some distance before it held; got the beach apparatus ready and kept watch all night. Schooner was valued at $1000, damage $250 by a broken fore mast and jib boom. The line was fired over the schooner at 7 p.m. The Captain*

November, 1911
Geo. W. Wescott

was grateful and said the vessel would surely have been lost had not the crew got there in time.

The next day, Partridge reported that the crew had returned to the station at 7:30 a.m., having spent the night watching the *Westcott*. The men went back to her at 11:00 a.m. to assist in moving her to deeper water and deploying an anchor, with snow still coming in squalls,

On the third of the month, the crew performed the drill for restoring the apparently drowned, then, probably with renewed interest, focused on the treatment of frostbite, and finished the day later by working around the grounds. On the morning of the fourth day, as light snow continued to fall, Partridge postponed the fire drill but sent men to help repair the schooner's mast, as her captain could not find anyone else to do the job.

In mid-November, when the South Manitou lookout thought he spotted a stranded schooner's light, the lifesavers soon located her less than a mile northwest of the station. After bringing the vessel's crew to safety, the surfmen made arrangements for the six men to travel to their home, having recovered some of their clothing. The rescued crewmen were taken aboard the steamer *Schlesinger* that had anchored in the harbor because of strong winds, but she soon departed for Milwaukee. The surfmen continued to work at the wreck, recovering lines, sails, spars, booms, and other gear from the wrecked vessel. A few days later, when the steamer *Crouse* came into the harbor, Acting Keeper Furst arranged for the steamer to tow the wreck to a safe anchorage.

November, 1911
Seneca

On November 23, 1911, the north island station was notified by telephone that a large steamer was stranded on the west coast. The lifesavers launched their surfboat and arranged to be towed by the mail carrier's boat to the site of the wrecked *Seneca*. Leaving the powerboat beyond the heavy surf, the keeper asked the ship's captain, whose own crew was dumping "mineral paint" overboard, what he wanted the surfmen to do. The captain requested that the lifesavers go to shore and tell his mate, who had already landed in the yawl boat, to telegraph for an Ann Arbor car ferry to pull his ship off the beach. However, while the lifesavers were still on land, the steamer was able to back off under her own power.

Just prior to closing the North Manitou station for the season, Keeper St. Peter reported that one of his surfmen on patrol had found a bunch of good shingles. Doubtless, the material was put to good use on the island.

By 1912, some of the issues associated with motorizing the service's rescue boats had been effectively resolved, and small, eight-horsepower gas engines were beginning to be installed in surfboats. That year, the Point Betsie and Sleeping Bear Point stations were assigned the passage's first motorized Beebe-McClellan surfboats, and the island stations received them about two years later.

A mail boat had landed in front of the Sleeping Bear Point station on a mid-January 1912 afternoon to deliver some passengers and pick up mail bags and freight. The station's no. 1, Charles Robinson, had used a plank from a bank of ice to enable the passengers to get to shore, but a man slipped off into the freezing, shallow water. Robinson, who was managing the station during its inactive period, was able to get him out of the water, and found him a suit of underclothing, a sweater, a pair of pants, socks, and shoes from the Women's National Relief Association's inventory at the station.

Only a few days later, when one might have expected life to be rather quiet at the shoreside station, the gasoline mail boat *Beatrice* hoisted a distress signal a little over a mile away, stuck fast in ice. Needing help to assist, Robinson got a surfman who lived near the station, as well as other members from his own family, to haul a small boat a quarter mile down the beach, where they launched it over icebergs and took the two men off the *Beatrice* and brought the mail bags, along with the boat's sidelights and compass, to shore.

Working at their jobs, the crews of the Manitou Passage stations, along with most of their colleagues in the service, were unlikely aware of an event on June 5, 1912, in the US Capitol that ultimately would alter their livelihoods. In what could be described as a "warning shot across the bow," a bill was introduced by US Senator Charles E. Townsend of Michigan to create a new federal agency, the US Coast Guard, comprised of the US Life-Saving Service and the Revenue Cutter Service. Although Congress took no immediate action on the initiative, an important study was commissioned by President William Howard Taft. Seeking to improve the government's economy and efficiency, the panel soon proposed another course of action: discontinuing the US Life-Saving Service, and reassigning its stations to the Bureau of Lighthouses.

Extensive debate over many months focused, among other issues, on the distinctly different responsibilities of these agencies irrespective of their coastal locations and their occasionally essential collaboration.

January, 1912

Beatrice

While Washington executives and legislators pondered reorganizing the federal government, the nation's lifesaving stations and lighthouses continued to be effectively served. Mid-June found Keeper Partridge's crew busy painting the stations' buildings. He welcomed back his no. 1, who had been excused from duty for two weeks owing to an arm injury.

As a noteworthy aside, the ring-shaped "summer" candy known as the "Life Saver" (or sometimes "LifeSaver") was born in 1912, named for the lifesaving flotation ring, which was a common life preserver for many decades, and prominently displayed aboard ships. Presumably, that included the ill-fated *Titanic*, which went down on her maiden voyage that April in the north Atlantic, with a catastrophic loss of passengers and crew.

In July, the South Manitou crew happened to observe a local resident fall off his gasoline boat. They quickly launched the surfboat and skiff and reached him within two minutes, but he had been injured in some way and had immediately sunk into deep water. They recovered him in about forty-five minutes, and reportedly performed resuscitation for three and a half hours, until a doctor arrived from mainland Empire and pronounced him dead.

In late August, the point's crew went to the aid of a boat being battered on the beach, securing it safely and removing the nine persons aboard. And that September, the point station's lookout burned a Coston signal in an attempt to warn off a schooner, but she failed to alter course sufficiently quickly to avoid crashing onto the beach. The lifesavers worked hard shifting her cargo of pine pickets, enabling the Canadian vessel, with her crew of fourteen, to slide safely into deep water.

At eleven o'clock one early October night, the station's patrol reported a steamer, the Cleveland-based *David Norton*, near shore about two and a half miles west of the station. The point crew immediately launched the surfboat and went to her. Carrying a load of hard coal from Buffalo to Milwaukee, she had struck a hidden rock and began to sink in thirty feet of water.

The crew ferried the mate to Glen Haven, where he could send word to her owners and notify wreckers, making several other needed trips until the wind picked up and the sea began to wash over the hull, prompting her crew of twenty-four to prepare to leave the ship. The lifesavers were able to land eleven crewmen with their power surfboat, then returned for the others. Not wanting to

October, 1912
David Norton

leave the boat, her master requested that the lifesavers stay by him that night, which they did, the wind and sea reaching gale-force at midnight.

Early the next morning, they made several trips to Glen Haven for messages. The wind and sea moderated during the afternoon, and a wrecking crew was able to reach the vessel and begin work. With the point's surfmen having had no sleep for forty-eight hours, they were happy to see their colleagues from South Manitou arriving to relieve them. Eventually, the wrecking company succeeded in refloating the vessel and towed her to the South Manitou harbor.

Only later it was learned that the South Manitou crew, having also heard the *David Norton's* distress signals, had attempted to go to the stricken ship, but when about halfway there, the engine of its power lifeboat had overheated and stopped. With a big sea running, a crew member became seasick, and when the men tried to sail to the wreck, they found that they were too far leeward to get there, so they returned to South Manitou to undertake engine repairs. From there, they had called the Sleeping Bear station, and heard that its crew was in the process of taking people off the wreck. This was another instance when the stations of the passage, with connected communications, could assist each other in responding to wrecks.

At North Manitou, John G. Sammet had replaced Telesford St. Peter, who served close to fourteen years in charge of the island station, and was transferred to Pentwater, Michigan for what would be his final station command.

April, 1913

Alice L.

About a week into the 1913 active season at North Manitou, a surfman on watch noticed that the local gas-powered boat *Alice L.* appeared to be stuck in ice more than six miles south of the station. Keeper Sammet, who was out on south patrol at the time, later recorded that the surfman, new to his crew, had "kept good watch of her and seeing she did not move reported same to No. 1 surfman."

Returning to the station, the keeper found his crew ready to respond to the nonmoving boat. Leaving at 3:00 p.m., the crew walked to the lighthouse, a distance of more than four and a half miles, and there met a gas-powered motor boat they had hired for ten dollars to enable them to reach the *Alice L.*, where they arrived at 5:30 p.m. It had been impossible to use any of the station's own boats for this rescue on account of the thickness of the ice.

The boat's own men had been unable to release her without assistance because "her wheel was too light to work in ice." But passing a line to them, the rescuers were able to tow her to Lighthouse Point, where her captain decided to remain in open water overnight. The lifesavers walked back to the station, arriving there at 9:30 p.m.

Sleeping Bear Point's Keeper Partridge reported on March 1, 1913 that he had received an order to take charge of the Charlevoix station by the tenth of that month. A week later, his no. 1, Charles Robinson, signed the point's daily log as acting keeper as Partridge headed north to his new assignment. The smooth transition of leadership was accomplished at the point, and just days later, Robinson officially became the station's keeper.

Keeper Sammet's log for April 23 reports that the crew deferred its International Code drill, and instead washed the walls in the station bedroom and dining room. In the afternoon, Sammet painted the floors of both rooms. Late the next month, Keeper Sammet continued his efforts to spruce up the station. He reported that the crew was taking up old sidewalk and trimming grass. He was painting the floor in the hall, and the crewmen were getting gravel.

Five days later, South Manitou's Keeper Kent recorded that his crew had launched the Mackinaw boat and made two trips to the mainland to bring two doctors, one from Leland and the other from Maple City, to treat No. 1 Surfman Furst's little boy, who was very sick.

On the last day of May, the Sleeping Bear Point lookout sighted a schooner, the *George W. Wescott*, four and a half miles northeast of the station, seeming to be nearly beached. The crew went to her in the power surfboat and found her in danger of getting caught on rocks, so they helped bring up her anchor, make sail, and tow her out of danger.

Upon returning to the station, the lookout saw her headed once again for the beach, so he burned a Coston signal. The ship's crew, apparently thinking they would clear the point, did not alter course and ran hard aground. The surfboat went to her again, where the men assisted in lightening her by shifting some of her cargo of flour and grain toward the stern. She then floated off and reached sufficiently deep water, where her captain dropped anchor and waited overnight before resuming her course to Glen Haven. Before doing so, however, the lifesavers again assisted the *Wescott's* own crew in heaving up her anchor and making sail, then monitored her until

May, 1913
George W. Wescott

Our Son, windjammer of old.
Leelanau Historical Society Museum.

she was at the Glen Haven dock, where she was to pick up a cargo of wood slabs.

In early June, the South Manitou crew responded to a request for help from a steamer that was towing a water-filled scow. Her crew had been bailing for several hours to keep the scow afloat. Led by Keeper Kent, the surfmen formed a bucket brigade and got about two feet of water out of her. They also corked numerous leaks, and sent a telegram to the owners to advise them of the activity.

On June 7, Sammet reported that his keeper's residence needed shingling, and that his crew was cleaning the house. He also wrote that a steamer had made two attempts to get alongside of Pickard Dock, but the sea and current were too strong. When the steamer blew four whistles, the lifesavers launched the power surf boat and went to the vessel, whose captain asked Sammet if he would take six passengers to shore, including a woman with three small children who were all seasick. Sammet brought them all to shore.

One morning in early August at 4:00 a.m., a launch that the North Manitou crew had previously assisted started to depart for her homeport of Pentwater when her rudder stalk was determined to be broken. The launch backed up to the beach where the rudder was unshipped, then repaired by North

Manitou's blacksmith shop and reinstalled, enabling the launch to proceed to home.

Two days later, the record shows, a North Manitou surfman was able to repair a launch's broken engine timer which had left the boat adrift in the passage until she happened to be discovered by a passing mail boat, whose captain towed her to the island station. And two days later, one of the surfmen took a resident island couple to where they could board the steamer *Manitou* for Chicago, using his own boat for this courtesy.

In mid-August, Keeper Sammet reported on the beach apparatus drill, and also that the crew was painting the inside of the surfboat and working on a locker for the crewmen's shaving mugs. Several days later, he reported that the crew was putting canvas on the ceiling of the powerboat's house to prevent dirt from getting into it. They were also wheeling sand away from the boat-launch track, and painting letters on that vital craft. Sammet's commitment to tidiness was exemplary!

Late that month, when they were not otherwise drilling, the crew was engaged in putting in shelving at their quarters for shoes, and in wheeling dirt and sod for the lawn.

Sammet reported that a rumor had circulated that a small steamer about forty or forty-five feet long had gone ashore at Gill's Pier, a mainland spot not far distant from Leland. It was later confirmed that the boat, crewed by one man, was a total loss after having wrecked while attempting to take a load of apples and cabbage from Traverse City to Manistique. The compass had broken, so he ran before the wind and wound up in the shallows where he dropped anchor, but the anchor line parted and the little schooner wound up on the rocks. The man had watched for an opportunity to jump off into about three feet of water, wading ashore.

Only about a week after that episode, there was a report from Leland that a seventy-seven-foot tug had hit the rocks at Gill's Pier, its crew swimming safely to shore. However, several days later, when a North Manitou surfman took his own boat to search for her, he found her about two miles south of Cathead Point, "burnt to the waterline," without further explanation.

In mid-September, Keeper Charles Robinson reported that his Sleeping Bear station had responded at night to a schooner's four blasts from her horn. The boat's crew could not free her anchor, but with the help of the surfmen the anchor was heaved up and they sailed away.

October, 1913
Petrel

In early October, the point's men responded to a telephoned alert that the schooner *Petrel* was in danger of pounding to pieces against the Glen Haven dock. Reaching her quickly, the men boarded her and moved her to an anchorage in deep water. A few days later, Robinson reported that he had sent a surfman to Glen Haven to examine the state of the telephone line, an electric storm the preceding night having burned out the cable and blown over two telephone poles.

Overall, the year 1913 saw an extraordinary number of crew and cargo losses throughout the Great Lakes, mostly resulting from a blizzard, driven by hurricane-force winds, that swept across the region from November eighth to the eleventh.

In its 1914 report, the service described that storm as "the most disastrous to shipping of any that has visited upon the region in a generation, if not in the entire history of lake navigation." Lake Huron led the Great Lakes' toll, with twenty-four vessels and 118 lives lost, and Lake Michigan claimed sixteen vessels and ten lives. Across the five lakes, as well as the Mackinac Straits and the Detroit and St. Mary's rivers, the storm built waves on Lakes Huron and Superior of close to forty feet, resulting in the loss or serious damage of seventy-one vessels and 248 lives.

In discussing the disasters from the fall blizzard, the lifesaving service reminded both high officials and the public that its charge and capabilities essentially were those of a "coast guard," and were not designed to serve vessels far from shore in the open sea. Its duties, the report elaborated, "consist mainly in warning the mariner away from inshore dangers and in performing rescue and salvage work when vessels are so unfortunate as to be driven ashore." The service emphasized that two-thirds of the vessels lost on the lakes in this extraordinary three-day storm were in open water, miles from land, and thus "beyond the reach of the line-throwing gun and the lifesavers' boats, and therefore outside the field of service endeavor."

Notably, not a single life was lost during the storm from the twenty-eight ships located within reach of the service's rescue forces and equipment. The hurricane occurred near the end of the navigation season, when some ships were in winter layup, but others were ferrying "products of mine, forest, field, factory, and mill" to ports where they would be needed until shipping resumed in the spring. The storm's southeastern track had hit mid- and southern Lake Michigan particularly hard.

As an example from one Michigan coastal community that was directly in its path, the service reported that at Port Huron, the hurricane had sand-filled a thirty-foot-wide, eight-foot-deep canal leading northeast into Lake Huron for one thousand feet of the waterway's length. "To accomplish this titanic task," the service wrote, "sea and wind had to lift untold thousands of tons of sand clear over a breakwater."

With its impact upon the Manitou Passage area being minimal, activities at the lifesaving stations were then focused on preparing for winter and the coming season. In late November, the Sleeping Bear Point's crew worked on the rollers in the power lifeboat which recently had been transferred to the station from Kenosha, Wisconsin. The men were still drilling that month with the boat, both with oars and the engine. Once when starting the engine, it was discovered that the intake pipe was frozen. They thawed it out and finished the drill, then made modifications to ensure the boat's proper performance.

At about the same time, the station received a call from D.H. Day, asking for assistance because a carload of potatoes had gone through the Glen Haven dock into the lake. Three surfmen went to the scene and fished out nine sacks.

On Christmas Day 1913, Keeper Sammet, whose north island station had remained open and fully crewed to the end of the month, reported that they did not drill with the beach apparatus on account of wet grounds. (The navigation season had apparently been extended by the unseasonably warm weather.) "Did not work but observed the day," he logged, but also reported to his superiors that he had visited the north patrol post to switch keys, so beach patrols were also still being conducted.

Five days later, he reported the passage of two steamers, but said the surfmen had not performed boat drill on account of freezing weather. Nonetheless, Sammet had his men working, scrubbing the woodwork and floors in their sleeping room and hall, preparing to lay up the station for winter on the following day.

The 1914 season was soon underway, with each station engaged in the opening preparations, and the rescuers were especially active early on. At Sleeping Bear Point, Keeper Robinson had the crew performing surfboat drill on the morning of April 7, noting in his log that according to the service's requirement, he had turned the steering oar over to his no. 1 for training purposes, while he took over the stroke oar himself. Afterwards, they drilled with international and Morse codes.

The pace picked up later in the day, when a telephone call came from Glen Haven reporting that the gasoline mail boat from South Manitou had been caught in a high north wind and sea and, not being able to make the island, had sought shelter at the Glen Haven pier. Once there, however, the boat could not come to the dock without fear of being pounded to pieces. The crew resourcefully fashioned rollers out of pound-net stakes they picked up off the beach. After getting the boat to the shore, the men worked together to roll her out of danger without doing any damage. (Two days later, after the weather had moderated a bit, the point's surfmen were called back to assist in relaunching the mail boat from its safe perch on the beach.)

In midafternoon, the point's surfmen started back to the station, where they were informed that a fish boat was caught in the ice a mile offshore with one man aboard "whose life was in great danger." Robinson got a team of horses from D.H. Day and after loading the station's rescue equipment into a wagon, the crew started out. They had gone about a mile and a quarter when the station received a call that other fishermen had managed to rescue the ice-marooned man.

Also on that day, D. H. Day called the North Manitou station from Glen Haven, saying that he had received word that a small boat with a man aboard who had been trying to go from the boat's home port of Frankfort to Manistique, on the lake's north coast, was caught in ice about a half-mile offshore. As the station's powerboat would not be effective in the ice, Keeper Sammet asked the owner of the mail boat, which had an iron-protected hull, if the crew could use it for the rescue attempt, and received his permission.

One of the surfmen offered the use of his own boat as well, and stayed outside the ice field to assist in the event the rescue craft itself needed to be pulled out. The surfmen found the marooned boat *Seavey* wedged firmly amidst the ice. "We run along the edge of ice," Keeper Sammet reported, and not being able to see any signs of life onboard or onshore, "we decided they had got the man ashore, as I had been informed that fishermen had left Leland with lines to give what assistance they could."

The lifesavers returned to the station. Sammet wrote, "Our boat...iced down quite heavy as we had a rough sea. As soon as we arrived [at about 8:00 p.m.]...we was informed that they got the man ashore about 3:45 p.m. The *Seavey* was in tow of the gas boat

Swan, bound for Manistique. They had a very short tow line [which] parted 4 times."

On the fifth try in rough sea, the *Swan* had headed for the North Manitou lighthouse, where the keeper and his assistants helped them haul the *Seavey* onto the beach. Sammet reported that the cost to the government of using the privately owned gas boat was ten dollars, while the surfman had donated the use of his personal boat "for the good of the service" in return for the ten gallons of gasoline the run had consumed.

Two days later, the *Seavey* was determined a total loss. However, the story does not end there. The *Swan* herself got "ground up" in ice several days later, then ran to North Manitou lighthouse, where her well-known owners, the Sharp brothers from Frankfort, pulled her onto the beach for shelter. The lighthouse crew later helped them relaunch and get them free of the beach, but their hull took on water so fast that they headed toward the North Manitou station, where they tried to pull her onto its beach because the pumping could not keep up with the leaks. They then were able to find horses to drag her out, for which there was no charge.

Not all of the station's surfmen had been able to assist because the station had received a message that the North Manitou mail boat *Alice L.* was also caught in ice about a mile north of Leland and needed their assistance. Keeper Sammet reported later that he had given Captain Sharp five gallons of gasoline because he did not have enough to get to Leland, where he had planned to purchase it. Soon thereafter, the lifesavers hauled *Swan* to a secure spot "as the Sharp Bros. decided to go home and come after her in June."

The *Alice L.* was again caught in ice and the subject of a North Manitou Island station's rescue about a year later, this time in a fresh wind and strong sea. The episode started on April 11, with a night telephone call from Mr. Day at Glen Haven to the station, alerting them that the boat was trapped amid ice a mile north of Leland. Keeper Sammet loaded gasoline, an anchor and line, towline, and jackets in the gas-powered mail boat *Rob*, launching her and clearing the beach at 8:45 p.m. They had gone about three miles when they discovered that the boat's batteries were failing, so they returned to the station, got a new set, and departed at about 10:00 p.m., in a rough sea and brisk wind, reaching the troubled boat at about 11:45 p.m.

Sammet wrote, "They found that the crew had set a fire on the

April, 1914
Seavey

beach close to the boat. Just before we got to the edge of the ice, we swung our lantern and was answered by a lantern on shore to one side of the fire, and the closer we got the faster they swung the light. Saw the boat stuck fast in ice possibly four or five hundred feet from shore, boat or ice not moving...took a run out from ice, after we run about two minutes they stopped swinging their light; decided all hands was on shore." The crew started back to the station, arriving there at 2:15 a.m. The next morning the station received word by phone that all hands and boat were safe, but could not find if the boat was damaged. The charge for the gas boat's use was again ten dollars.

In early May, Keeper Robinson received instructions to fly the American flag on Mother's Day, relaying that order to the island stations by phone. Ten days later, Robinson's crew met the Point Betsie crew by surfboat to take the new district superintendent, Gus Lofberg, to the Sleeping Bear station to supervise the crew's performance of some drills. He continued his inspections through the district and was then delivered to the South Manitou station, where he was previously the keeper.

When Sleeping Bear Point's watch hollered that the station's smokehouse was on fire just before Independence Day, the crew put out the blaze with an extinguisher and several buckets of water.

On an August day, the South Manitou lookout saw a steamer displaying a distress flag, adrift about three miles south of the station. The crew was quickly underway, and upon arriving discovered that the steamer's boiler had exploded, fortunately without hurting anyone. The crew got a line to her and started towing; soon the Sleeping Bear Point crew also arrived on the scene by power surfboat, and the steamer was safely towed to a dock in the south island's harbor.

In early October, Keeper Kent reported that he had sent his no. 1 to Empire for supplies and to take the South Manitou surfmen's wives and children on a day's outing, as they had not been to the mainland for months—or, as the wives might have put it, they had been stuck on an island, gazing at the shoreline across the passage for much too long.

Late that fall, the Sleeping Bear Point crew was called upon to help find two drowned bodies in nearby Glen Lake. The keeper sent two surfmen with dragging equipment, but they were unable to locate them after two days of searching.

A gas boat, the *Agnes*, provided the final two records of the North Manitou Island lifesavers' rescue activities, only about two weeks apart and involving the same boat. On the morning of October 24, the surfman in the lookout discovered the *Agnes* had broken away from her anchorage during the night. Because of a brisk wind, Keeper Sammet was unable to see the full length of the beach from the lookout. He called the keepers of both the Sleeping Bear Point and South Manitou lighthouse stations to see if they had spotted the boat, and learned that the *Agnes* was on the island's beach, a mile and a half from the light.

November, 1914
Agnes

"Given a brisk north wind and rough sea, we decided we would not be able to pull her off the beach with the power surfboat," he wrote, so they got a team and wagon from a resident to haul planks, lines, and tackle to pull her out. They left the station at 7:00 a.m. and arrived at the site an hour later, pulling the *Agnes* onto the beach, and returned to the station later that morning. He said that the boat's starboard side had a couple of broken planks and others were "chewed up." He opined that it would have been impossible to get her back into the water with the power surfboat, given her condition and the high seas.

Then, on the night of November 5, a surfman rang an alarm and reported that the *Agnes* was on fire. The crew responded with fire extinguishers, and after using them up, quenched the rest of the flames with sand. With the boat on the beach close to the station's premises, the owner had been draining the engine and the gas from her tank for the winter. "After having everything pretty well drained," Keeper Sammet wrote, "he started the engine. The engine backfired and ignited gas in [the] bottom of [the] boat. No damage to boat."

At mainland Sleeping Bear Point, Keeper Robinson and his family faced the typical challenges of a nineteenth-century winter. His children and others residing west of the village of Glen Haven had to hike a trail across the edge of the dune twice daily, to and from school. This trek gained considerable notoriety following the Robinson family's 1914 Christmas Eve. They attended a party in Glen Arbor, and the festivities apparently ran late that night. Making their way back over the dune, they paused at the patrol post, where Charles checked his watch in the light of a match. It read 2:00 a.m. They then hustled down the slope to their residence. A story published two decades later in the November 2, 1934 issue of *The Grand Rapids Press* related the subsequent startling event:

At the late winter daybreak, the first-rising member of the family called the others from their beds with a horrified cry that Sleeping Bear Point was gone. Incredulous, they tumbled out to see. Gone it was. There stood the mountain, as serene and majestic as it had been the day before, but the end had been shorn away as sharply as if sliced by a giant knife, so the great ridge ended in a sheer wall of sand perhaps 40 feet high. Where before a tongue of sand dotted with fish shanties and drying racks had reached northeastward into the bay, there was only gray water. Sometime between 2 a.m. and daybreak, Lake Michigan noiselessly sucked down some 10 acres of land with everything on it, including a large area which the Robinsons had traversed.

Son Dale Robinson, whose drowning in 1934 in nearby Platte Lake occasioned this recollection, said that he and his brothers had followed their own footsteps from the previous night to a forty-foot precipice where the skeleton of an old, sand-buried ship lay exposed by the steep sandy shoreline's sudden collapse. Similar natural landslides have happened at least twice near the Sleeping Bear shoreline since 1914.

America's Esteemed Surfmen Become Respected US Coastguardsmen

Several years of debate culminated in 1915, in a stressful transition for US Life-Saving Service personnel throughout the country. The agency's leaders had continued to voice concern over Congress's failure to grant the compensation increases for the station's experienced (and thus most valuable) personnel and its retirees, as they had repeatedly requested. As the service had reported to Congress at the close of fiscal 1914, "The veteran surfmen of the service—those whose annual enlistments cover periods running back 20 or 30 years and whose experience and skill have been the mainstay of the service—have been rapidly falling out of the ranks." Surely with regret, the service's leaders apparently felt compelled to sound a dire warning that a "class of men signally lacking in every essential of the capable surfman has replaced them." This was a disturbing trend that did not escape notice, nor did another marked change, the rapid expansion of recreational powerboating over the prior decade.

Whereas in 1904, eighty-eight recreational motorboat accidents accounted for just 11 percent of all reported marine casualties, in 1913 alone there were 1,035 such events, constituting 60 percent of all marine accidents, with the reduced number of commercial crises putting seamen in jeopardy. Were a disaster to occur, however, the rescuers' response, in stronger and more powerful rescue craft, would be faster and safer than in the past.

The remedy the nation's policymakers had in mind for addressing these trends, in the interest of both economy and efficiency but with little support from veteran lifesavers, was the creation of a new agency, the US Coast Guard, consisting of the forces of the US Life-Saving Service and the Revenue Cutter Service (formerly the Revenue Marine from which the lifesavers earlier had been separated). Federal legislation to define the composition and organization of the new Coast Guard was approved on January 28, 1915, and the transformation began almost immediately.

The current Manitou Passage lifesaving station keepers: Charles Robinson at Sleeping Bear Point, Allen Kent at South Manitou, John Sammet at North Manitou, and Edwin E. Bedford at Point Betsie, opened their stations for the 1915 active season, quickly receiving notice that the official name of the service was now the "United States Coast Guard." Within the service's ranks, district superintendents, station keepers, their no. 1 surfmen, and others became Coast Guard-commissioned officers, warrant officers, and regular enlisted men, although many station leaders commonly continued to be identified by their veteran men, and by themselves, as the "keeper" or the "captain."

On South Manitou, Keeper Kent wrote that he was beginning the spring season with the same members (and their respective number designations) as in the prior year. "All day was used up in reading all orders and instructions," he added, as well as studying the Coast Guard's enlistment procedures.

Five days later, station activities were somewhat more typical, starting with an inspection at 8:00 a.m., followed by cleaning house. In the early afternoon, however, the lookout discovered that a large storage barn situated near the harbor's dock was on fire. The crew took buckets to the scene, but because the hose would not reach far enough, they were unable to combat the barn's own blaze. They could only wet down nearby dwellings as sparks repeatedly ignited them, resulting in the loss of much grain and farm equipment. Cancelling their routine beach patrols, the surfmen stood guard through the night, with the wind blowing sparks toward the buildings.

North Manitou's Keeper Sammet was soon transferred to the St. Joseph, Michigan station, being succeeded by Swedish-born Nels Palmer, who had served previously on the Charlevoix station's crew. (Five years later, Palmer would move to the Ludington Coast Guard station, where he would serve until 1934, becoming that station's longest serving chief.)

During the month of August, members of the two island and Sleeping Bear Point crews were examined by a medical officer at Manistee in preparation for their acceptance into the new Coast Guard.

Only six months after Congress's enactment of the organic Coast Guard legislation, the agency reported that the legislative reorganization of the nation's lifesaving operations was accomplishing its objective of enhancing efficiency by the "rehabilitation of the personnel concerned." Not many of the distinguished "storm warriors" of the past likely appreciated the application of the term "rehabilitation."

With due recognition of the distinctive accomplishments of the US Coast Guard and the deep public respect with which it has been held for more than one hundred years, its creation marked a significant departure from the culture, though not the operations, of the original, independent American lifesaving experience. An important gain for the crews, however, was that the reorganization made them eligible for retirement benefits, for which General Superintendent Kimball had so long campaigned. It is a bit ironic that with this victory came his own involuntary retirement from federal service, after more than a half-century's distinguished, unparalleled leadership.

While the station chief's formal titles had changed, their stations' essential tasks continued. On South Manitou, Kent reported having conducted a surfboat drill under oars, as well as a beach apparatus drill utilizing the life car, on August 31, 1915. He also noted that the day's report was the last that he (and other keepers) would be making on the customary form, as his next day's entry was to be made on a replacement developed by the Coast Guard. The surfmen's typical activities were unchanged, as two days later he recorded that the crew was preparing to repair damage to the power surfboat, and that the beach apparatus drill also had been performed (for the second time that week).

At Sleeping Bear Point, Keeper Robinson also reported at the end of August that his crew had launched the Beebe-McLellan self-bailing surfboat and drilled under sail. He noted that this exercise had gone badly; the crewmen were said to be working in the boat-house a couple of hours later, drying the gear.

On September 1, Sleeping Bear Point's Keeper Robinson recorded the enlistment of Frankfort's "native born citizen" George N. Bernier as his Coast Guard station's surfman no. 7. He also provided a list of his entire crew, by their number, along with their next of kin, starting with his no. 1, Patrick J. McCauley. Nos. 1 and 5 were married; the others were single.

In mid-November, Kent reported weather conditions on the south island every four hours of the twenty-four-hour day during a southeast gale, noting that his crew was remaining alert to vessels that were seeking the harbor's shelter.

At Point Betsie, Captain Edwin Bedford retired in 1918, reporting in the log that he was turning over all of the station's public property temporarily to surfman no. 1, Ludwig Hendricksen. However, its responsibility for rescues was sharply reduced by the nearby Frankfort Harbor station's high-powered boats. The point station was destined to become officially inactive only three years after the Coast Guard had built a handsome new structure in 1917 to replace the lifesaving service's aging building.

Under its reduced status, the Point Betsie station had very limited personnel, and served primarily as an observation post toward Platte Bay and the passage in coordination with the active, fully-staffed Frankfort station, despite unsuccessful appeals from some residents for the point station's return to full, active status.

New Realities and Memories

The Depression, navigational improvements, and other changes ultimately resulted in the decommissioning, in mid-December 1937, of the Coast Guard station at Point Betsie. Its final officer-in-charge dutifully, and likely with more than usual sentimentality, reported draining its water system, shutting down its furnace, and shuttering its windows. A long and rich tradition of the service to Lake Michigan mariners and residents had come to an end. The classic building and surrounding land, cherished for the past seventy-five years by private owners, is situated across the road from the county-owned, volunteer-operated Point Betsie Lighthouse and other public museum structures.

The closures of the other Coast Guard rescue stations serving the Manitou Passage soon followed; North Manitou Island in 1939, South Manitou Island and Sleeping Bear Point in 1958 (the latter after a 1931 relocation and a 1944 wartime closing). A boating-season-only Coast Guard station remains at Frankfort Harbor, with the larger station at Manistee now serving much of the northeast Lake Michigan coast. Essential coverage is also provided throughout the region by high-speed Coast Guard Air Station helicopters based at the Traverse City airport.

The 1915 administrative restructuring of lifesaving services proved to be something of a forerunner, as in 1939, President Franklin D. Roosevelt, by executive order, moved the nation's lighthouse personnel into the Coast Guard for reasons of administrative efficiency. That shift, too, caused a loss of professional identity that lightkeepers of long tenure felt deeply.

Simply put, the nation's primarily coastal-based lightkeepers, through the generations being justifiably proud of their identity, were rather uneasy about their place within the seafaring Coast Guard. As managerial changes are typically unsettling, particularly to veteran employees, similar concerns had persisted within the lifesavers' ranks for a time, but the restructurings gradually gained

Point Betsie's light yet shines.
Author's 2021 image.

acceptance. From today's viewpoint more than a century later, the US lifesavers' and lightkeepers' stories initially may be "just history" to some people, but they undeniably hold a noble, courageous, and essential place in the American maritime experience, and should inspire our nation.

Among many notable changes throughout the second half of the twentieth century, the South Manitou Island Lighthouse ceased operation in 1958, the Grand Traverse light was automated and mounted on a separate steel tower in 1972, and in the spring of 1983, the Point Betsie station—the last light on Lake Michigan's eastern shore to be served by resident keepers—was also automated, its final personnel being sad to surrender their service post. All US coastal navigation lights now operate automatically, and are maintained periodically by nonresident technicians.

Regrettably, some of the old lenses were destroyed decades ago when their lighting systems were modernized; many of the surviving optics are features of museum settings such as Point Betsie Lighthouse, under the ownership of the Coast Guard's curatorial staff. Even lenses displayed in museums require periodic professional service, which is best performed by increasingly scarce, talented consultants who are retired from the Coast Guard.

In two other major federal bureaucratic restructurings, the Coast Guard became part of the newly created Department of Transportation in 1967, and moved again in 2003 into the multifaceted, now heavily burdened Department of Homeland Security, where it is the only military element. (Under law, it could be placed under the navy's control if circumstances justified it.)

At Sleeping Bear Dunes National Lakeshore, the protection and interpretation of the Manitou islands and much of the passage's mainland dune-lined coast are the responsibility of the US Department of the Interior's esteemed but budget-strained National Park Service, the park's professional staff, and its enthusiastic volunteers.

The beautiful Manitou Passage's natural features and the national lakeshore's historic restorations, as well as the separately owned Point Betsie and Grand Traverse light stations, are protected places where visitors learn, experience, and appreciate memories of critically needed lifesaving service provided to generations of Lake Michigan mariners.

In honor of all guardians of the passage's past.

"Goodbye"
Leelanau Historical Society Museum.

Acknowledgments

Special thanks are certainly in order with respect to the completion of this, my third Lake Michigan northeastern coastal history. I am indebted to numerous individuals for their counsel, assistance, and support.

I much appreciated the readings of the initial draft text by Roger Dewey, my colleague for ten years on the board of The Friends of Point Betsie Lighthouse; by Bill Herd, who devoted much of his career and his retirement to the establishment and successful operations of the Sleeping Bear Dunes National Lakeshore; by Grant Brown, Jr., author of *Ninety Years Crossing Lake Michigan*, an insightful account of the year-round, ninety-year operations of the Ann Arbor Railroad ferries; and by Frankfort neighbor Bruce Campbell Ogilvie, who recently wrote *Dead Reckoning*, a unique memoir of his father's service on US Liberty ships conducting convoys on the dangerous North Atlantic during World War II.

I benefited from JoAnne Cook's comments regarding Anishinaabek culture, which is important to our region's history and contemporary life. I also wish to thank the Leelanau Historical Society Museum, in Leland, Michigan, on the Manitou Passage shore, for the availability of numerous images that illustrate this text, as well as other picture sources that are also credited. And I want to acknowledge the Point Betsie Lighthouse and the Boathouse Museum, with which I have been involved for many years. Through contributions of many contributors and volunteers, the site now provides visitors a unique opportunity to learn of the dedicated services provided Manitou Passage mariners and residents by the talented crews of our nation's lighthouse and lifesaving services. Those men, along with their families, have an important place in our rich maritime heritage.

On a more personal note, I cannot adequately express enough appreciation to my own family members who assisted me throughout my several years' research and production of this account of the official guardians of Lake Michigan's famous Manitou Passage. My wife Peggy aided me enormously at the outset by assisting me in photographing extensive documents for later study during several visits to the Chicago facility of the US National Archives. More recently, she has been through the text and photos numerous times with her artistically trained eyes. Throughout the development of the work, my son-in-law Nando, along with his daughter Mia, generously assisted me through digital challenges I confronted in the preparation of the text and images; without them, I simply could not have completed this project.

Truthfully, my entire family experienced this endeavor, one way or another, over a long time. To my wonderful Peggy, our daughter Annie, her Nando and their daughters Mia and Andrea, and our daughter Susie, her husband Matthew and daughter Sylvia, all of whom have shared in it, I give you my sincere thanks.

The judgments that this account required, as well as any errors of omission or commission, are the burden of its researcher and author.

Notes and Bibliography

US Government:

US Life-Saving Service. Annual reports, FY 1876-1915. Washington, DC. Accessed primarily through HathiTrust.

US Life-Saving Service. Records of the stations at Michigan's North Manitou Island, Point Betsie, Sleeping Bear Point, and South Manitou Island, 1876-1915. US National Archives and Records Administration regional office, Chicago, IL.

US National Archives and Records Administration. Lighthouse records.

Books:

Anderson, Charles M. *Isle of View: A History of South Manitou Island.* Frankfort, MI: J.B. Publications, 1979.

Crowner, Gerald E. *The South Manitou Story.* Mio, MI: The Print Shop, 1982.

Dennis, Jerry. *The Living Great Lakes: Searching for the Heart of the Inland Seas.* New York: St. Martin's Press, 2003.

Furth, Glenn C. *My Point of View.* April 1992.

Goudschaal, Claudia D. *Destination: Leelanau: Boats Sailing Leelanau Waters, 1835-1900.* 2009.

Hatcher, Harlan. *The Great Lakes.* New York: Oxford University Press, 1944.

Hawley, Jonathan P. *Point Betsie: Lightkeeping and Lifesaving on Northeastern Lake Michigan.* Ann Arbor, MI: University of Michigan Press, and Traverse City, MI: Petoskey Publishing Co., 2008.

Hawley, Jonathan P. *From Artisans to Artists: Betsie Bay's Historic "Island" Story.* Grand Rapids, MI: Chapbook Press, 2014.

Karamanski, Theodore J. *Schooner Passage: Sailing Ships and the Lake Michigan Frontier.* Detroit: Wayne State University Press, 2000.

Noble, Dennis L. *Lighthouses & Keepers: The US Lighthouse Service and Its Legacy.* Annapolis, MD: Naval Institute Press, 1997.

Noble, Dennis L. *That Others Might Live: The US Life-Saving Service, 1878-1915.* Annapolis, MD: United States Naval Institute, 1994.

O'Flynn, Joseph P. *Nautical Dictionary.* Boyne City, MI: Harbor House Publishers, Inc., 1992.

Plumb, Ralph. *Lake Michigan*. Manitowoc, WI: Brandt Printing and Binding Co., 1941.

Quaife, Milo M. *Lake Michigan*. Indianapolis, IN: The Bobbs-Merrill Co., 1944.

Ratigan, William. *Great Lakes Shipwrecks & Survivors*. Grand Rapids, MI: William B. Eerdmans Publishing Co., 1977.

Richardson, Ross. *The Search for the Westmoreland: Lake Michigan's Treasure Shipwreck.* Traverse City, MI: Arbutus Press, 2012.

Rusco, Rita Hadra. *North Manitou Island: Between Sunrise and Sunset.* BookCrafters,1991.

Sapulki, Wayne S. *Lighthouses of Lake Michigan: Past and Present.* Manchester, MI: Wilderness Adventure Books, 2001.

Shanks, Ralph, Wick York, and Lisa Woo Shanks, ed. *The US Life-Saving Service: Heroes, Rescues and Architecture of the Early Coast Guard.* Petaluma, CA: Costano Books, 1996.

Shelak, Benjamin J. *Shipwrecks of Lake Michigan.* Black Earth, WI: Trails Books, 2003.

Stonehouse, Frederick. *Wreck Ashore: The United States Life-Saving Service on the Great Lakes.* Duluth, MN: Lake Superior Port Cities, Inc., 1994.

Swayze, David D. *Shipwreck! A Comprehensive Directory of Over 3,700 Shipwrecks on the Great Lakes.* Boyne City, MI: Harbor House Publishers, Inc., 1992.

Thompson, Mark. *Graveyard of the Lakes.* Detroit: Wayne State University Press, 2000.

Vent, Myron H. *South Manitou Island: From Pioneer Community to National Park.* Springfield, VA, 1973.

Wakefield, Lawrence and Lucille. *Sail & Rail: A Narrative History of Transportation in the Traverse City Region.* Traverse City, MI: Village Press, 1980.

Warner, Gene. *The Manitou Passage Story: An Indefinitive History of the Settlement of Northeast Lake Michigan.* BoysMindBooks.com, 2011.

Weeks, George. *Sleeping Bear: Yesterday and Today.* Franklin, MI: Altwerger and Mandel Publishing Co., 1990.

Wilkinson, William D. and Commander Timothy R. Dring, USNR (Retired). *American Coastal Rescue Craft: A Design History of US Coastal Craft Used by the United States Life-Saving Service and the United States Coast Guard.* Gainesville, FL: University Press of Florida, 2009.

About the Author

Dr. Jonathan P. Hawley, a resident of Frankfort, Michigan for twenty years, along with his wife, artist Peggy Hawley, earned his PhD in political science at the University of Missouri-Columbia. His career included university teaching; ten years' staff service in the US House of Representatives, during which he worked toward the establishment of Michigan's Sleeping Bear Dunes National Lakeshore; and nearly two decades of corporate public affairs consulting. Upon moving to Frankfort, Jon became a founding board member of The Friends of Point Betsie Lighthouse, serving throughout his ten-year tenure as vice president and president during the historic light station's restoration and the construction of its museum. A retired member of the board of the Grand Traverse Regional Community Foundation, he serves on the board of Frankfort's Benzie Shores District Library, and is a Rotarian. Jon is the author of *Point Betsie: Lightkeeping and Lifesaving on Northeastern Lake Michigan* (2008), *and From Artisans to Artists: Betsie Bay's Historic "Island" Story* (2014).

9 781954 786486